IMAGES
of America

POLAROID

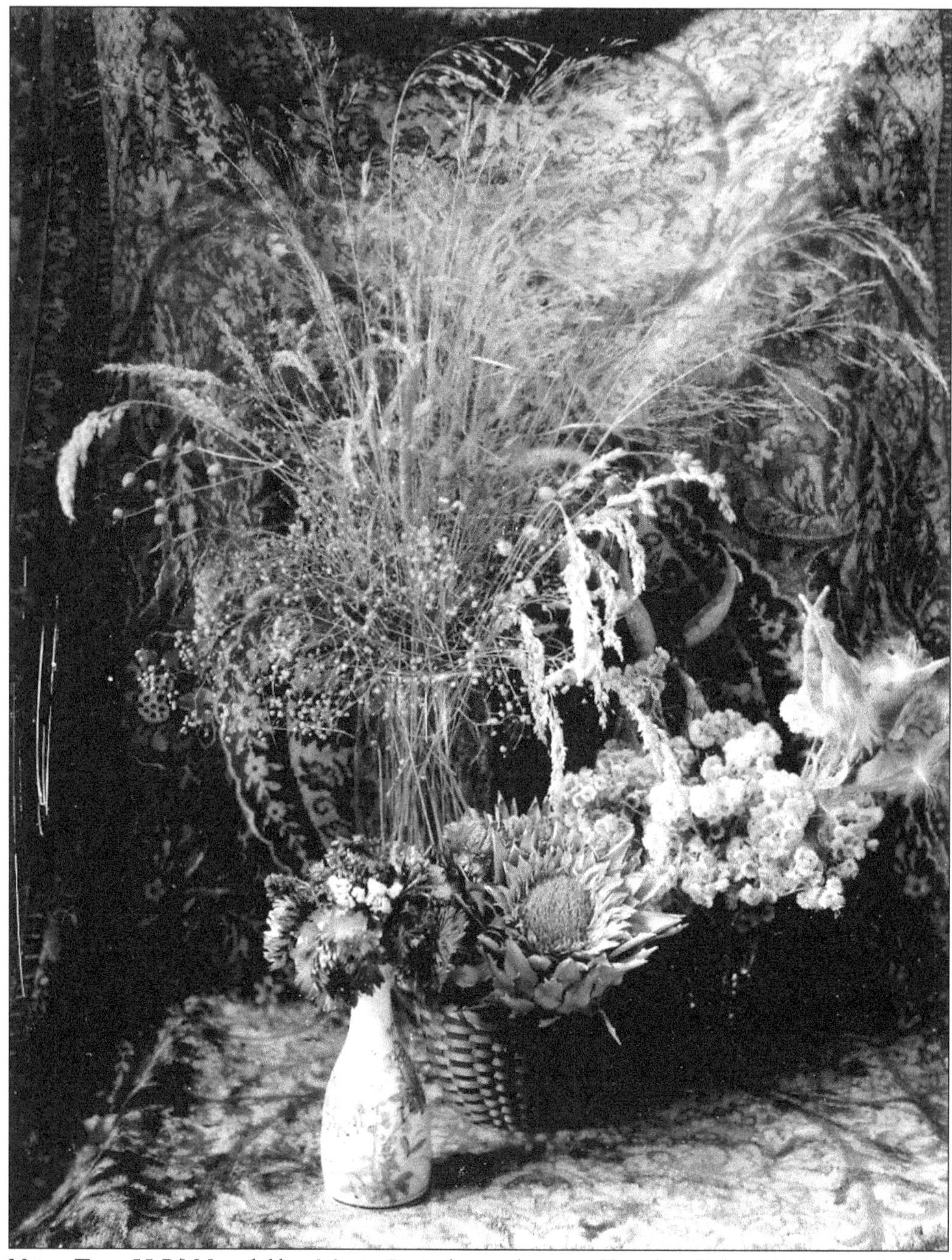

Using Type 55 P/N Land film, Marie Cosindas made one of her first Polaroid black-and-white images, *Still Life II*, in 1961.

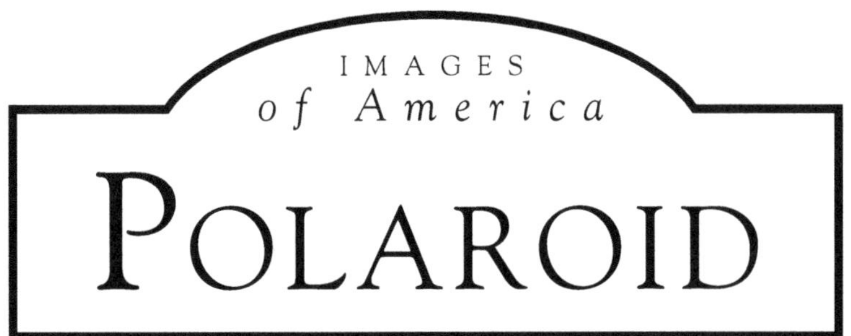

Alan R. Earls and Nasrin Rohani
Foreword by Marie Cosindas

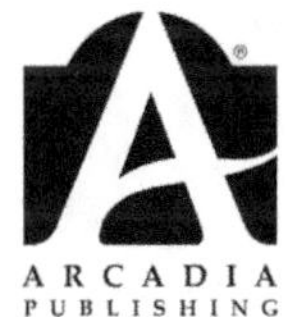

ISBN 978-1-5316-2179-7

Published by Arcadia Publishing
Charleston, South Carolina

Library of Congress Catalog Card Number: 2004110656

For all general information, contact Arcadia Publishing:
Telephone 843-853-2070
Fax 843-853-0044
E-mail sales@arcadiapublishing.com
For customer service and orders:
Toll-free 1-888-313-2665

Visit us on the Internet at www.arcadiapublishing.com

Acknowledgments

The authors are grateful to Polaroid Corporation and especially appreciate the assistance of Skip Colcord, director of corporate communications. Unless otherwise noted, all of the images were provided by the Polaroid Corporate Archives and are reproduced here with Polaroid's permission. Our special thanks go to Marie Cosindas, who was generous with her time and thoughts and who kindly permitted several of her photographs to be included here. The photographs by Marie Cosindas reproduced here have her copyright. For background material about Edwin Land and Polaroid's history, we relied primarily on archival records from the extensive resources of the Polaroid Corporate Archives. In addition, the following books were particularly useful: *Insisting on Impossible: The Life of Edwin Land, Inventor of Instant Photography*, by Victor McElheny (Perseus Books, 1999); *Land's Polaroid: A Company and the Man Who Invented It*, by Peter Wensberg (Houghton Mifflin, 1987); *The Polaroid Story*, by Mark Olshaker (Scarborough House, 1978).

No book of this scope could fail to acknowledge the work of Polaroid's longtime company photographer, Roy Jacoby. The vast majority of the images included here dating up to 1960 are his work. Finally, we are indebted to Kaia Motter and Arcadia Publishing for their patience and helpful insights.

Contents

Foreword

It was a chance meeting with Stanford Calderwood, Polaroid's vice president of advertising and marketing, in 1961 at an event honoring Minor White, a renowned figure in the world of photography. I was about to travel to Yosemite to participate in my first workshop with Ansel Adams. Calderwood asked whether I had a Polaroid four-by-five back for my camera. As yet unfamiliar with the capabilities offered by Polaroid's new medium, I showed little enthusiasm for the suggestion. Nonetheless, I was sent a four-by-five Polaroid back to use with my Linhof camera, along with some black-and-white film similar to the film Adams was using for his workshops.

As it turned out, those first black-and-white images on Polaroid film influenced my life. However, I continued to rely mostly on conventional film and gained valuable experience working with Adams in the field and in the darkroom. Observing my work, Ansel said, "You work in black and white but think in color."

In 1962, Polaroid invited me to experiment with its new instant color roll film. A new era began. By 1965, I was working almost exclusively with four-by-five Polacolor, and a year later I became a color consultant with Polaroid and worked with Howard Rogers, inventor of Polacolor.

Seeing the images and then being able to adjust the colors by using various methods that I had explored extensively produced amazing results. With Polaroid film, the photograph became a collaboration between myself and my subjects. We both shared in the experience of making the photograph together. I became liberated from the darkroom, and it was as though I were holding the darkroom in the palm of my hand.

Eventually I learned more about this new medium and the company that had spawned it and began to know and work with the company founder, Edwin Land. I learned that my experience was not an accident. Land was a visionary in every sense. Although primarily absorbed in science and the business of running a science-based enterprise, Land also thought deeply about the art of photography and its potential transformation, as he thought deeply about almost everything he encountered in life. He believed that industry should exist at the intersection of art and science, and he made a commitment to creativity by supporting photographers and their use of Polaroid's new products.

For me and for many other photographers coming into our own at the time, Land and Polaroid opened doors and sent us in new directions. *Polaroid* brings to life these decades of excitement. Land and his associates, the many people of Polaroid, and the innovations they made, which recast so many aspects of daily life, are here in candid and intimate images.

The success of Land and Polaroid has left a deep and positive impact on the world and on those of us who knew them. Their story is told here in its most accessible form—through photography.

—Marie Cosindas
Boston, January 2005

Bostonian Marie Cosindas, a leading figure in the 1960s wave of experimental color photography, began her career as a painter. However, a pivotal trip to Greece, the influence of teachers such as Ansel Adams, and the richness and stunning immediacy of the then new "instant" color films being introduced by Polaroid led her to put aside the brush and apply her compositional talents to the realm of photography. Over the succeeding years, Cosindas has created a rich oeuvre of work, much of it using Polaroid films. Highlights of her career include her first solo exhibition at the Museum of Modern Art in 1966. This was the first time that Polaroid color film was shown in an exhibit at the museum. In 1978, Tom Wolfe wrote the essay for her first book, Marie Cosindas: Color Photographs, *published by the New York Graphic Society. Cosindas continues to work in Boston. Her photographs are included in the permanent collections of museums worldwide.*

Introduction

Nothing in the annals of American business quite compares to Polaroid. Thanks to the almost wholly original work of its founder, Edwin H. Land, and its key researchers, Polaroid again and again amazed the world with products that barely anyone had dreamt of let alone tried to produce.

"I have long aspired to make our company a noble prototype of industry, penetrating in science, reliable in engineering, creative in aesthetics and wholesomely prosperous in economics." —Edwin H. Land.

Polaroid became all of that and more, thanks to Land's ideas and persistence. Polaroid's contributions to the field of polarization, to photography, to cameras, to film, and to a host of other areas were unique and pioneering.

When Land invented his first synthetic sheet polarizer in 1928, it was almost as stunning an achievement as the invention of the laser some three decades later at Bell Labs. Polarized light could now be experienced and applied by researchers and even by the general public. And, by launching Land-Wheelwright Laboratories in 1932, Land made sure Polaroid was the sole supplier of products that used polarization.

Light-polarizing filters, sunglasses, desk lamps, the Dermascope, light-conditioning windows for trains, 3D movies, Vectograph three-dimensional photography, training simulators, goggles—all emerged in short order from the company Land built.

Land was born in Bridgeport, Connecticut, in 1909. In his youth he was already infatuated with optics and science in general. He entered Harvard in 1926 but after his freshman year left to pursue research into polarizers on his own in New York City. Existing polarizers were made from herapathite, a crystal of iodine and quinine salts developed by a 19th-century researcher, William Bird Herapath. The crystals were difficult to grow to a size that would make them truly useful. By 1928, Land had developed the idea of simply aligning vast numbers of microscopic crystals in a polymer sheet and created the first synthetic sheet polarizer—a breakthrough. In 1934, at the age of 25, Land was issued his first patent.

Harvard permitted him to continue some of his research using its facilities and from that arrangement, Land and his Harvard physics instructor, George Wheelwright, launched Land-Wheelwright Laboratories in 1932, initially in a barn in Wellesley Hills, Massachusetts, and later in the Back Bay section of Boston, and finally in Cambridge, where the company remained headquartered for more than half a century.

The name for Land's breakthrough polarizing sheet, Polaroid, was suggested by Clarence Kennedy, a Smith College art professor and the first company consultant with whom Land worked in the 1930s on three-dimensional photography. Polaroid was incorporated in 1937 to acquire the assets of Land-Wheelwright Laboratories and to develop and manufacture commercial products. The new company was financed by fresh investments of $750,000, from leading Wall Street financiers such as James Warburg, J. P. Morgan, Averill Harriman, the firms of Schroeder Rockefeller and Kuhn and Loeb, as well as several others.

Thanks to growth in World War II and the success of instant photography a few years thereafter, by 1950, the company employed 429 people, occupied 115,000 square feet, and had net sales of nearly $6.5 million. By 1958, the company was employing 2,500 in 500,000 square feet, with sales approaching $90 million.

The decades that followed witnessed similar growth, as ever more capable and affordable photographic technologies emerged from the imagination of Land and the laboratories of Polaroid.

But that was by no means the whole story. Land was always involved in the world around him in many other ways and made sure that Polaroid was, too. For instance, in 1944, Land helped write *Science, the Endless Frontier* for the National Science Foundation, a document that laid the foundation for postwar government support of research.

Throughout the 1950s and beyond, Land was intimately involved in advising the government and a succession of presidents on matters relating to science. His role was particularly critical in advocating for the creation of the U-2 spy plane and in leading the design and development of the camera which it carried. Land was awarded the Presidential Medal of Freedom in 1963 and the National Medal of Science in 1967.

Land earned 537 patents in his lifetime, second only to Edison at the time. He was awarded 16 honorary degrees and received honors from many national and international scientific and photographic societies. He was elected to the American Academy of Arts and Sciences, National Academy of Science, National Academy of Engineering, British Royal Society, and many others.

In 1980, Land founded and endowed the Rowland Institute for Science, a private non-profit institution, to provide an environment for scientists to pursue basic scientific research. Following his retirement from Polaroid in 1982, he took up full-time work on his color vision research at Rowland himself.

Even that was but a pause in the story, as Land continued to garner honors and work diligently in science up to his death in 1991. For its part, Polaroid continued to innovate even without Land. A hostile takeover was successfully thwarted in 1988, and Polaroid beat back Kodak's entrance into the instant photography market with an epic patent infringement lawsuit initiated in 1976 and finally concluded in its favor in 1991. The $900 million settlement was the largest in the history of patent infringement cases at the time.

Today, Polaroid Corporation still designs, develops, manufactures, and markets instant and digital imaging products and related products. The company's principal products are instant cameras and instant film, which are marketed worldwide. In addition to its principal products, the company designs, develops, manufactures, and/or markets photographic hardware accessories for the instant photography market. The company's other products and services consist of eyewear, principally sunglasses, and secure identification systems for commercial applications. The company also performs contract manufacturing for third parties and licenses its brand and technology to third parties.

One

The Vision and Passion of Edwin Land

In his own way, the handsome boy genius Edwin Land was as iconic as Einstein for Americans of a certain age. Born into a well-to-do Connecticut family, Edwin Land seemed determined to achieve greatness from an early age. While still a college student (he attended Harvard but never graduated), he threw himself into one of the most daunting puzzles available within one of the most intriguing provinces of science at the time—the polarization of light. Building on tantalizing but incomplete discoveries forgotten or overlooked by others, Land focused his sharp mind and tireless efforts on weaving a molecular screen that would comb light until only light waves in one plane were left. However, this trick, useful for many kinds of scientific research but also applicable almost anywhere humans experienced light, would become more than a noteworthy scientific paper or a brief headline in a journal if the material could be mass- produced.

That is what Land did, producing a comparatively inexpensive, polymer-based sheet polarizer that permitted polarization to be experienced on a large scale. On that sound footing, he then moved ahead to tackle a host of related, similar, or simply interesting challenges—usually with a commercial application in sight on some distant promontory. For example, over his long career, Land worked with varying degrees of technical and commercial success on areas such as stereo photography, 3-D movies, missile-guidance systems, reconnaissance cameras and film, gunnery-training simulators, and (as an adviser to the government) spy planes and spy satellites. Using his polarizing techniques, he spent years advocating for an automobile lighting system that, had it been adopted universally, would have vastly improved the safety of nighttime driving.

His greatest success, the development and advancement of instant photography, was sparked by his young daughter's asking why she had to wait to see photographs. Land, too, wondered why. So, pushing the limits of chemistry and straining the resources of his still small company, Land and his research team made instant photography a reality by 1947. Never one to rest on his laurels, Land was soon pushing for the next revolution, the development of instant color film in 1963, and followed that triumph with his greatest technical achievement, the SX-70 camera and film system in 1972.

All of these accomplishments brought Land wealth and made Polaroid a household name and a darling of Wall Street. But that was never enough. Land, the passionate entrepreneur and scientist, always saw new things to do—often where no one else noticed. For instance, starting in the 1950s, Land developed heterodox theories about the nature of vision, challenging the received wisdom (still taught today) that color perception is the result of objects reflecting only certain wavelengths of light. He believed he had proved—and others have since come to agree—that vision is more complex than that.

But above all, Land was not the kind of genius popularly skewered today as a nerd. A true visionary, Land understood the impact and influence of his ideas. Like a renaissance man, he had wide interests and contacts. Besides being an avid reader of science and philosophy, he enjoyed the company of artists and people of accomplishment from all walks of life. He could communicate and lead as surely as he could envision solutions to technical problems. And his company, diverse in talent across gender and even racial lines, was a reflection of his own pursuit of dreams and visions.

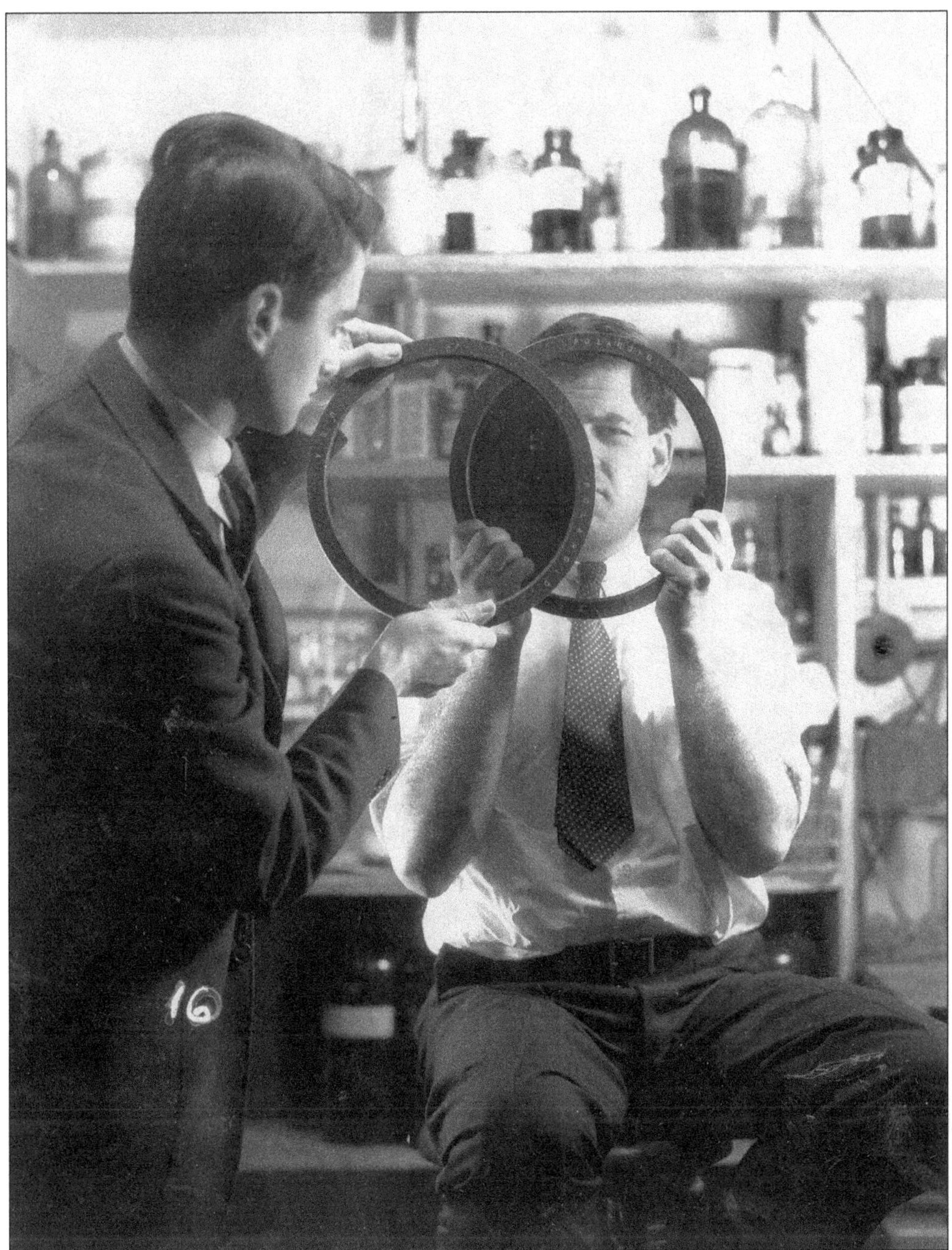

Edwin Land, the inventor of synthetic polarizer and the founder of Polaroid Corporation, is shown in 1936 with Nick Rogers holding polarizers to demonstrate the polarization of light. The intersecting circles became Polaroid's logo, and "Polaroid" became a trademark in 1935.

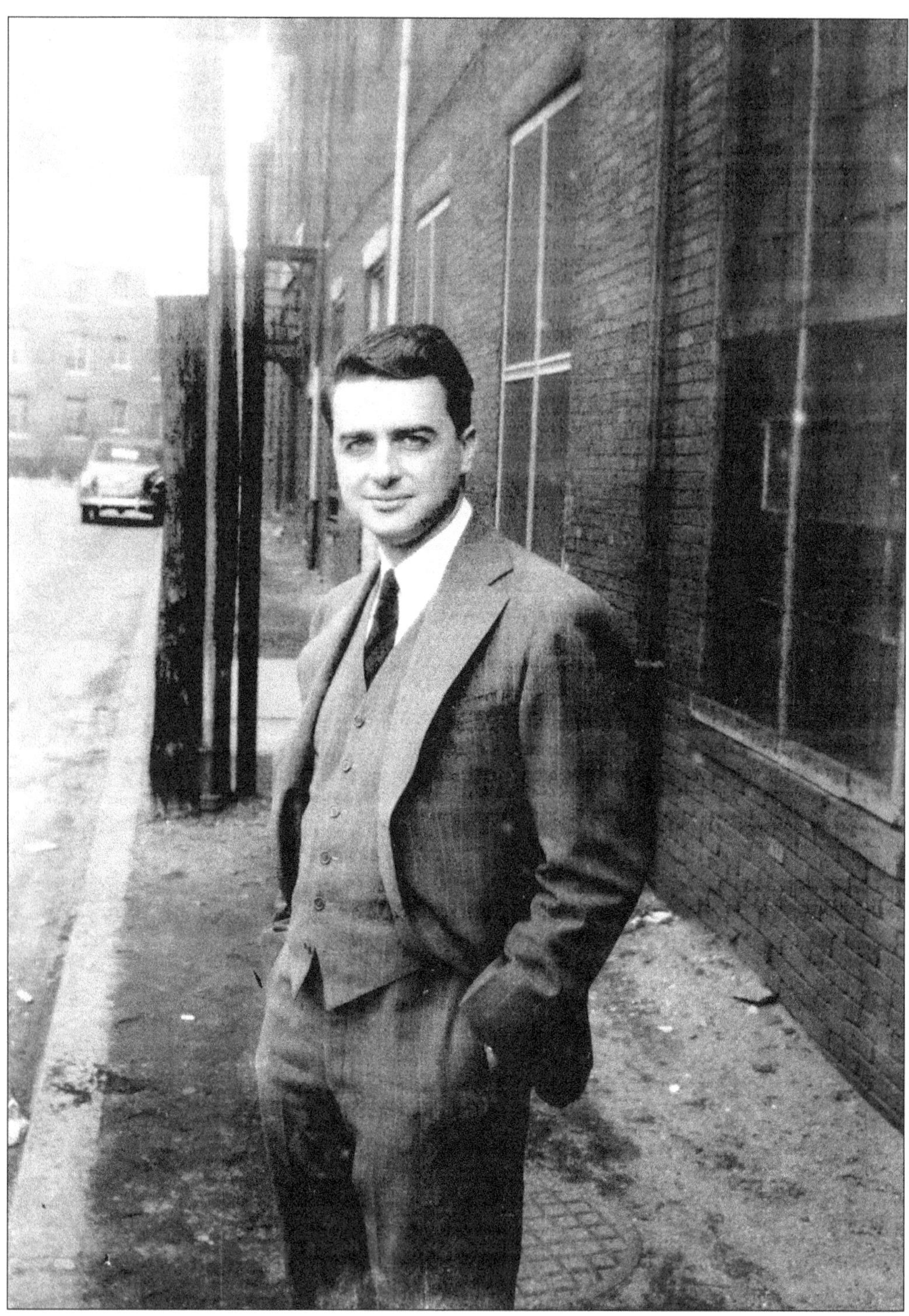

This 1947 test photograph shows Land outside his Osborn Street laboratory in Cambridge, where he invented instant photography. Here, he worked and often ended up sleeping. In the same historic building, Alexander Graham Bell made his first "long-distance" telephone call from Boston to Cambridge.

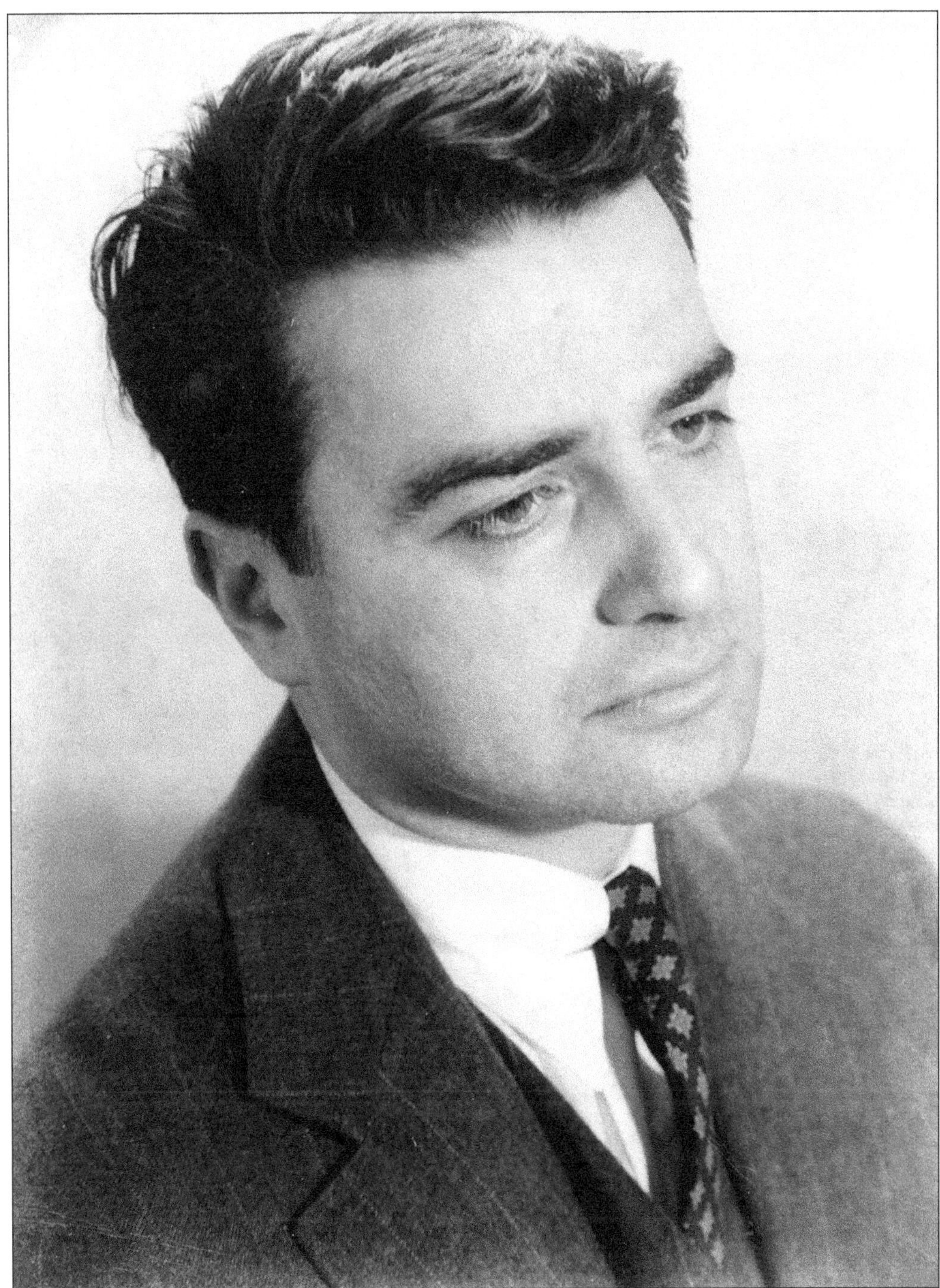

This 1947 laboratory test photograph, taken by researcher Meroë Morse, shows Land in his lab, looking tired, reflective, and somewhat less self-possessed. Land, the inventor, was himself a frequent subject of test photographs. This helped ensure the secrecy surrounding the development of instant photography.

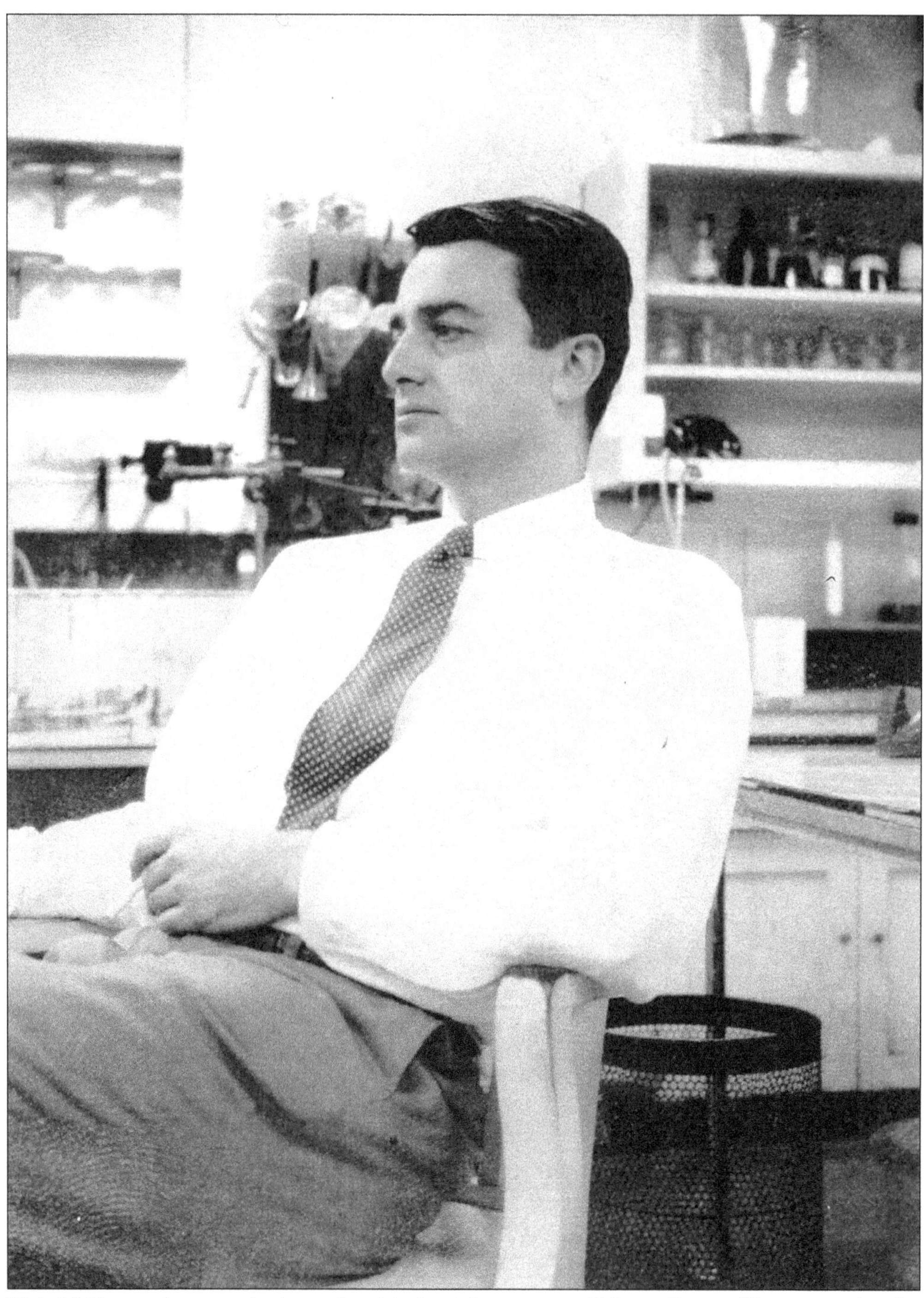

This 1948 test photograph shows Land in his laboratory at Osborn Street. "Do not undertake the program unless the goal is manifestly important and its achievement nearly impossible." —Edwin H. Land.

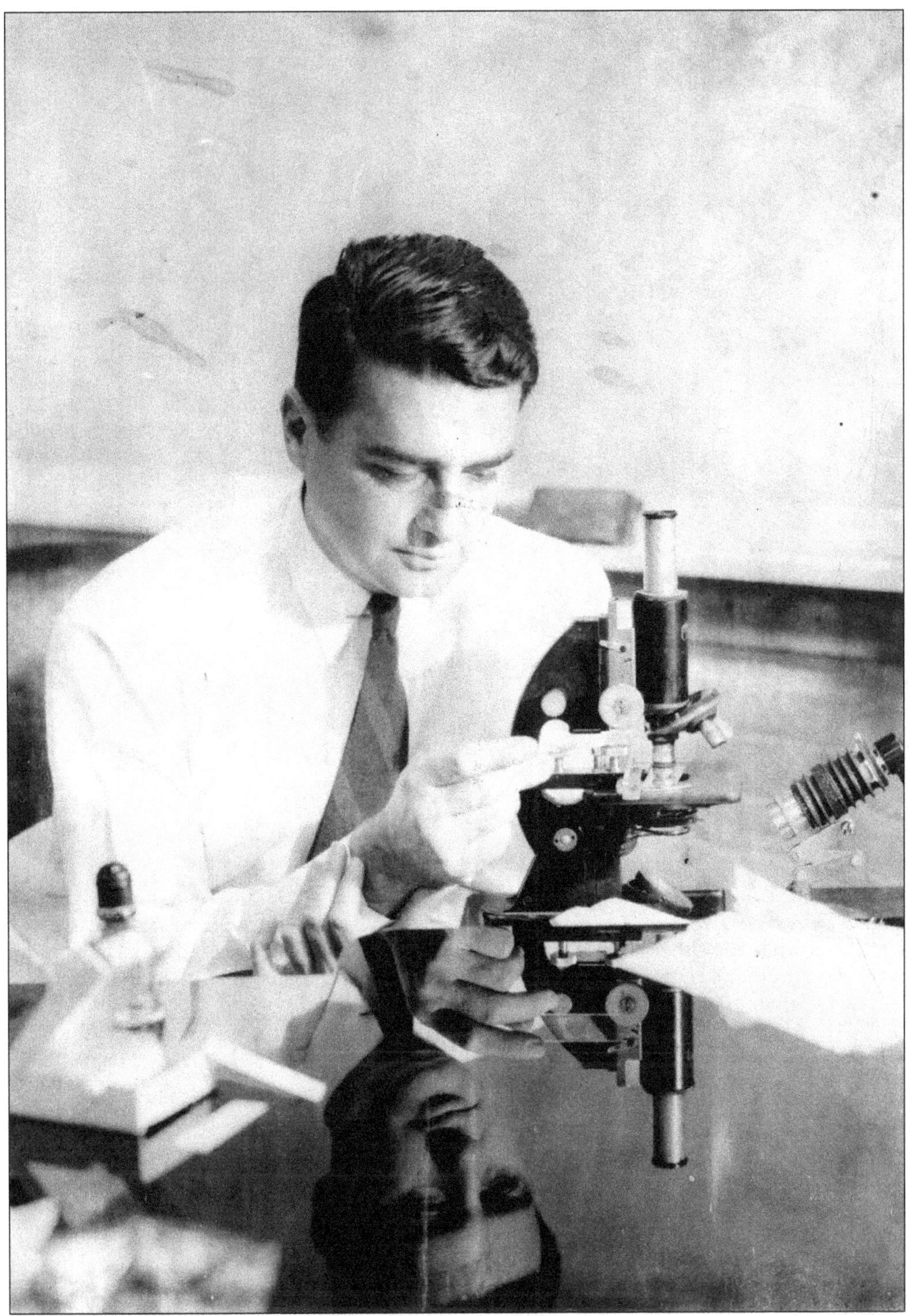

In this 1946 laboratory test photograph, another taken by Meroë Morse, Land is absorbed in work with a microscope.

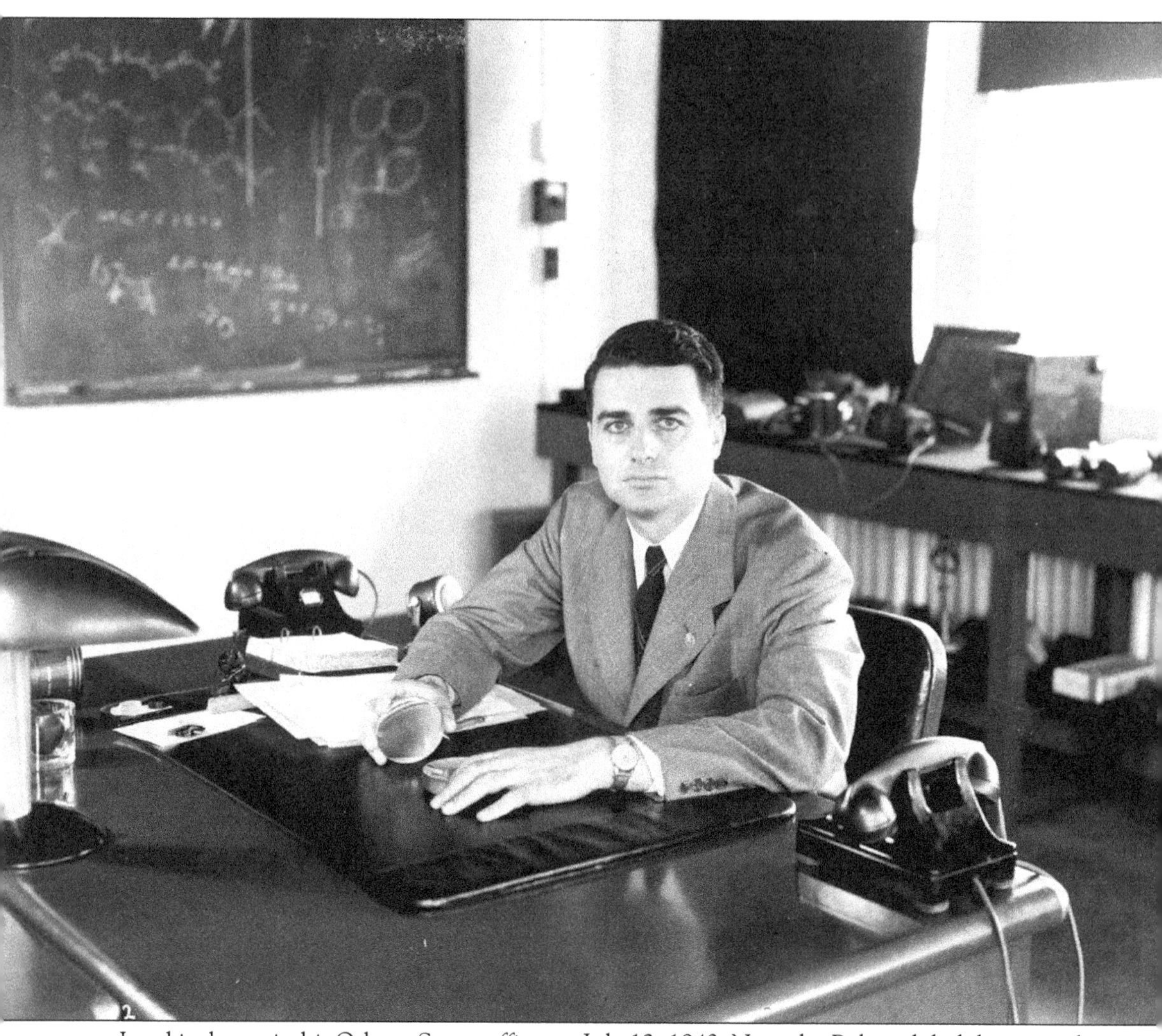

Land is shown in his Osborn Street office on July 12, 1943. Note the Polaroid desk lamp on the table and the polished optics in his hand. "Do not do anything that anyone else can do readily." —Edwin H. Land.

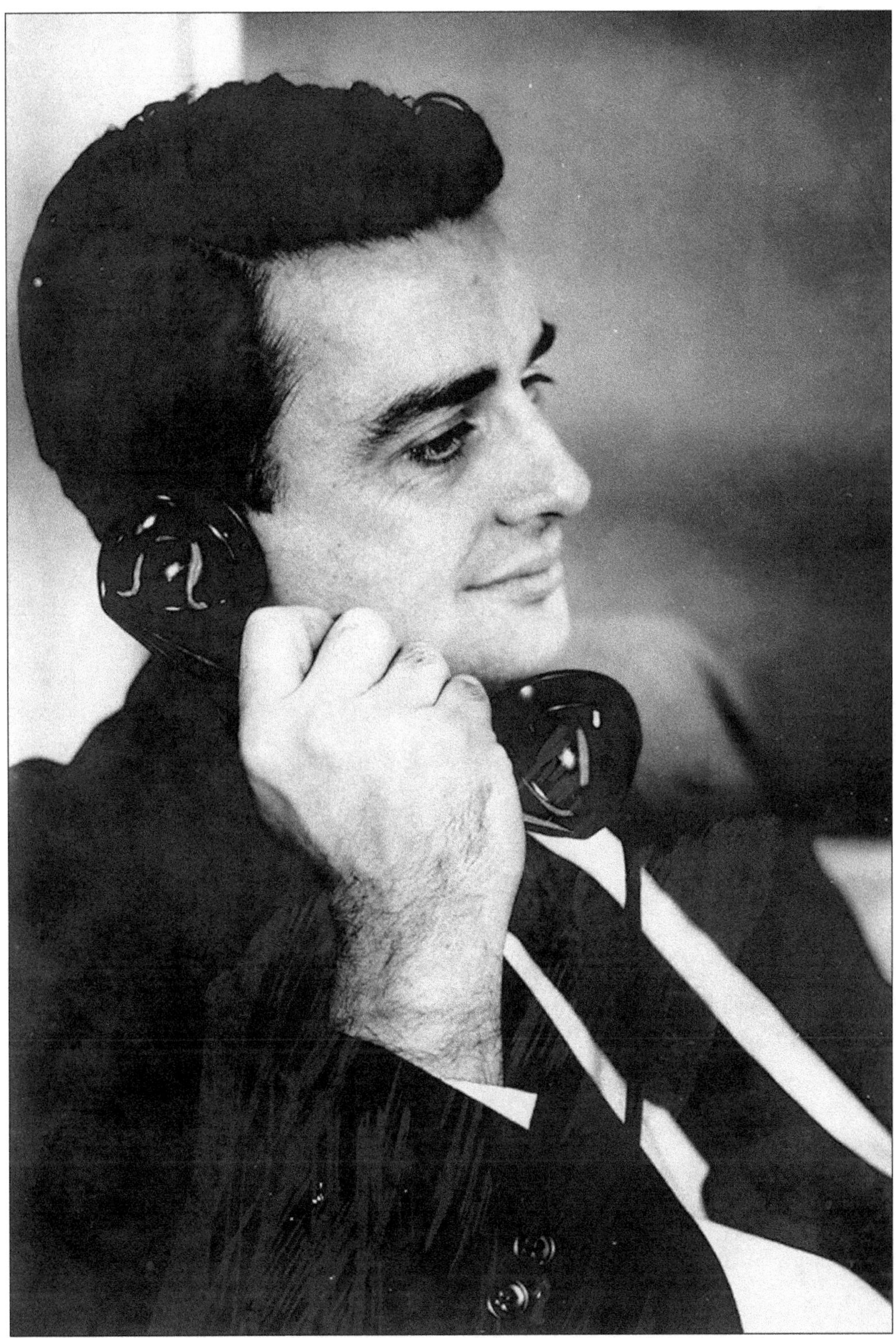

Edwin Land is on the telephone in his office. This Polaroid test photograph from 1945 is one of the earliest images of Land on instant film.

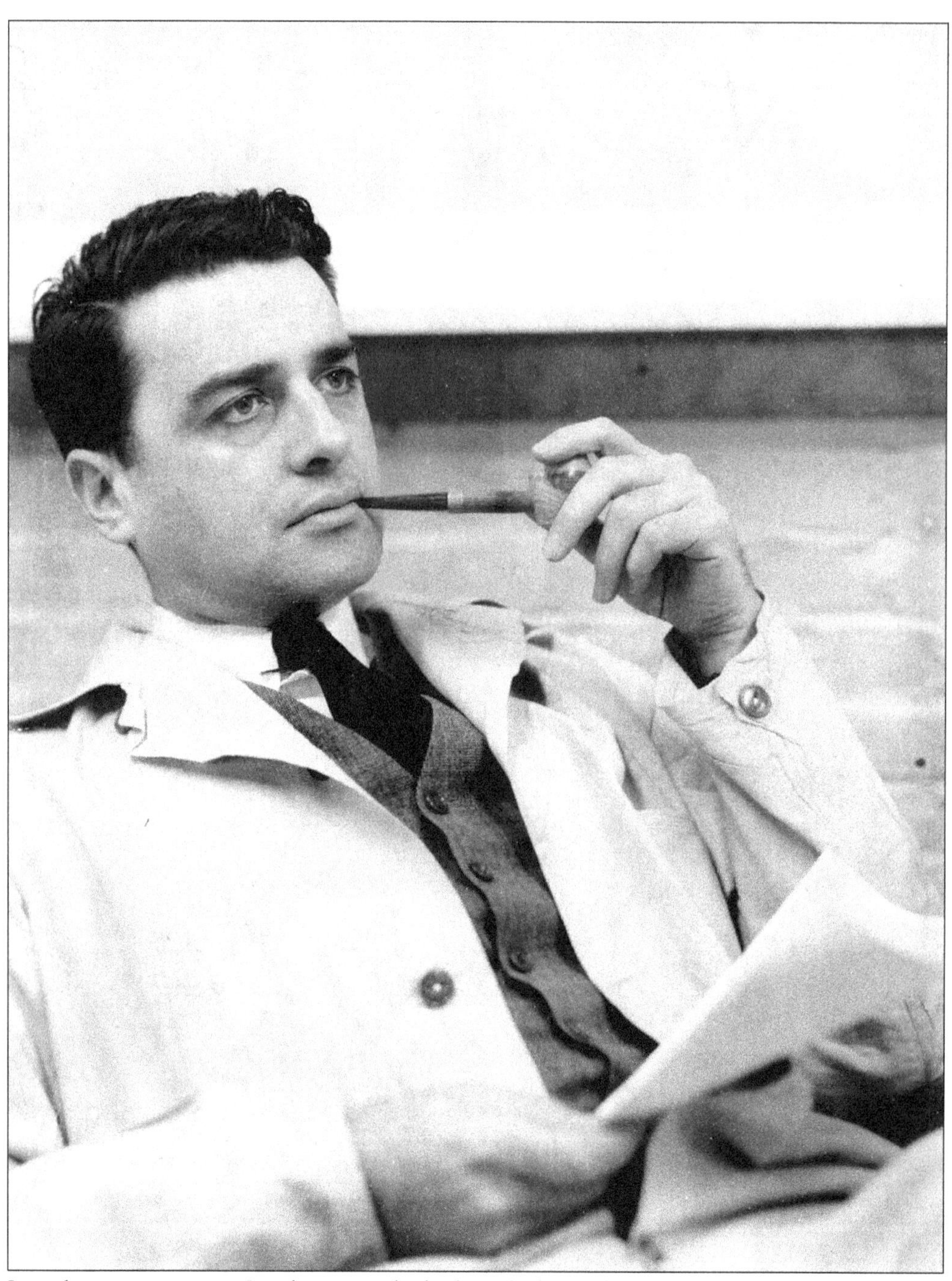

In a characteristic pose, Land seems to be looking far beyond the immediate challenges he and his company are facing. At the time this 1947 test photograph was taken, Land had committed the company and most of its resources to the development of instant photography.

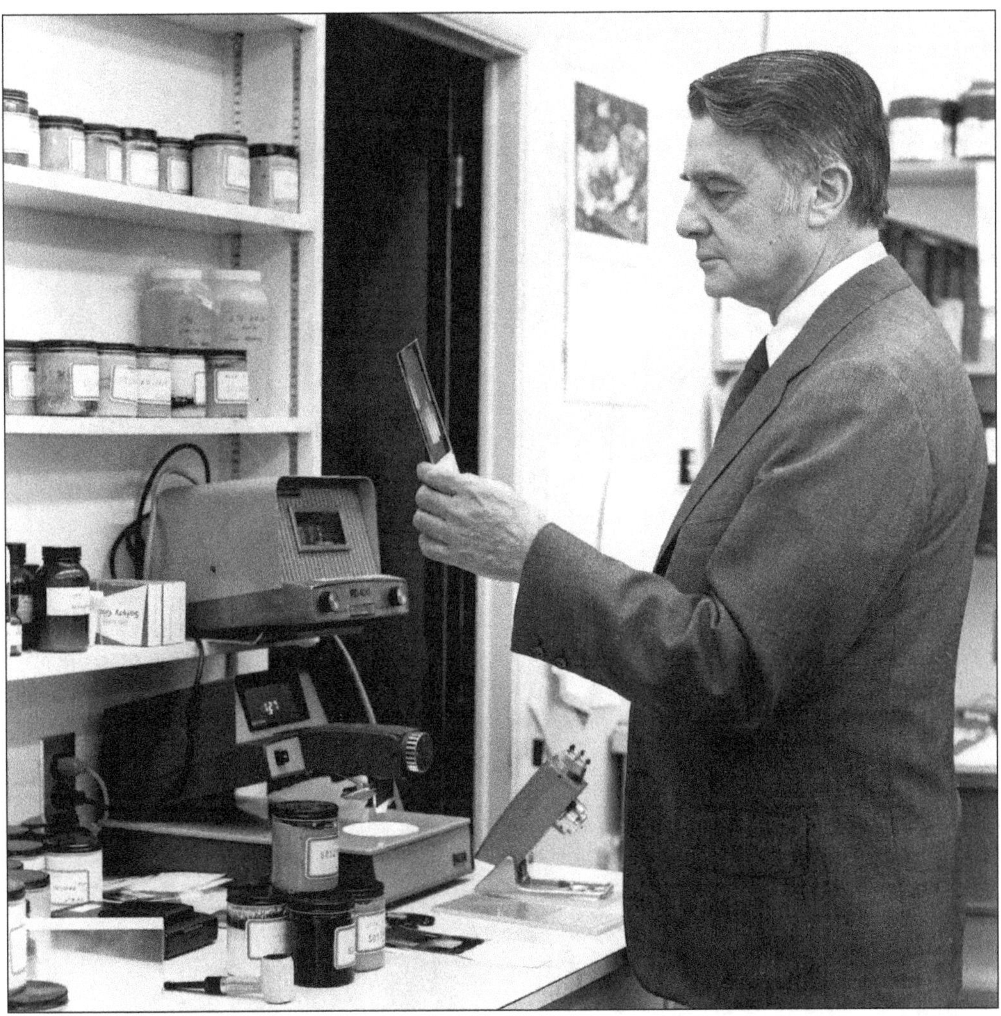

Land was still often a creature of the laboratory, as this photograph reveals. "The second great product of industry should be the rewarding working life for every person." —Edwin H. Land.

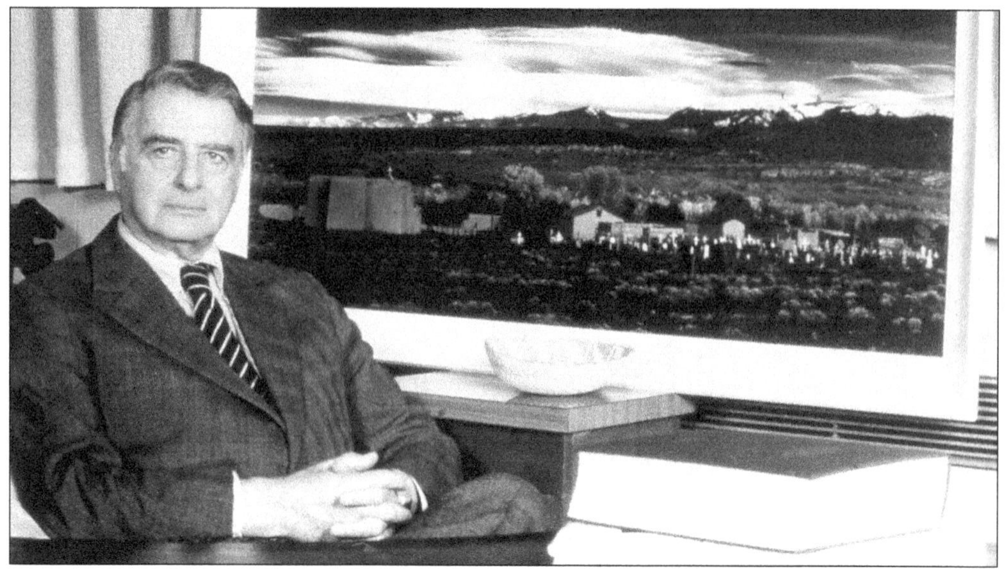

"Industry at its best is the intersection of science and art." —Edwin H. Land. Land is shown here in his office with one of the more famous western landscapes captured by black-and-white master Ansel Adams. Adams and his wife, Virginia, became friends with the Lands and often hosted them on vacations. Adams became fond of Polaroid as a photographic medium and provided a high-profile endorsement of instant photography. Land stated, "Ansel Adams transformed the photography of nature into an art free of sentimentality. His faith, talent and insight have taught and inspired all of us."

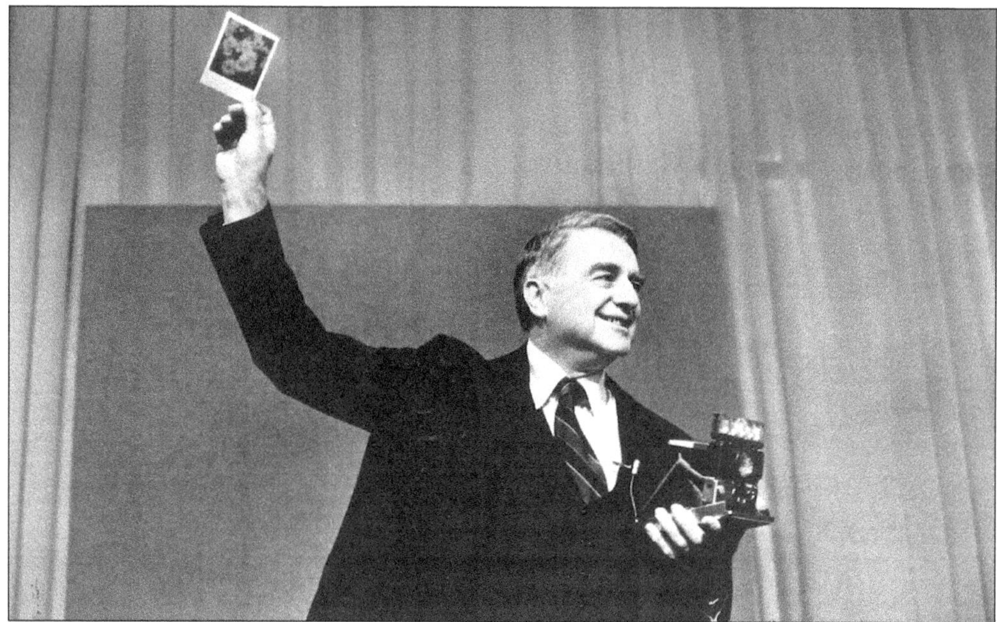

"I have long aspired to make our company a noble prototype of industry, penetrating in science, reliable in engineering, creative in aesthetics and wholesomely prosperous in economics." —Edwin H. Land. In this photograph, Land looks exuberant as he demonstrates the new SX-70 Time Zero film at the 1979 annual meeting.

Two

Land's Curiosity Shop

Like many other people of exceptional talent, Edwin Land could work alone, single-mindedly, and without difficulty for long periods. But unlike some, he could also work well collaboratively. As the polarization technology he invented moved from the laboratory to large-scale commercialization, Land found he needed others, and he learned the new role of entrepreneur and manager. Launching the business that eventually grew into Polaroid began with the formation of Land-Wheelwright Laboratories, an enterprise first started at the suggestion of Land's colleague George Wheelwright, a Harvard physics section leader who also provided the initial funding.

On the strength of Land's patents and continued innovations in polarization, Land-Wheelwright quickly showed signs of becoming a success with products for the scientific market and a contract to produce polarized sunglasses with the American Optical Company. In the offing were 3-D movies, based on polarization, and the exciting but never-to-be-fulfilled prospects of installing Land's glare-reducing night-driving polarized headlamps on every car in America.

Land's gift for publicity matched his technical talents, and his products regularly got top billing in newspapers and magazines. High-profile applications for the likes of Helena Rubenstein, the New York Museum of Science and Industry's permanent exhibit demonstrating the application of polarized light in 1935, and the Chrysler exhibit at the 1939 New York World's Fair helped ensure that the company became increasingly familiar to the general public. But profitability was elusive, and more money was needed to sustain development of new markets and new products. So Wheelwright approached some private investors on Wall Street and came away with a multiyear financing deal that ended up sustaining the company into the war years.

Still, when the 50-employee company incorporated in 1937 under the name Polaroid Corporation, net sales totaled only $141,000. Indeed, it was only in 1941, with the first trickle of defense contracts beginning to pour in, that the company topped $1 million in sales. However, the Land-Wheelwright years and the first years of Polaroid set the pattern for what was to come: products that were fresh and imaginative based on patented technology that competitors could not touch. And Polaroid was no longer just Edwin Land and a laboratory. It was a company with a unique culture, ready to thrive on new challenges, no matter how daunting.

In a 1978 letter to shareholders, Land wrote: "Fifty years after we undertook to make the first synthetic polarizers we find them the essential layer in digital liquid-crystal. And thirty four years after we undertook to make the first instant camera and film, our kind of photography has become ubiquitous."

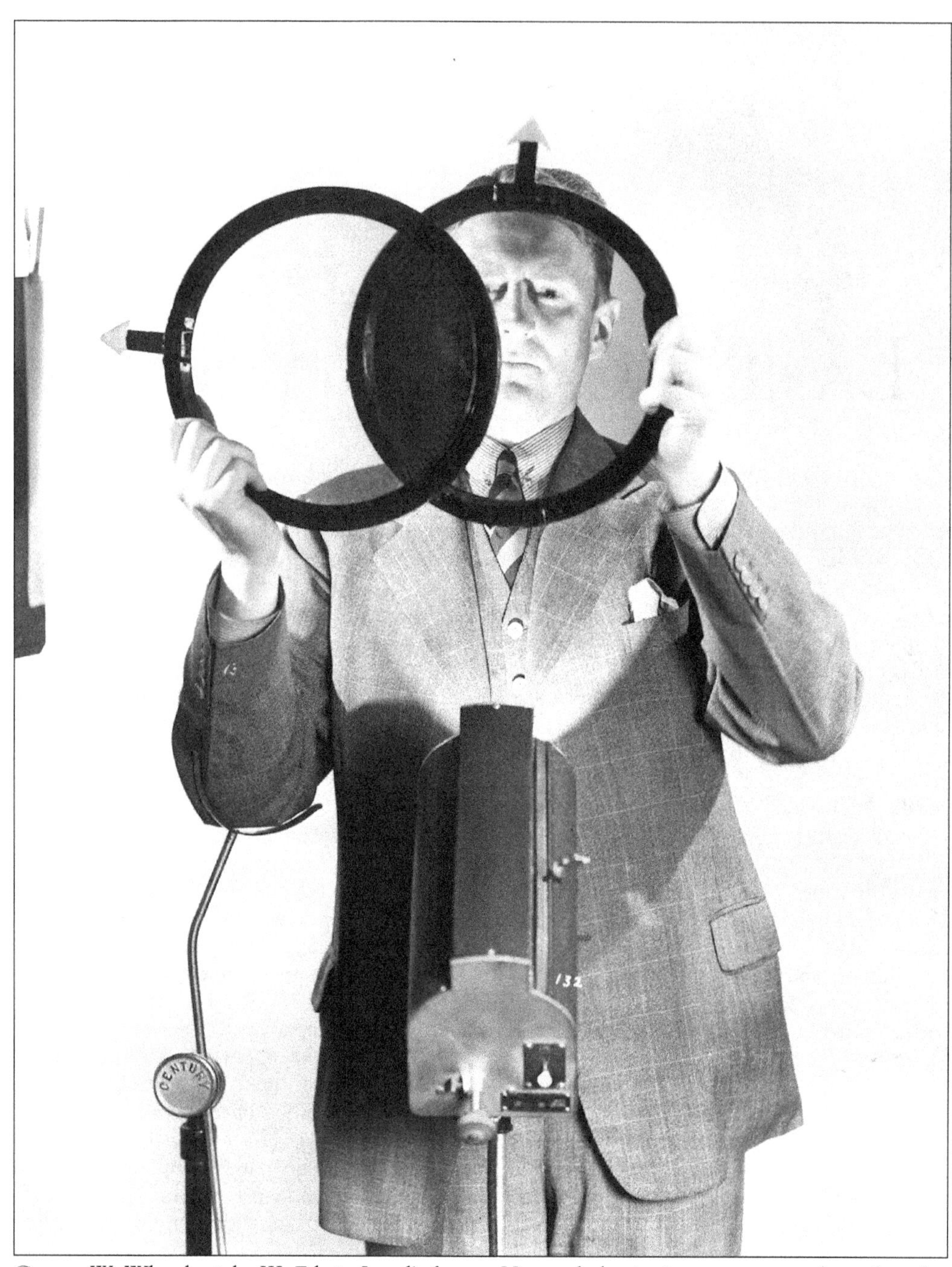

George W. Wheelwright III, Edwin Land's former Harvard physics instructor, was the cofounder of the Land-Wheelwright Laboratories, which was incorporated in 1933 to manufacture polarizers and develop commercial products. Wheelwright helped provide initial funding for the company and, in the 1930s, attracted key investors. In this photograph, he is holding large polarizing filters with axes denoted by the projecting arrows on each.

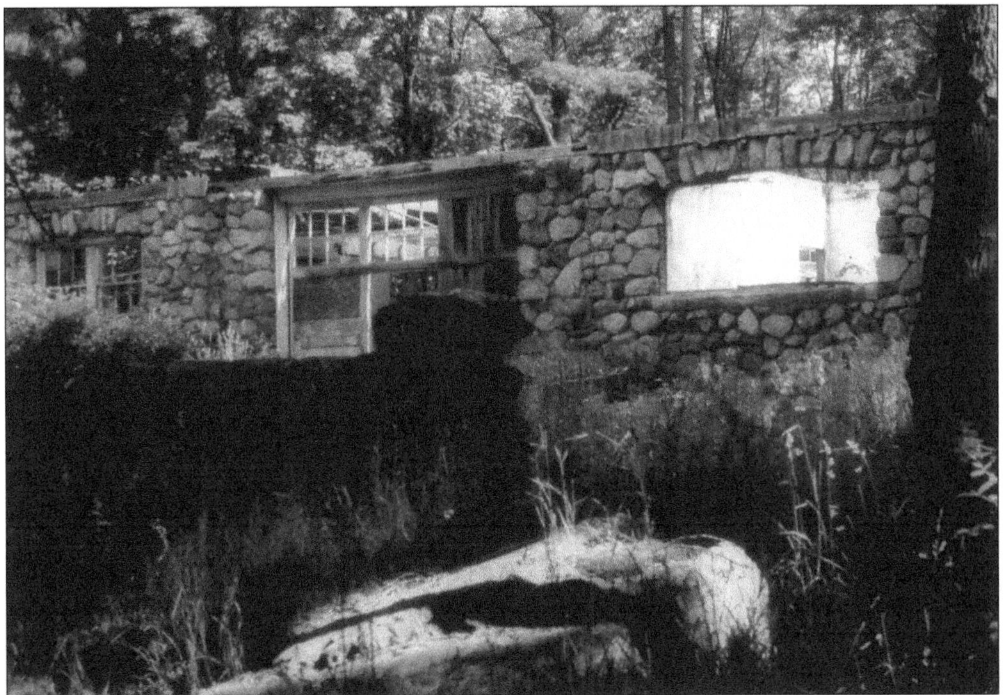

Land-Wheelwright Laboratories moved its first one-room shop on top of the Harvard Square garage to this Wellesley Hills dairy barn to set up its first laboratory.

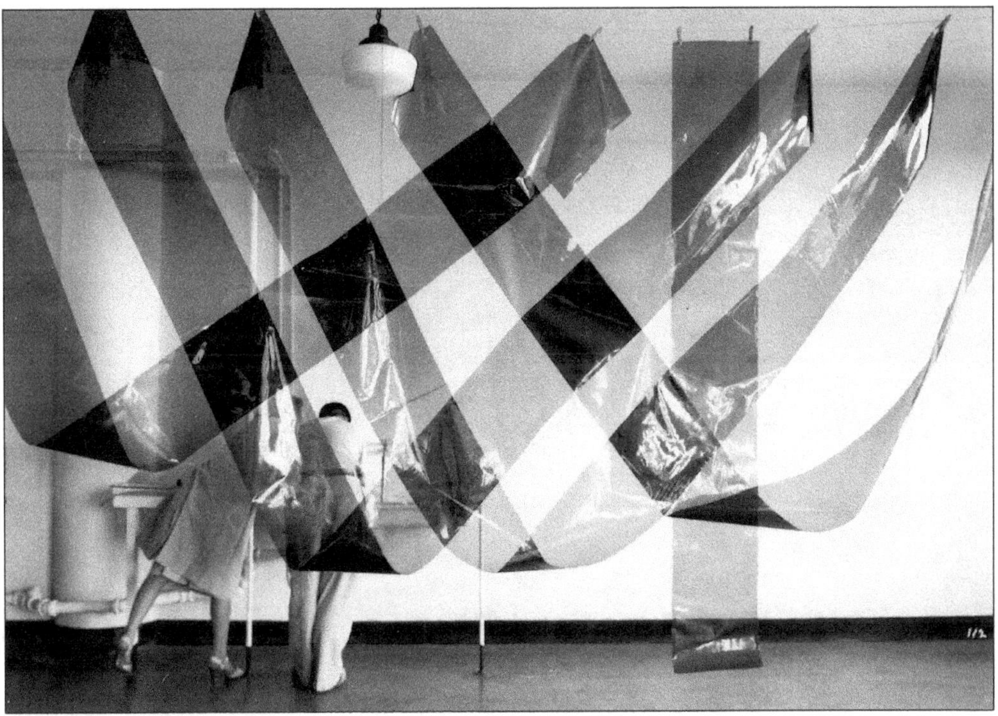

Polarizing strips are hanging from the wall while lab employees work.

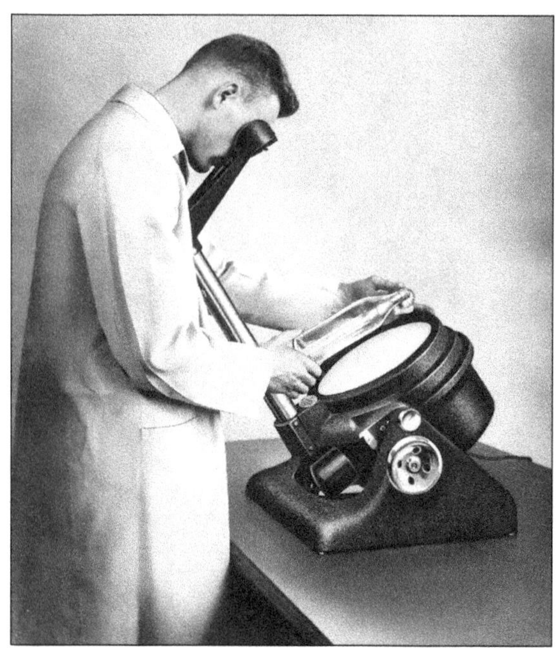

The Polariscope was developed to detect strains in materials like glass and certain plastics. The strained areas appear colored when seen by polarized light. In a 1938 photograph, Al Bachelder is testing a large bottle.

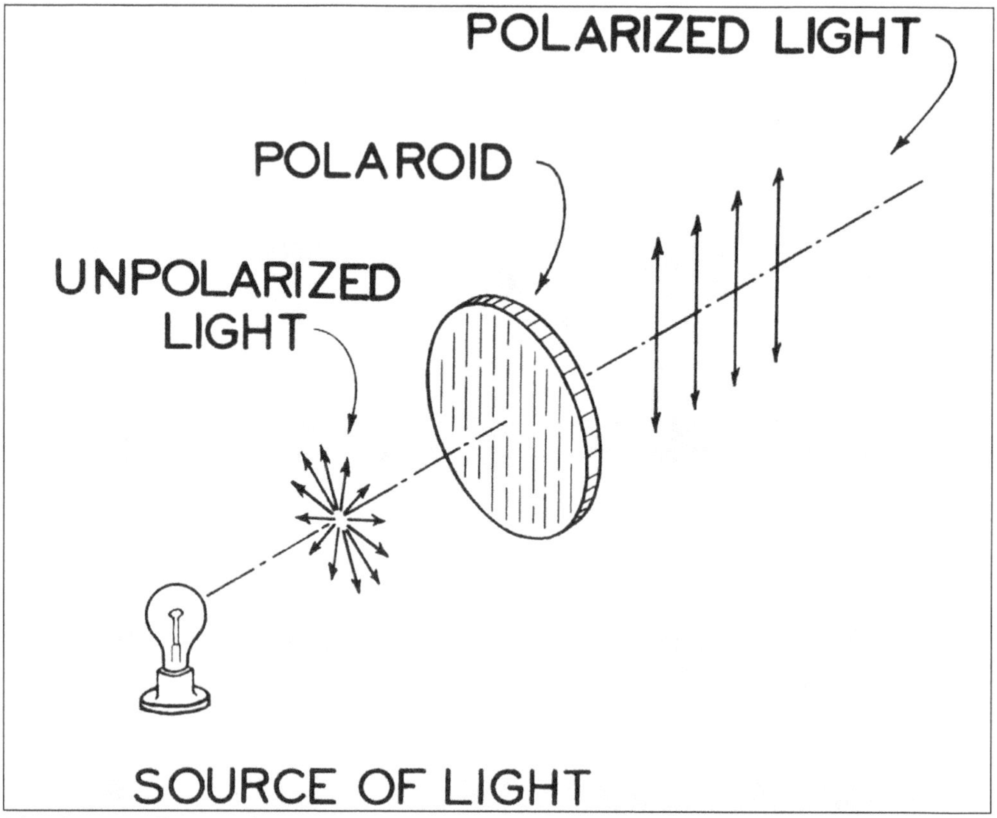

POLARIZED LIGHT

POLAROID

UNPOLARIZED LIGHT

SOURCE OF LIGHT

This diagram illustrates how normal unpolarized light, in this case from an incandescent lamp, tends to scatter at right angles to a given ray. By contrast, only light waves operating in one plane are able to pass through the polarizer.

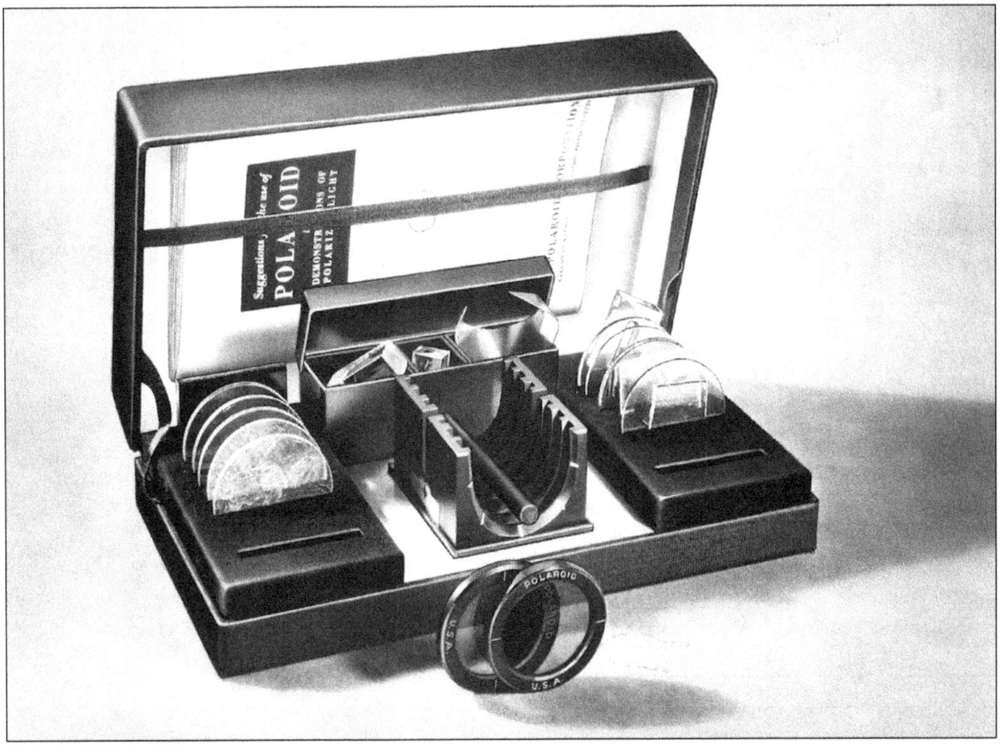

Land-Wheelwright Laboratories sold school kits to demonstrate the polarization of light. This example is from 1938.

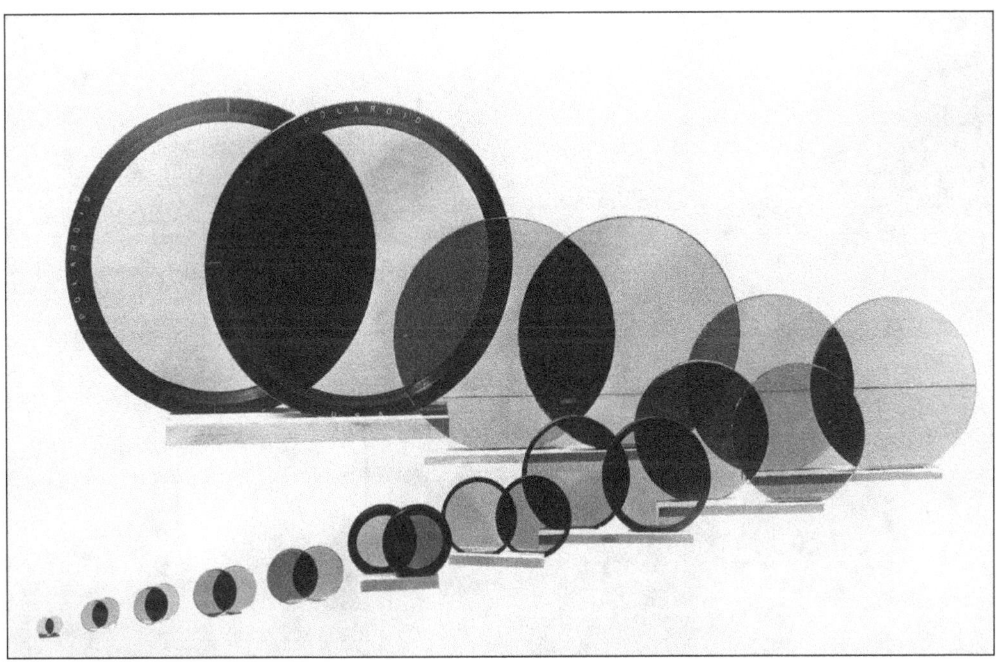

This display of polarizing filters showcases the largest to the smallest of the products manufactured by Polaroid. They were produced in many colors, shapes, and sizes.

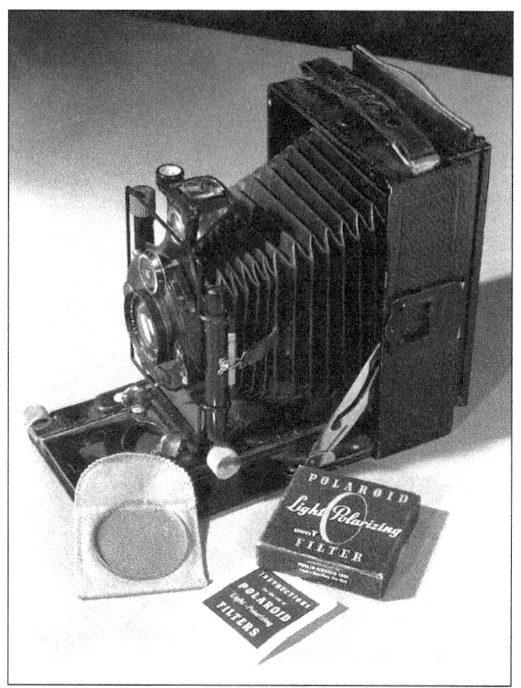

The first order for light-polarizing filters was signed with Kodak in 1934. This order was filled by Edwin Land, Helen Land (his wife), Ernest Calabro, Bob Blake, and George Wheelwright.

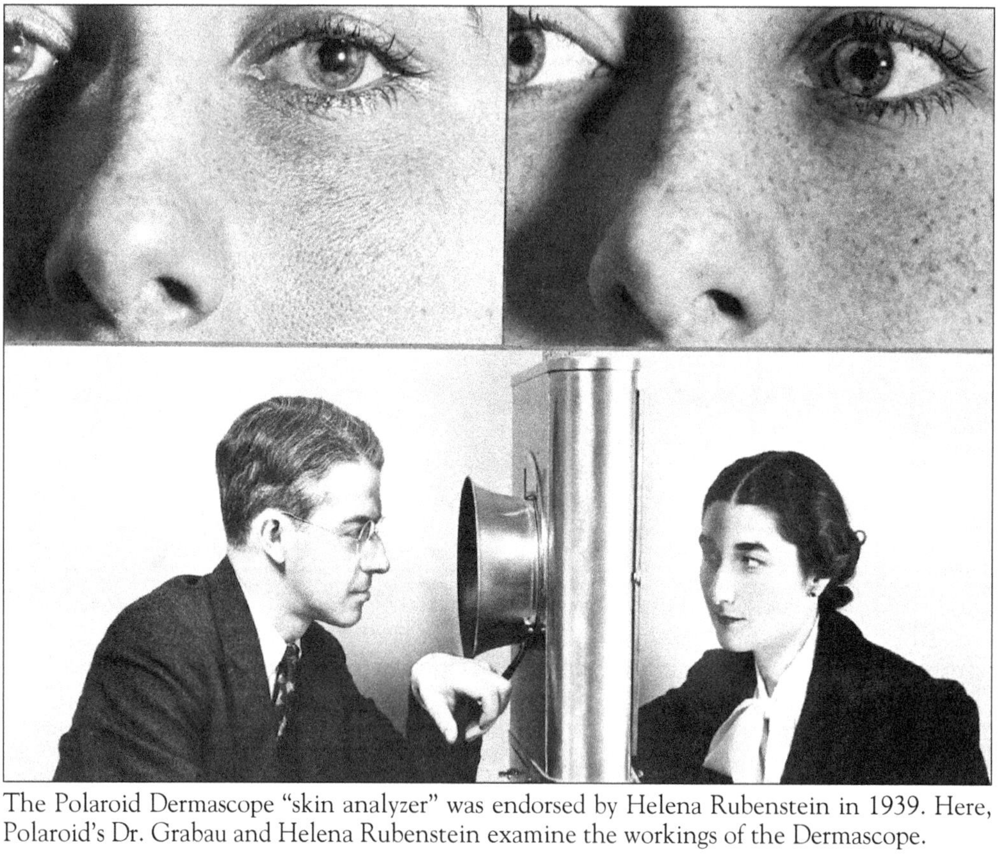

The Polaroid Dermascope "skin analyzer" was endorsed by Helena Rubenstein in 1939. Here, Polaroid's Dr. Grabau and Helena Rubenstein examine the workings of the Dermascope.

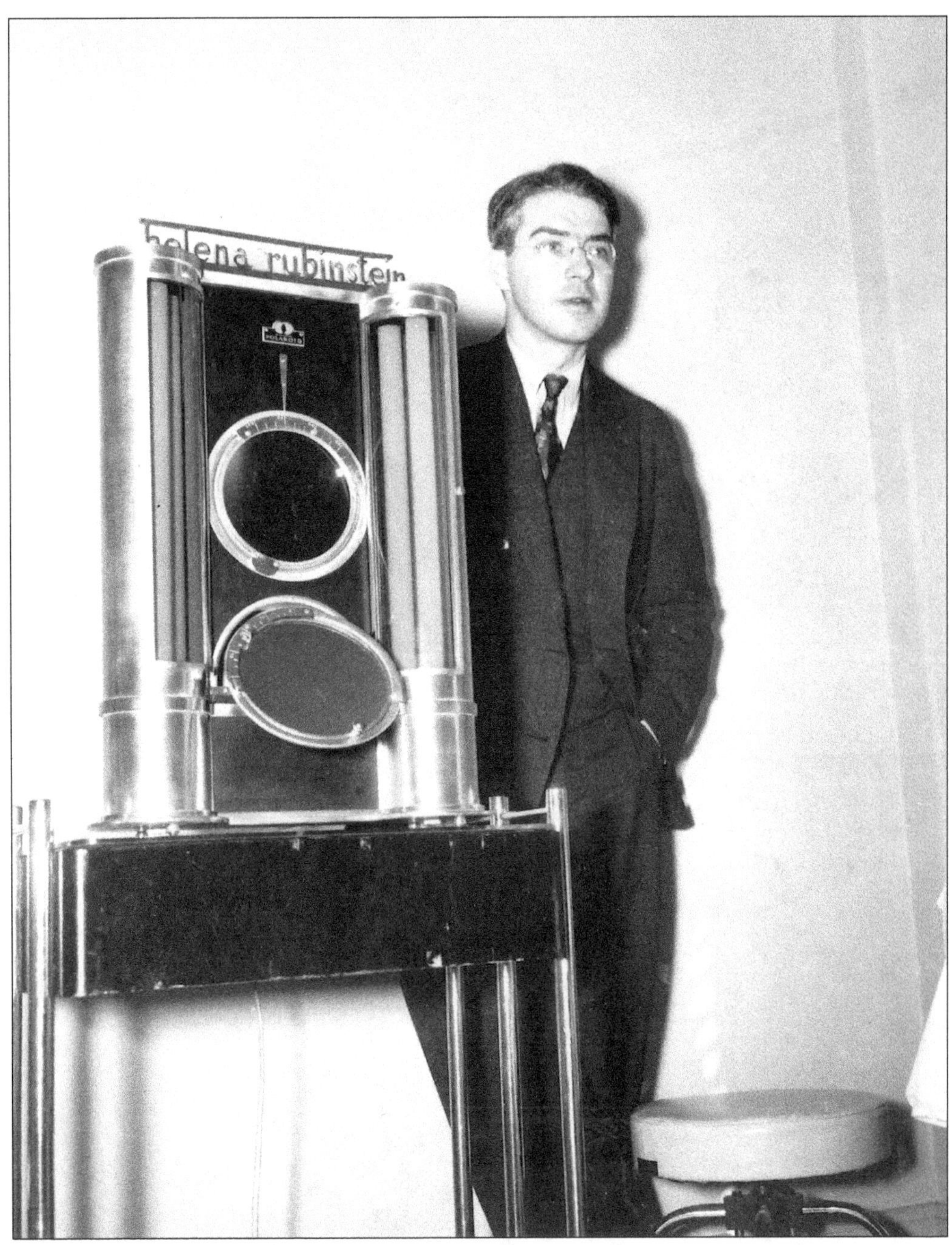

Dr. Grabau stands beside the Dermascope.

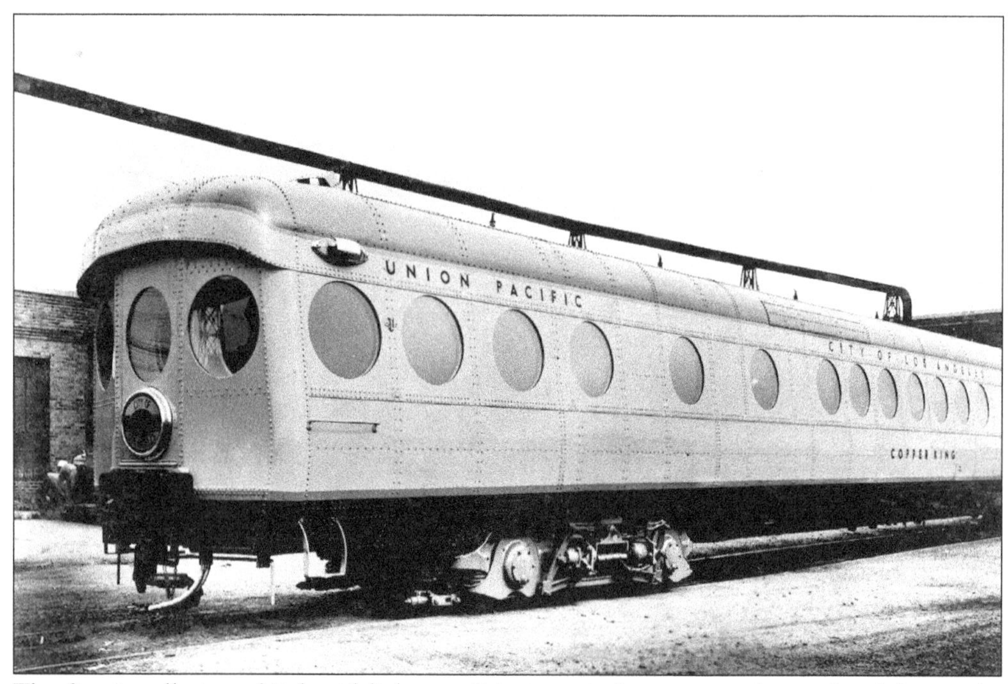

The first installation of Polaroid light-conditioning windows was made on the club car of a Union Pacific streamliner in 1938.

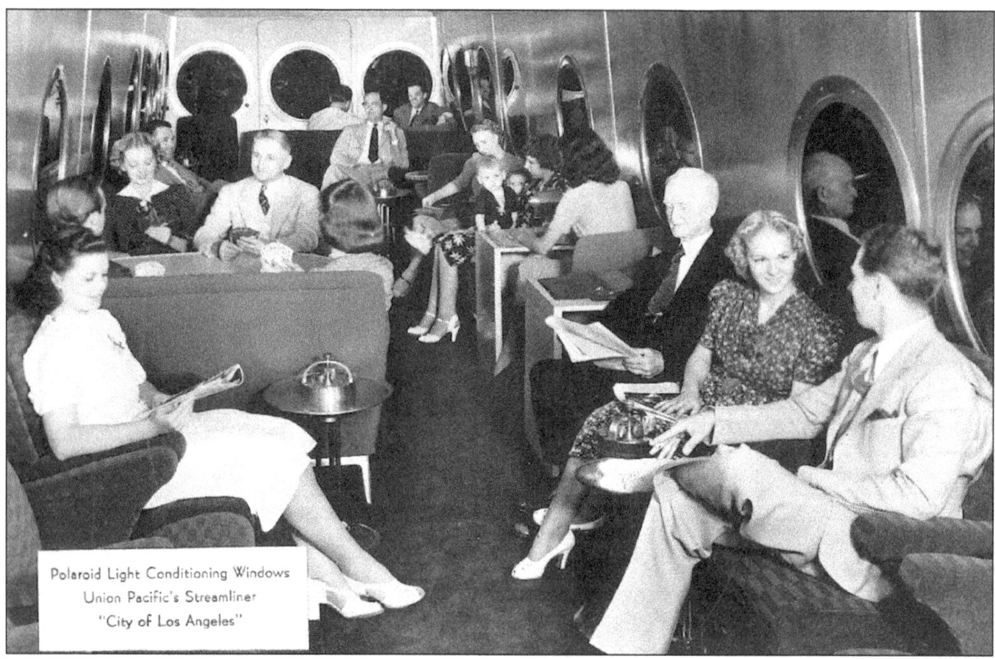

This view of the interior of the Copper King—a club car in Union Pacific's *City of Los Angeles* train—shows the passengers surrounded by Polaroid light-conditioning windows. Each window has two polarizers. The outer one is fixed. When the axis of the inner polarizer rotates, the window darkens until it blocks out all light.

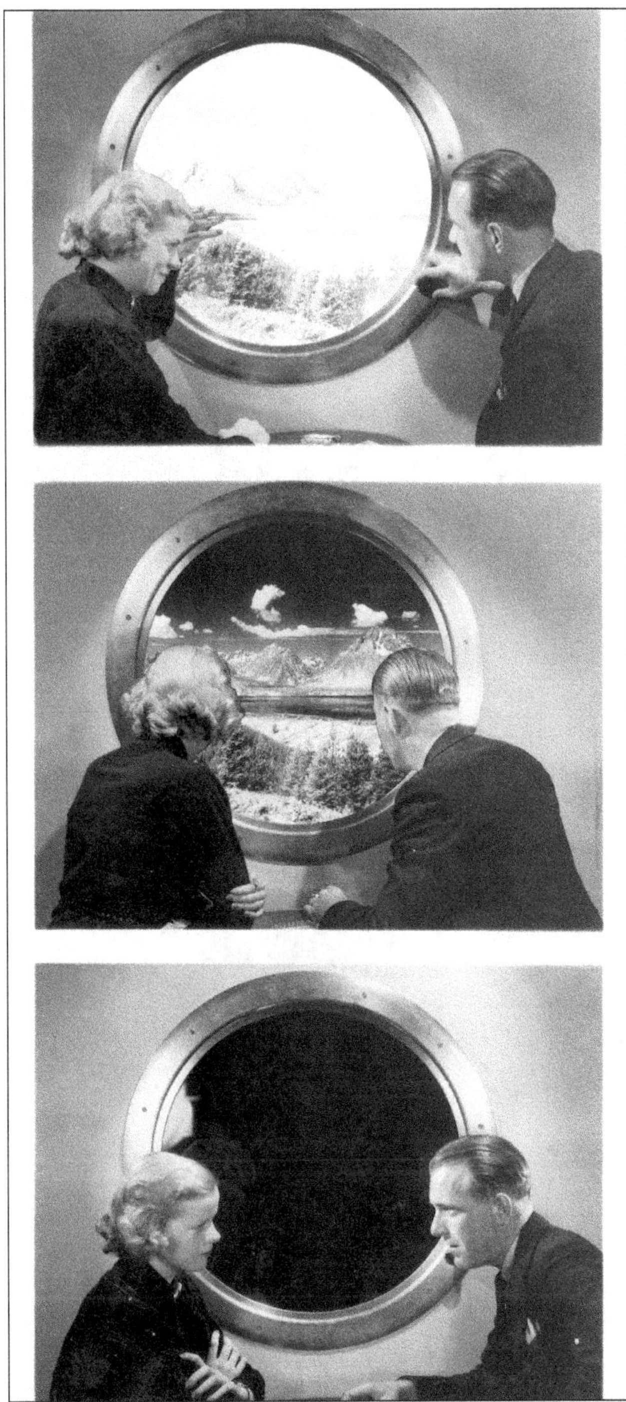

In these advertising photographs, the wonders of the Copper King polarizing windows are clearly demonstrated. In the first view, the outside is deemed "too bright." In a second view, with a turn of the control knob of the Polaroid light-conditioning windows, the brilliance is brought down to a more comfortable level. For passengers who want privacy or even less light, a further turn of the knob cuts off the view entirely in the third view.

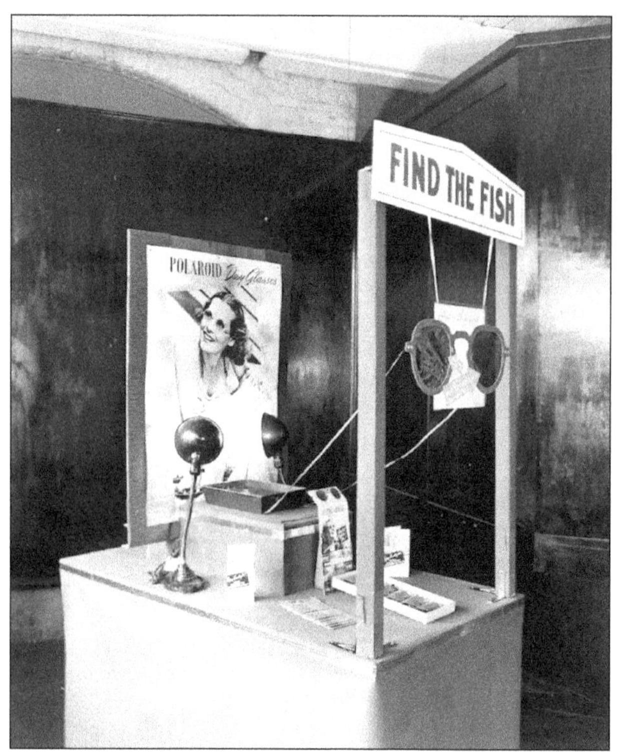

Entitled "Find the Fish," this window display of Polaroid day glasses appeared in 1941 at the company's Albany Street facility in Boston. When Edwin Land in 1935 displayed his invention to a representative of the American Optical Company, he placed a bowl of goldfish beside the window so the sun shone through, the glare making it impossible to see the fish. He then placed his sheet polarizer in front of the bowl so that the swimming fish could be seen clearly. The demonstration helped convince American Optical to work with the fledgling firm. This display reprises that key moment for visitors to the facility.

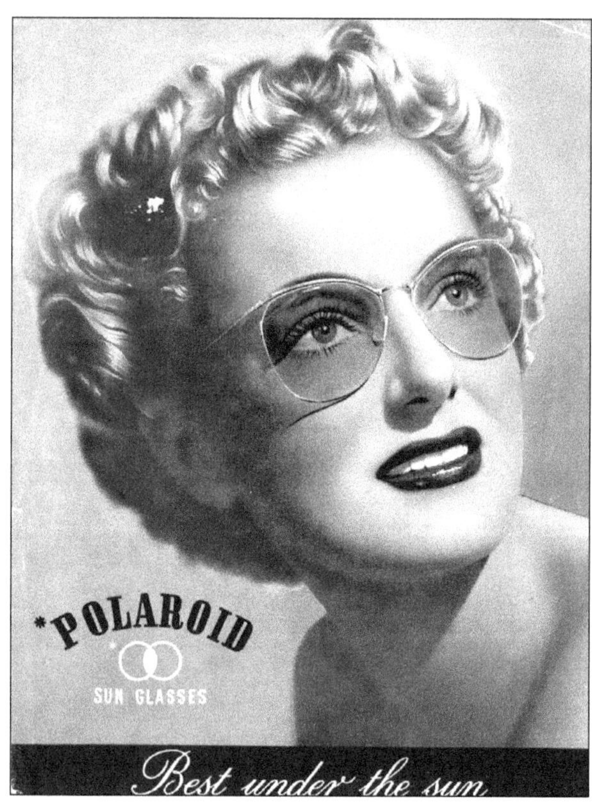

This color pamphlet extols the virtues of Polaroid sunglasses.

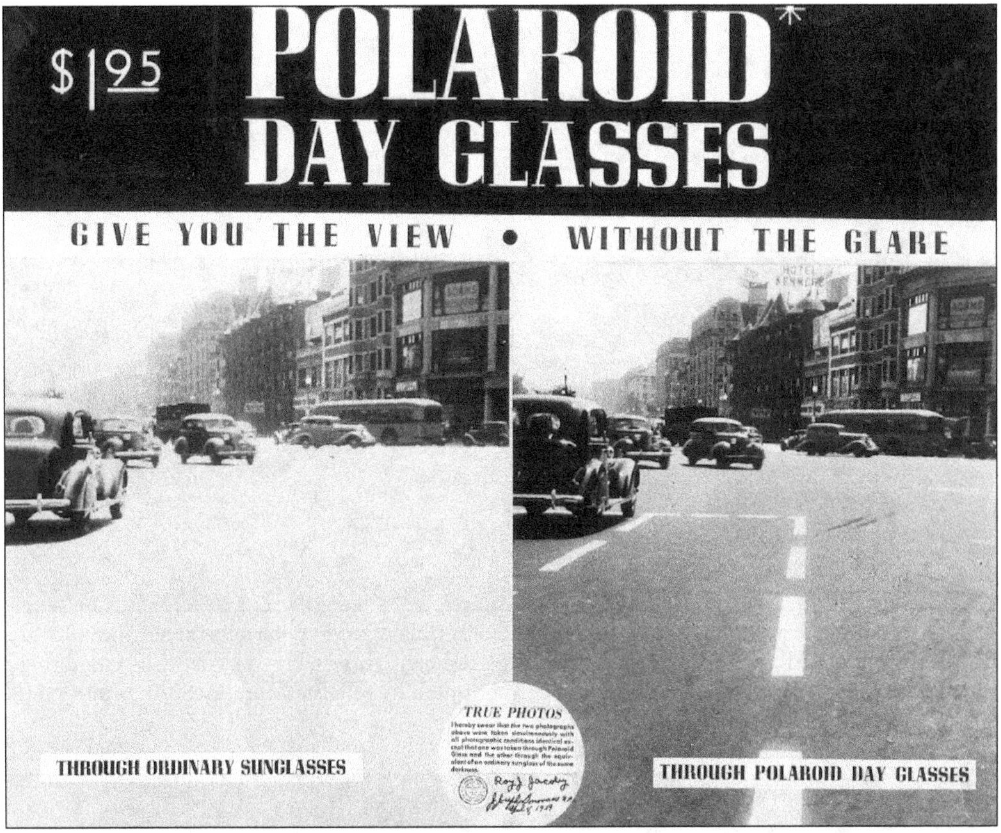

$1.95 **POLAROID***
DAY GLASSES

GIVE YOU THE VIEW • WITHOUT THE GLARE

THROUGH ORDINARY SUNGLASSES

TRUE PHOTOS

Roy J. Jacoby

THROUGH POLAROID DAY GLASSES

The advertisement for Polaroid day glasses shows traffic and glare in Boston's Kenmore Square. Notice the "certification" as to the authenticity of the photographs, signed by company photographer Roy J. Jacoby.

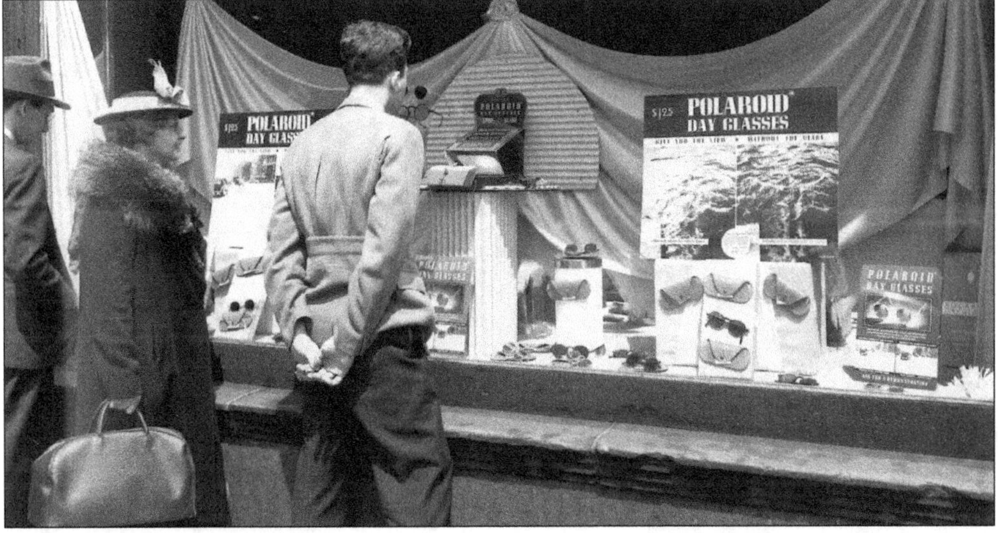

This June 1939 display of Polaroid glasses at a pharmacy shows the prominence and popularity of the company's products at the time.

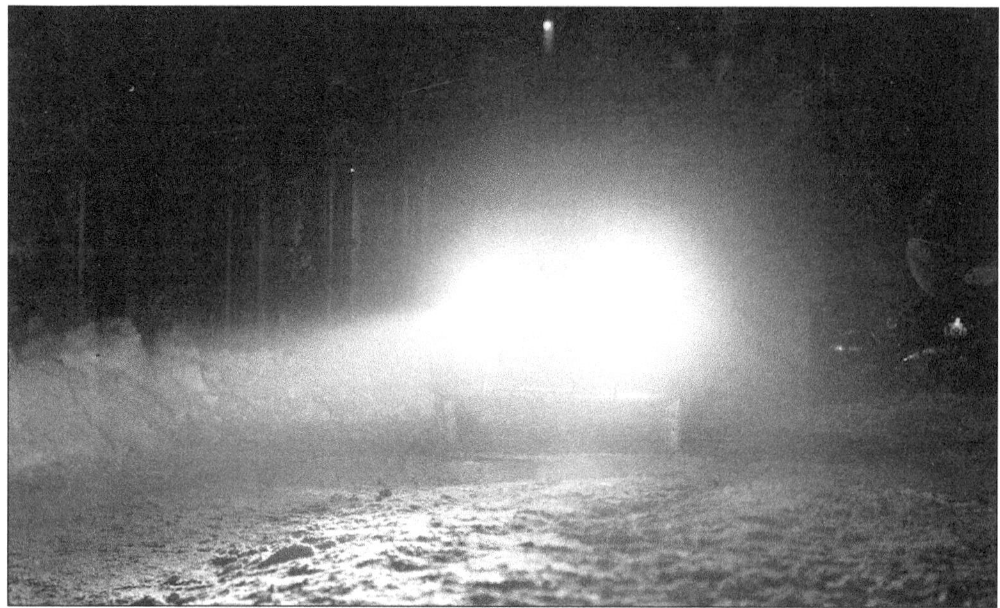

This sequence of photographs demonstrates the potential of Land's polarizers for automobile use. Land-Wheelwright Laboratories tested its antiglare headlights at Harvard Yard in Cambridge in 1936. In this photograph, glare from the conventional headlights of an oncoming car renders nearly everything else in the scene invisible.

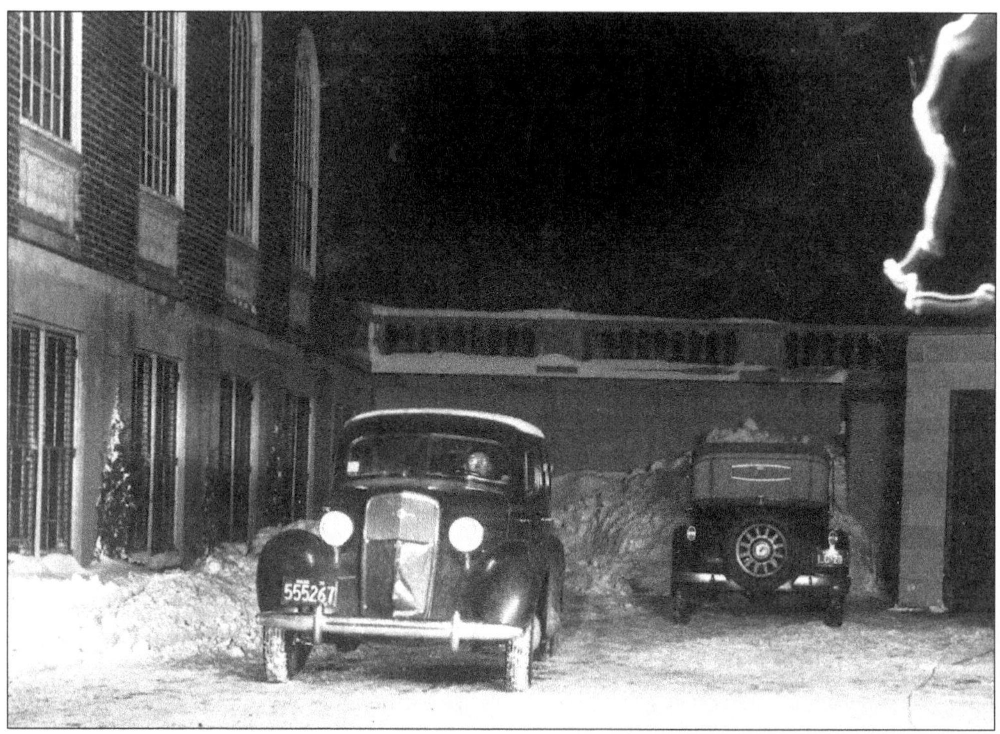

This Ford coupe is equipped with polarizing antiglare headlights that eliminate glare and improve visibility.

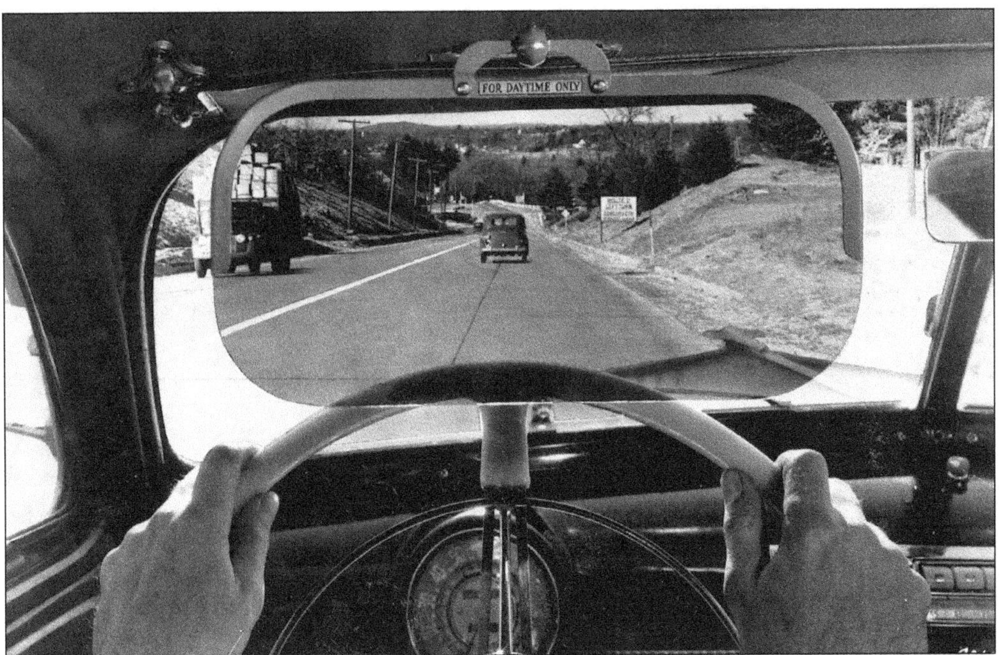

The Polaroid day driving visor was introduced in 1945 to eliminate glare from the sun. This view shows clearly how the visor could enhance daytime driving. The view is of Route 2 at Crosby's Corner on the Concord-Lincoln line, heading west.

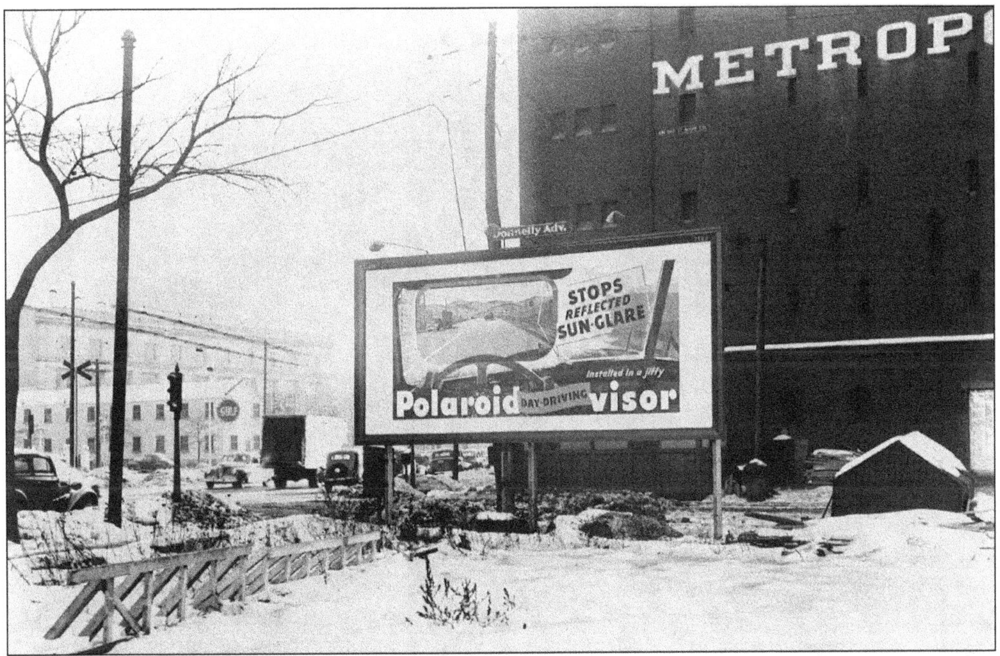

This wintertime view shows a billboard on Massachusetts Avenue in Cambridge, near the Massachusetts Institute of Technology (MIT) campus, advertising the Polaroid day driving visor. The Metropolitan Storage building remains a landmark on the site to this day.

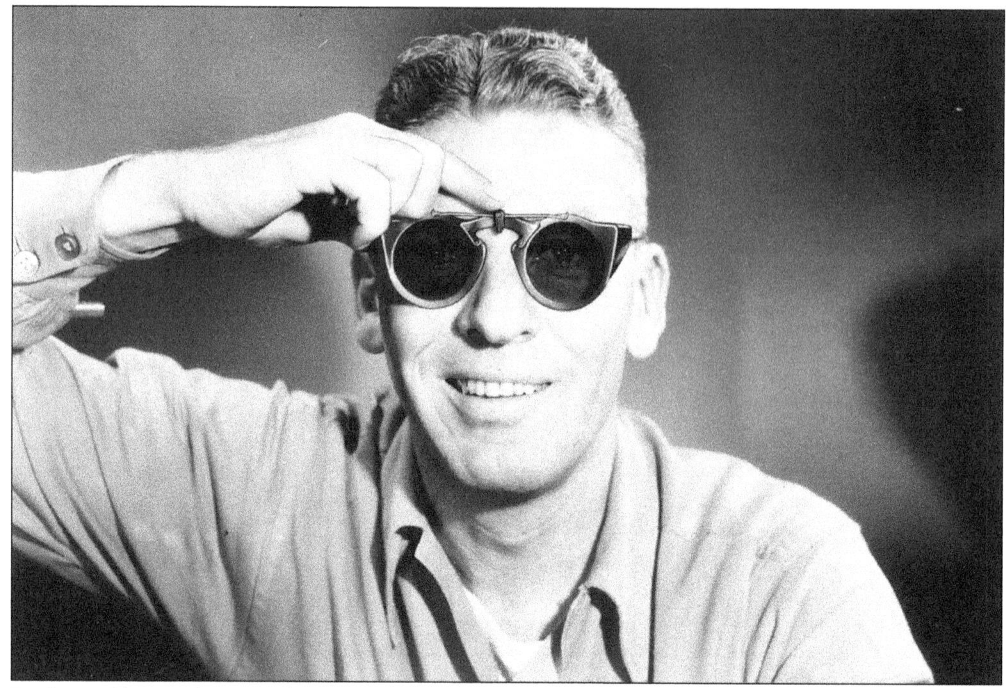

In this publicity photograph, a model has his finger on the adjustment lever of a pair of variable day glasses. This is the "normal" position—a flick of the finger can completely lighten or darken the apparent tint using the polarizing effect.

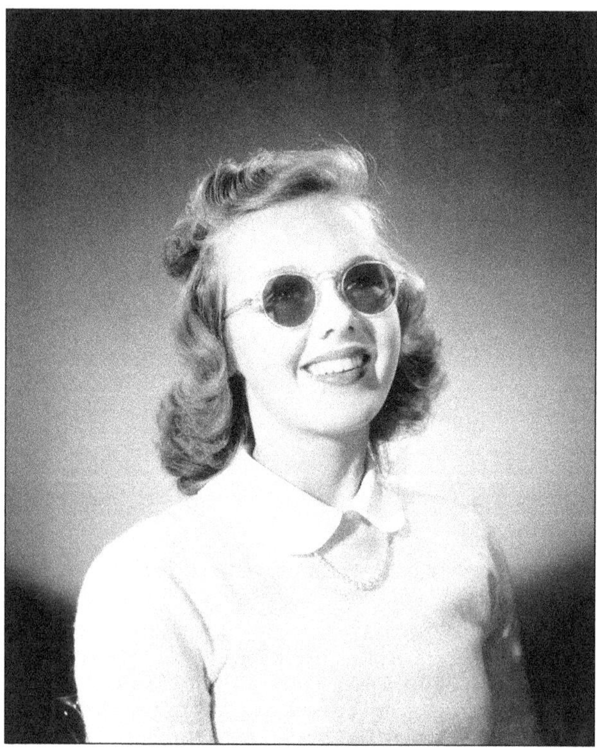

The American Optical Company signed a license agreement to use the polarizers for the manufacture of sunglasses and began selling them in December 1936 for $3.75 a pair, as shown in this publicity shot.

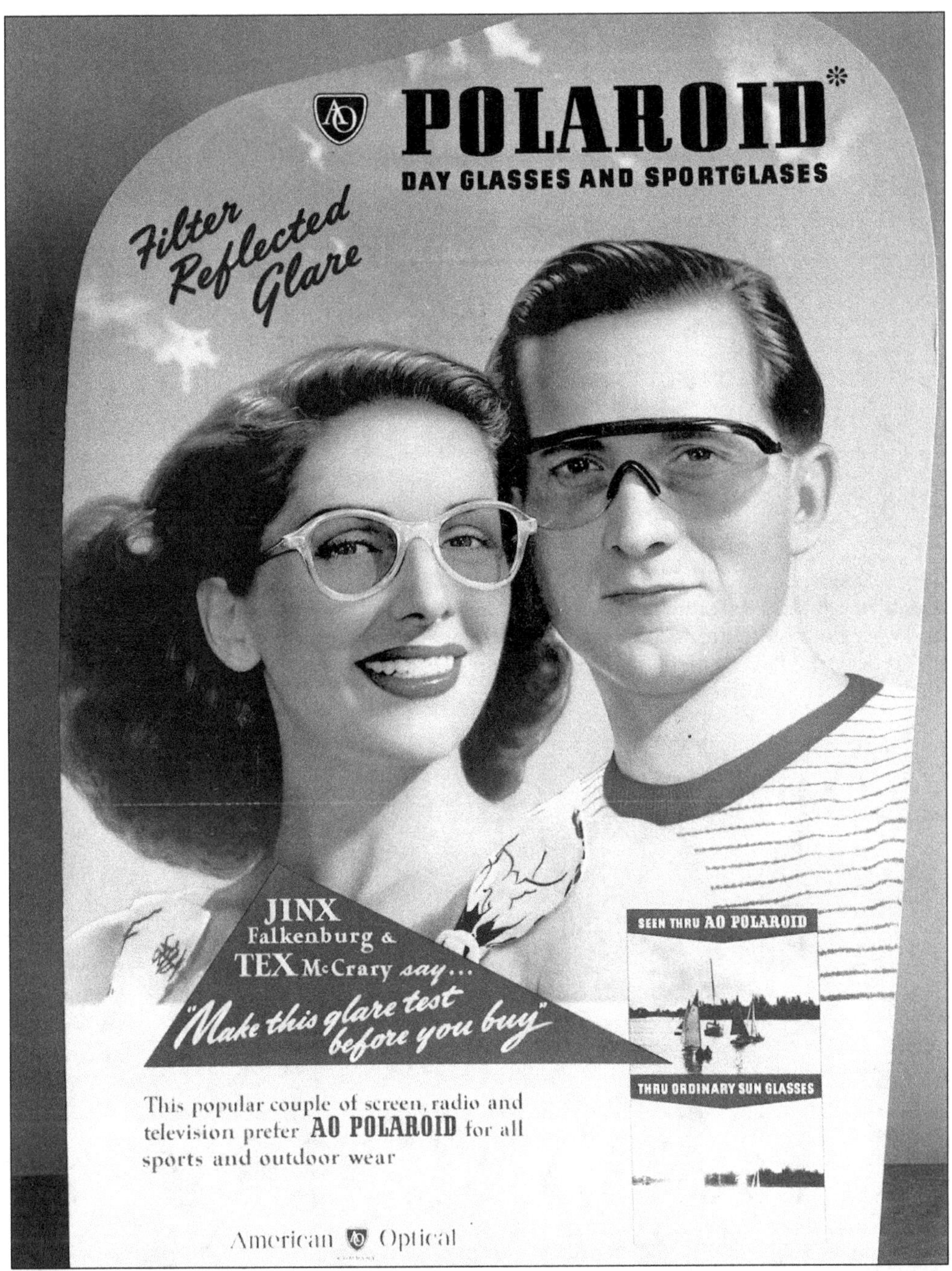

Right from the start, Polaroid employed the star power of celebrities for its publicity at every opportunity. Here, Jinx Falkenburg and Tex McCrary—radio and television personalities—show off Polaroid day glasses and sport glasses. The glasses were manufactured by the American Optical Company, located in Southbridge, Massachusetts. American Optical was then one of the largest makers of eyeglasses and other optical products in the world.

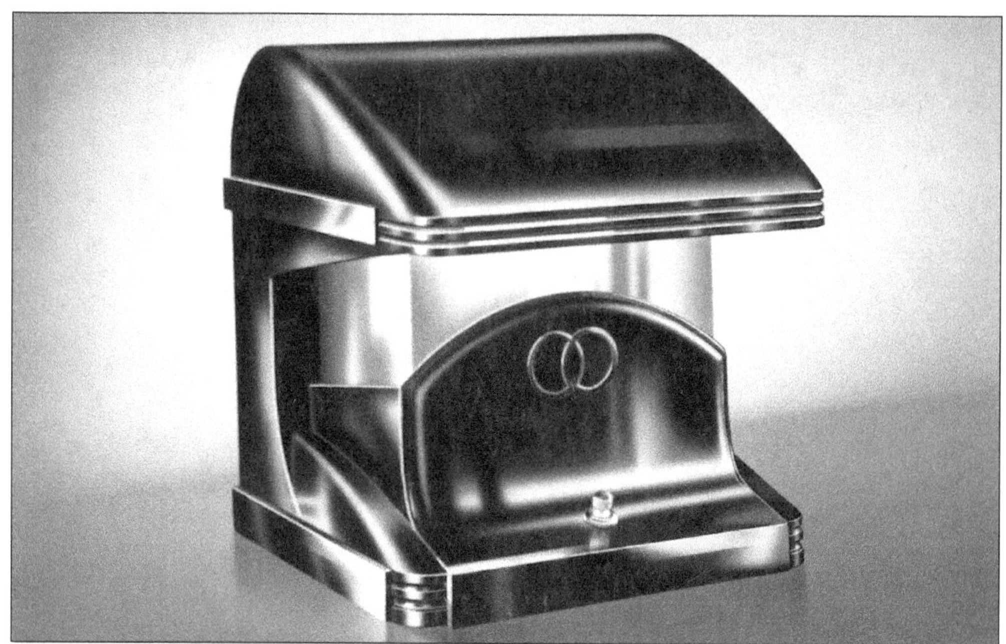

In 1938, Polaroid introduced several desk lamps using a polarizing sheet to eliminate the reflected glare. This Polaroid desk lamp was designed by Charles Baratelli and Prof. Clarence Kennedy.

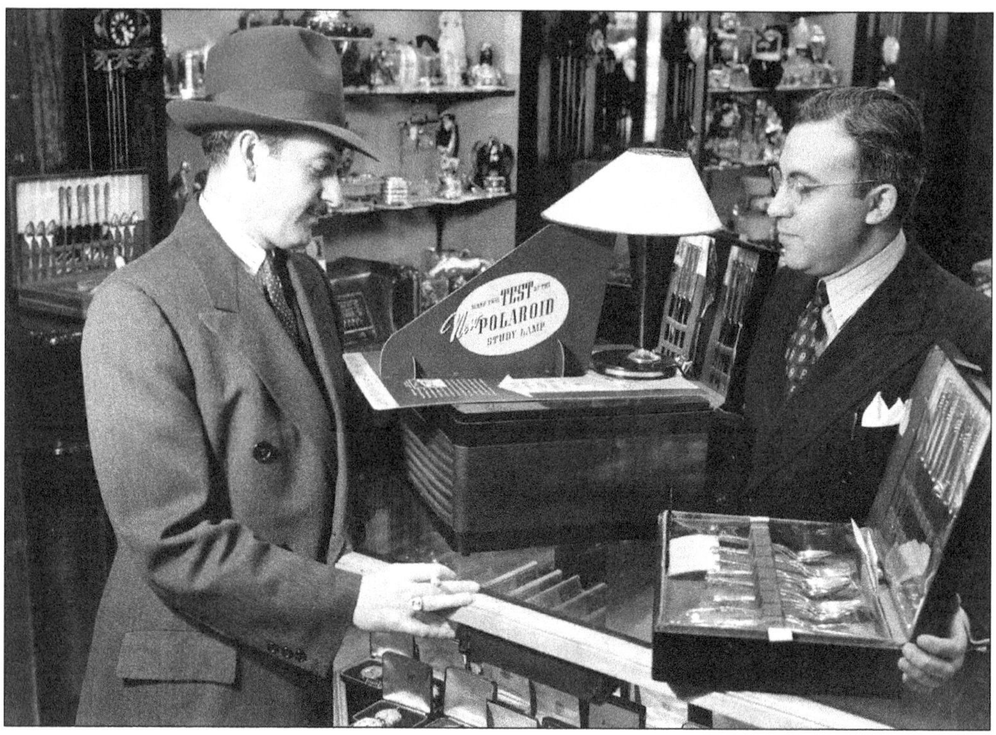

A Polaroid study lamp is being demonstrated here in the surroundings of high-priced luxury goods.

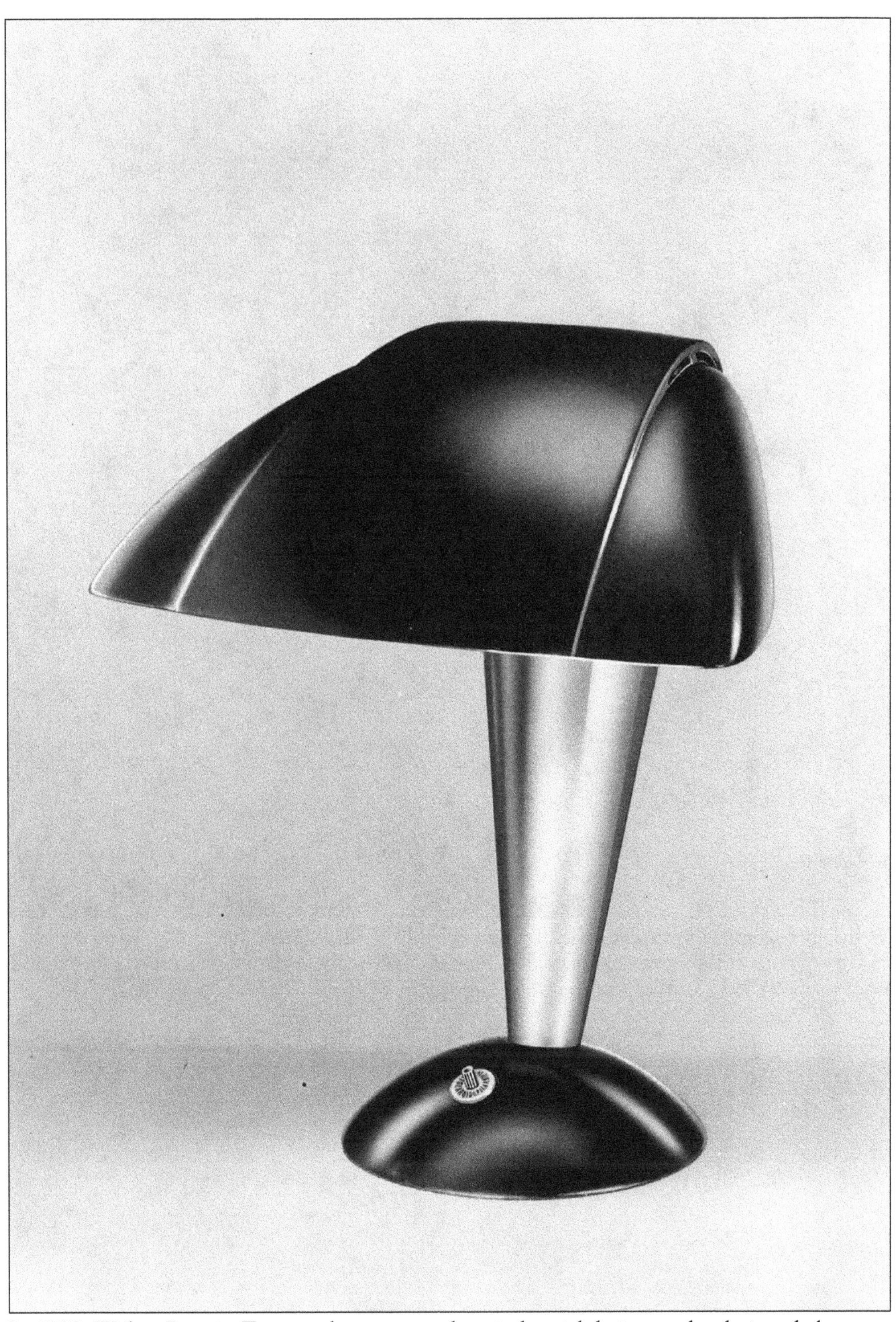

In 1939, Walter Dorwin Teague, the great art deco industrial designer who designed glassware for Steuben and gas stations for Texaco, redesigned the Polaroid desk lamp. Polaroid continued to incorporate the finest design in its products throughout its history.

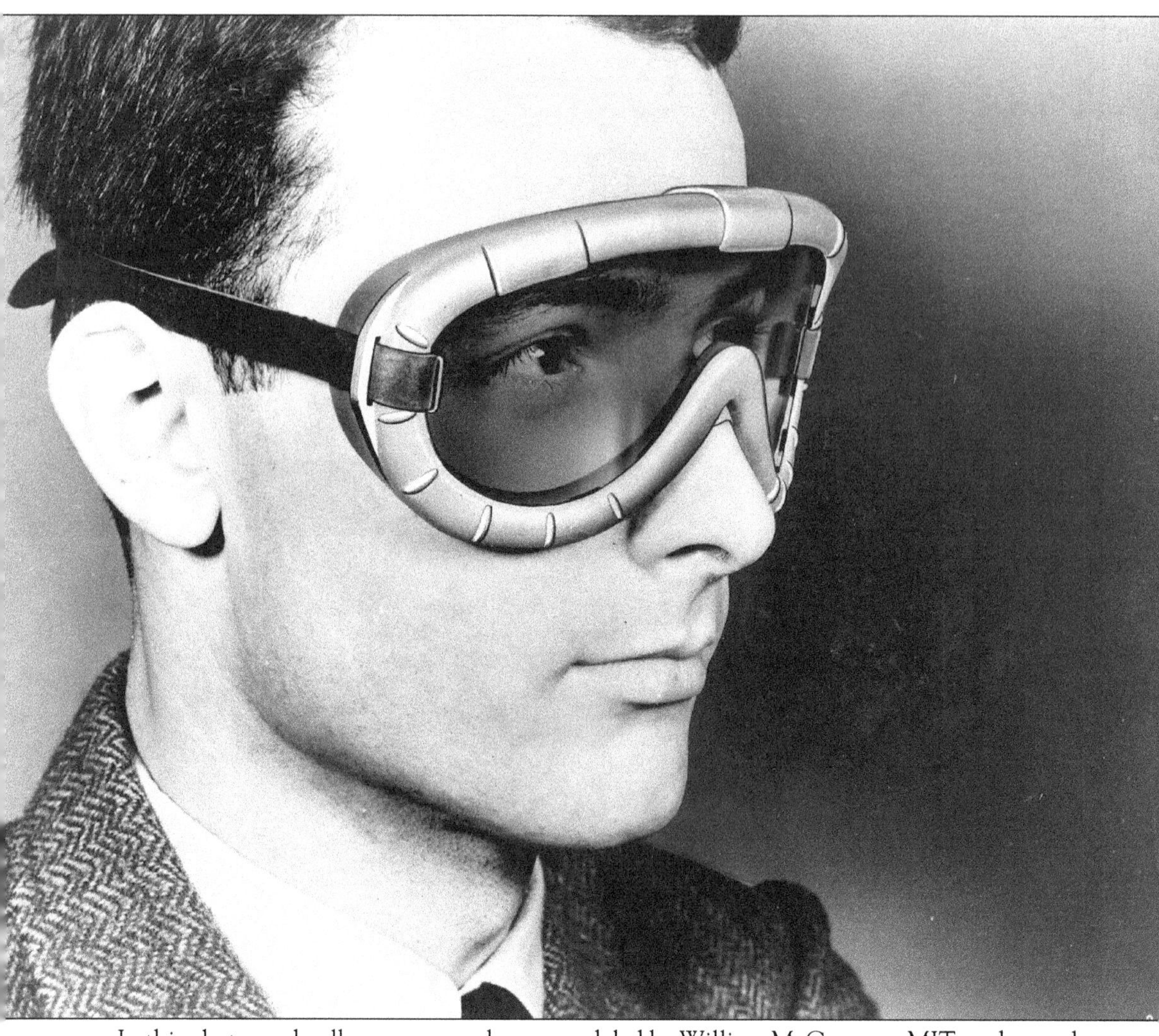

In this photograph, all-purpose goggles are modeled by William McCune, an MIT graduate who joined Polaroid in 1939 to head the quality control department. McCune succeeded Edwin Land as president in 1975 and retired from the company in 1991.

Three

Quality and Quantity
Polaroid and the War Effort

The World War II years changed Polaroid. Like many other companies swept up in the demands of the war, Polaroid grew by leaps and bounds. In fact, famously, the company took over part of the landmark Necco (New England Confectionery Company) building on Massachusetts Avenue in Cambridge for a period of time to accommodate its dramatically expanded manufacturing requirements. Thanks to the company's capable management—Edwin Land had evidenced talent here as well—and the growing technical expertise of the company, Polaroid was able to deliver products of many kinds to the armed forces. Many of them used the company's polarizing techniques. Polaroid's growth during the war was phenomenal. Hundreds of women filled out the ranks at Polaroid—as they did at companies across the country. And the products they turned out were crucial to providing a combat edge to Allied forces: training devices, gun sights, goggles, infrared night viewing devices, polarizing and color filters for range finders and periscopes, and Vectograph materials for making three-dimensional aerial photographs.

Still, while Land was determined to support the war effort, he was also anxious to return to civilian projects. Indeed, at the war's end he voluntarily handed off some promising government programs, such as the Dove guided missile, to other companies so he could return the company to pursuit of its own destiny. There could be no looking back. Polaroid was no longer a tiny start-up. It was a young, maturing company to be reckoned with.

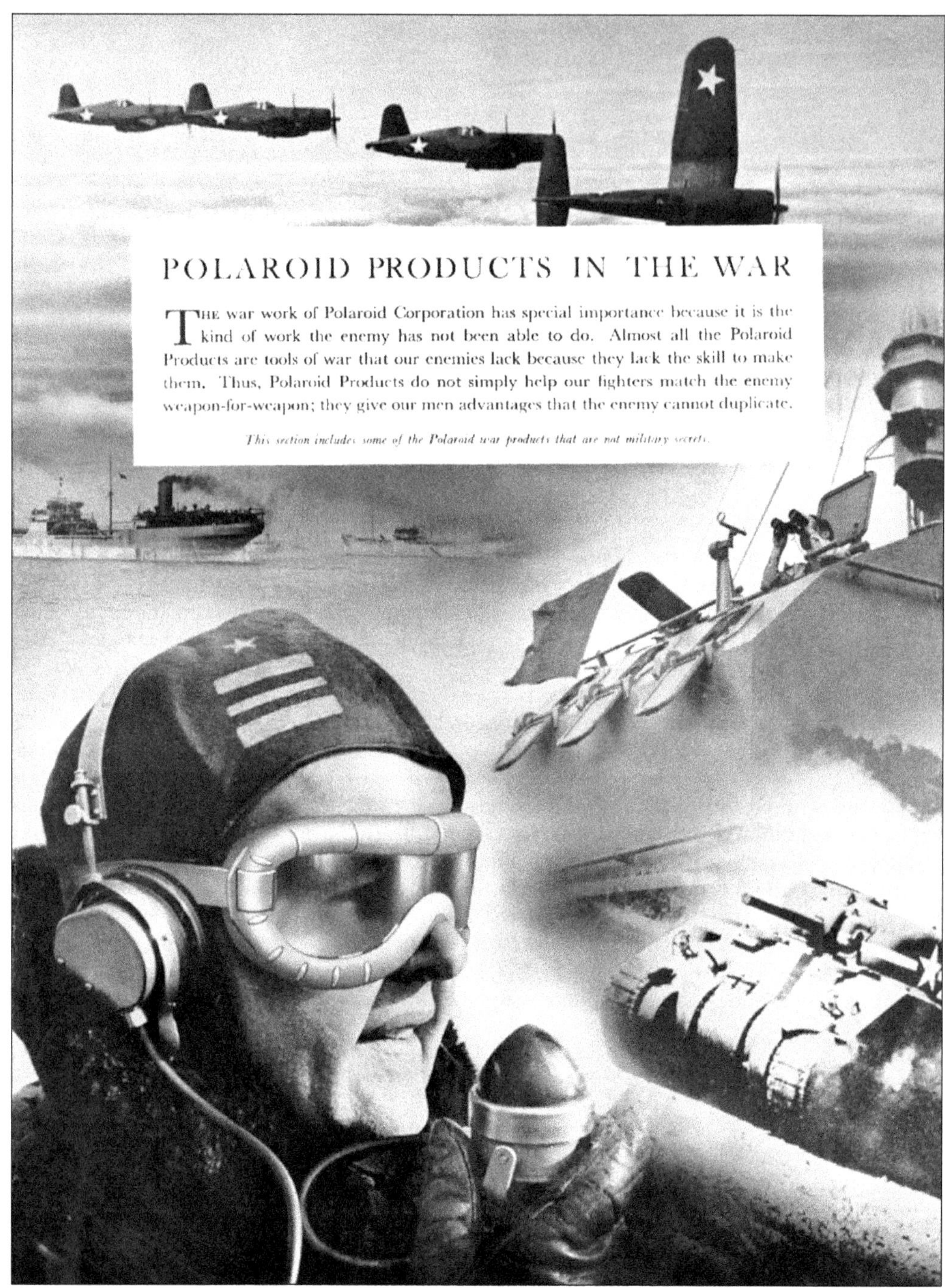

POLAROID PRODUCTS IN THE WAR

THE war work of Polaroid Corporation has special importance because it is the kind of work the enemy has not been able to do. Almost all the Polaroid Products are tools of war that our enemies lack because they lack the skill to make them. Thus, Polaroid Products do not simply help our fighters match the enemy weapon-for-weapon; they give our men advantages that the enemy cannot duplicate.

This section includes some of the Polaroid war products that are not military secrets.

Polaroid products in the war are dramatically showcased in this 1943 Polaroid handbook.

Polaroid all-purpose goggles were standard equipment for millions of U.S. military personnel. The goggles sharpen the vision by protecting the eyes against wind, dust, and glare. Different lenses may be inserted in the frame. In this 1942 photograph, Gen. George S. Patton is wearing a pair of the goggles.

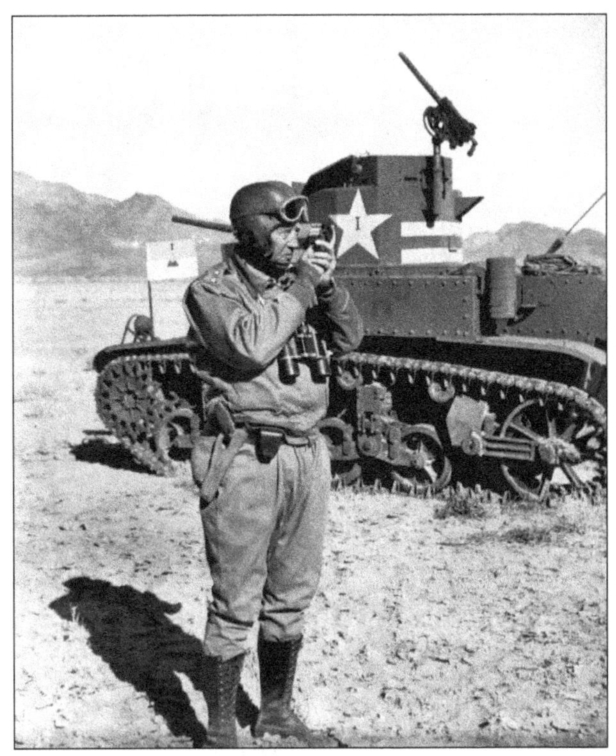

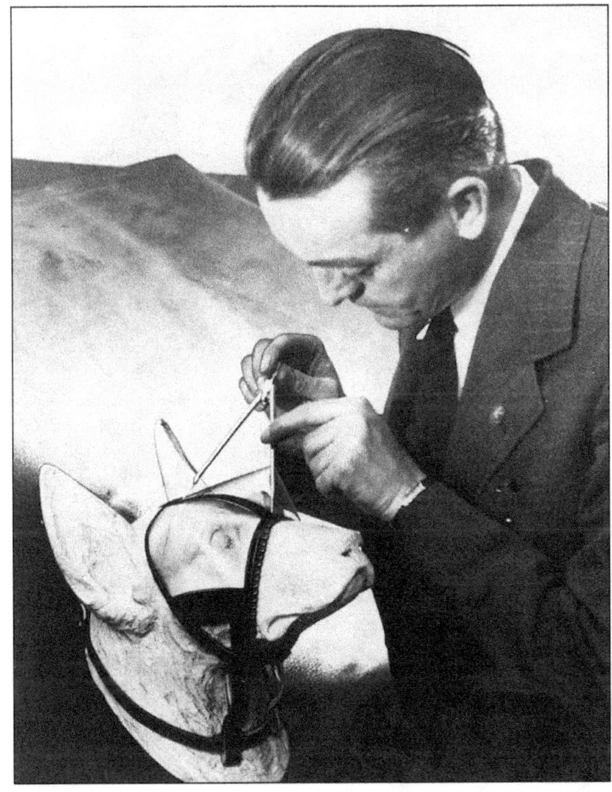

Polaroid's products were widely used in wartime—even by canines. Here, the measurements of a set of dog goggles are confirmed on a model of a dog's head. The goggles protected the eyes of many of the 10,000 dogs trained for military service during the war.

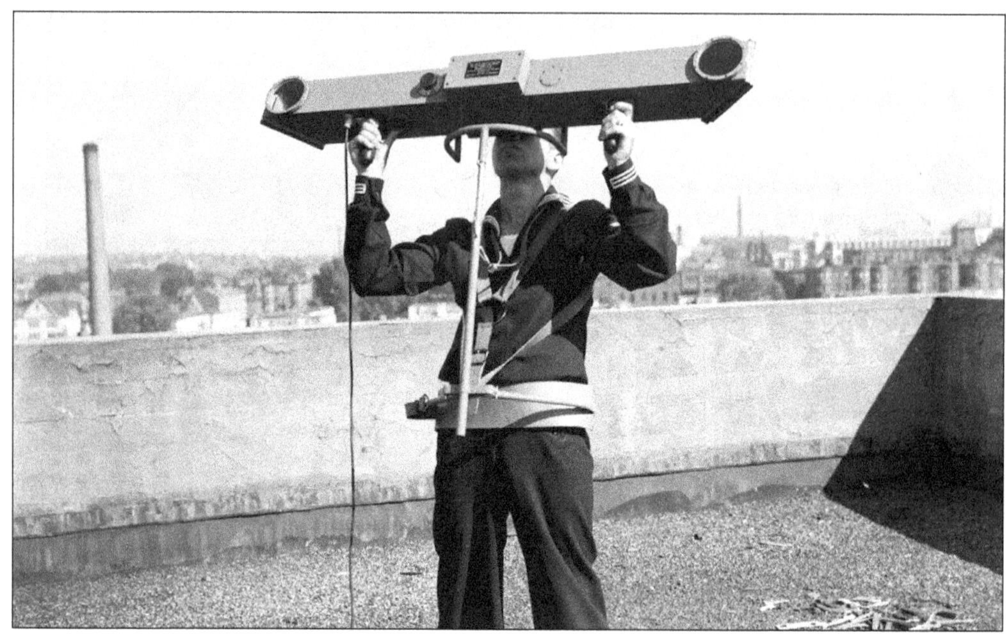

A navy seaman tests a 43-inch range finder on the roof of Polaroid's building at 730 Main Street in Cambridge.

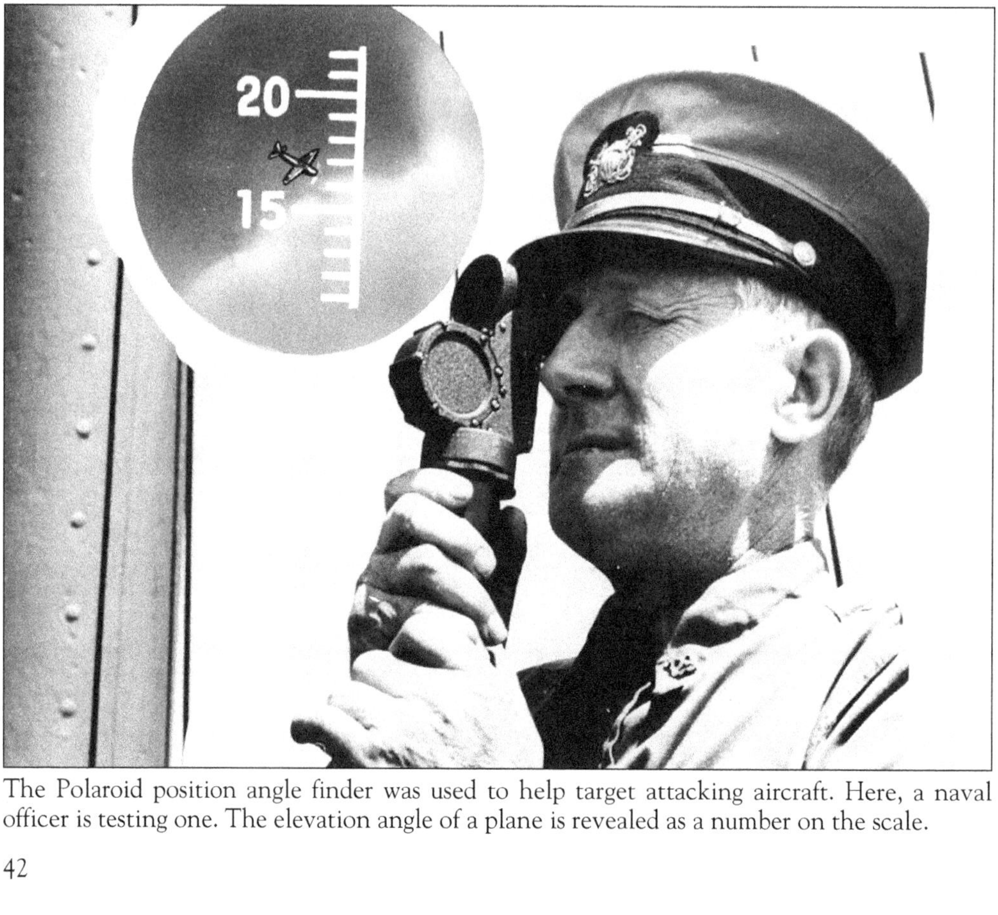

The Polaroid position angle finder was used to help target attacking aircraft. Here, a naval officer is testing one. The elevation angle of a plane is revealed as a number on the scale.

The Polaroid machine-gun trainer was manufactured in 1941. This picture, taken at South Boston Naval Training Center in 1943, shows a gunner trainee in a Polaroid training device that provided stereoscopic motion picture technology and sound to provide realistic simulation of tracer bullets and hits scored on a target. In addition to offering realism, the system saved the military millions of dollars in ammunition that would have been used for training. The technology used in the product was a forerunner of the arcade games that emerged in the 1970s and 1980s.

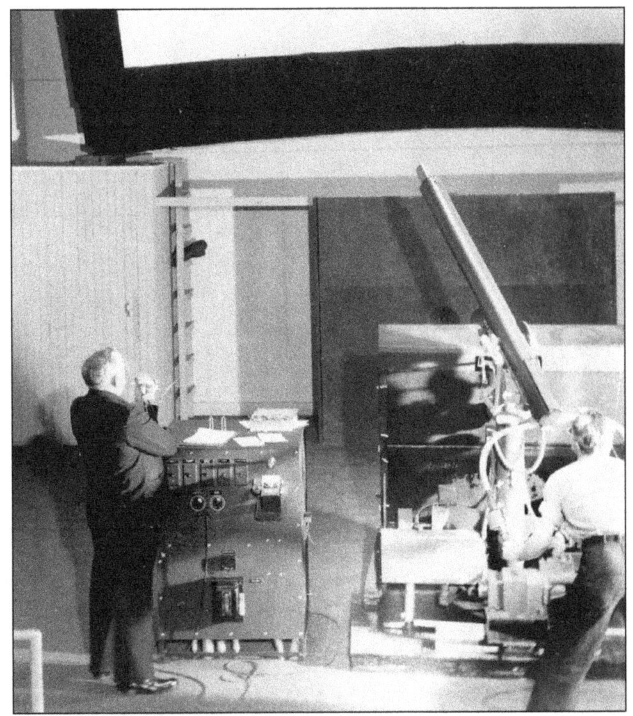

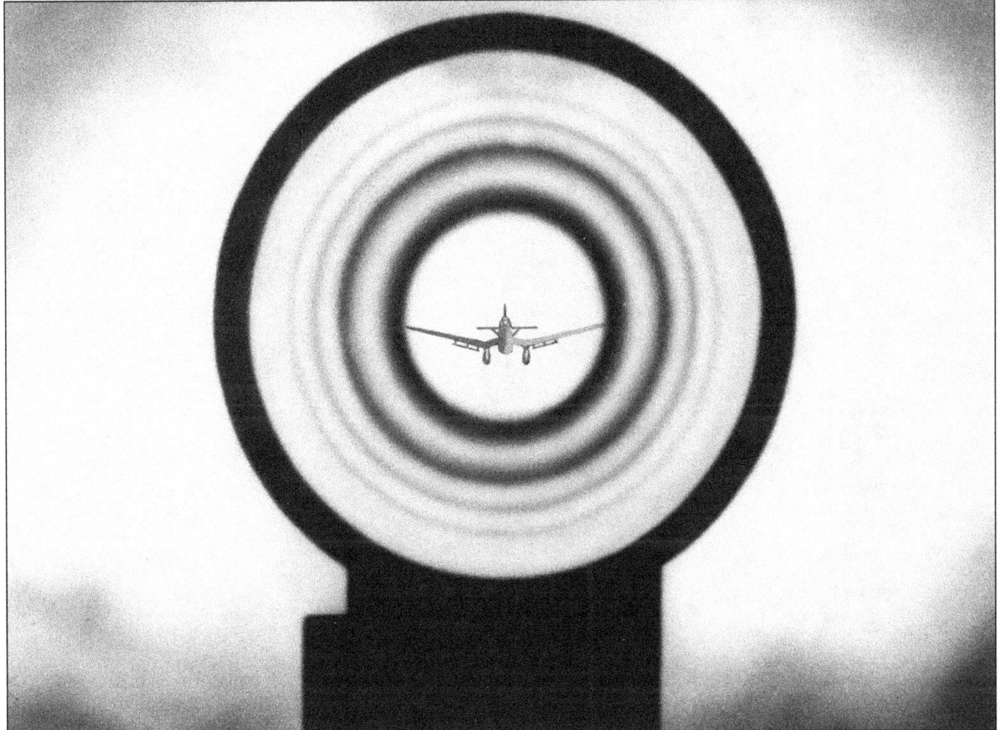

A Polaroid ring sight, designed to enhance firing accuracy, displays a frontal view of a German Ju-87 dive bomber.

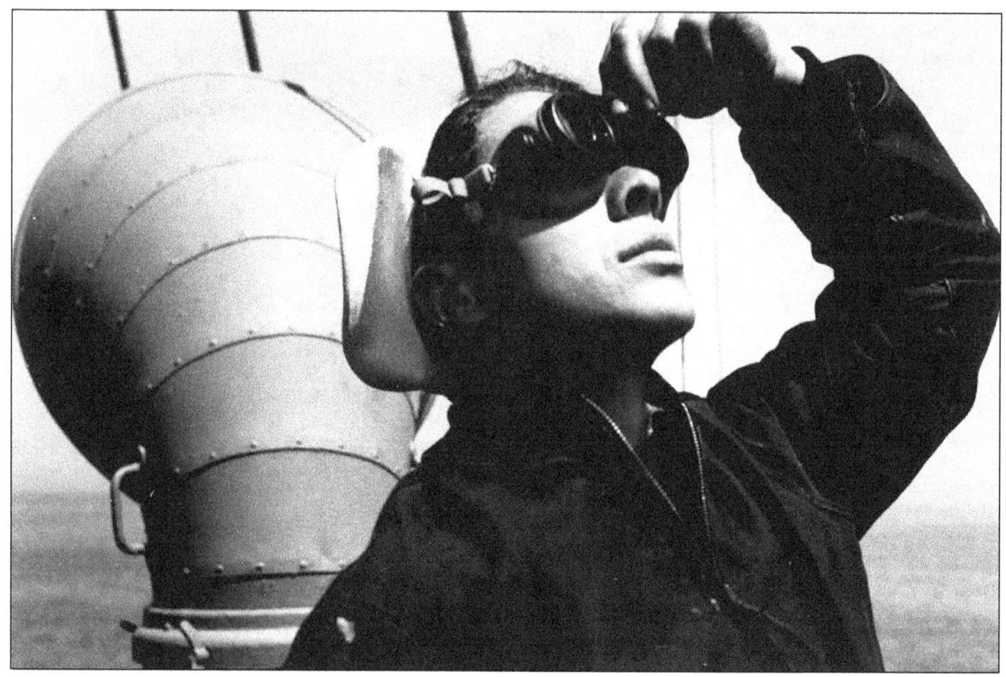

A twist of the knob on the Polaroid variable density goggles controls the amount of light. This 1943 photograph shows a sailor adjusting the light.

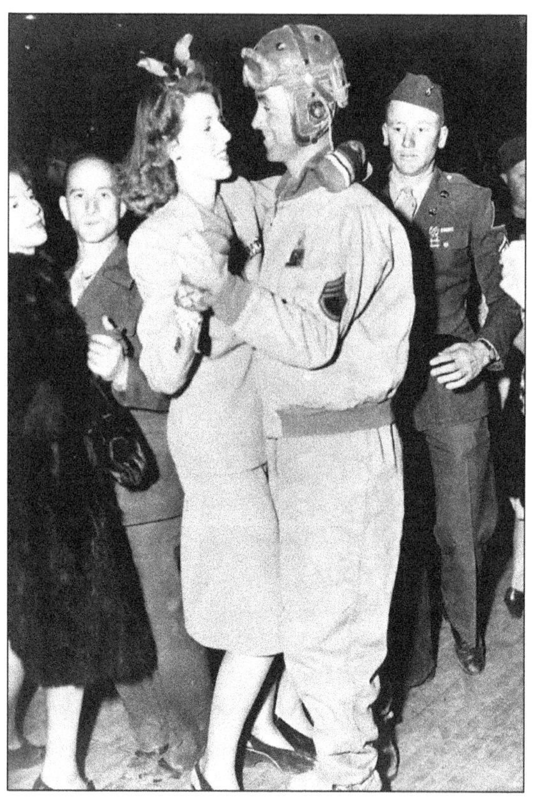

Even while dancing, this soldier keeps his Polaroid all-purpose goggles on over his tanker's helmet.

A sailor uses a Polaroid range finder on a 20-millimeter antiaircraft gun.

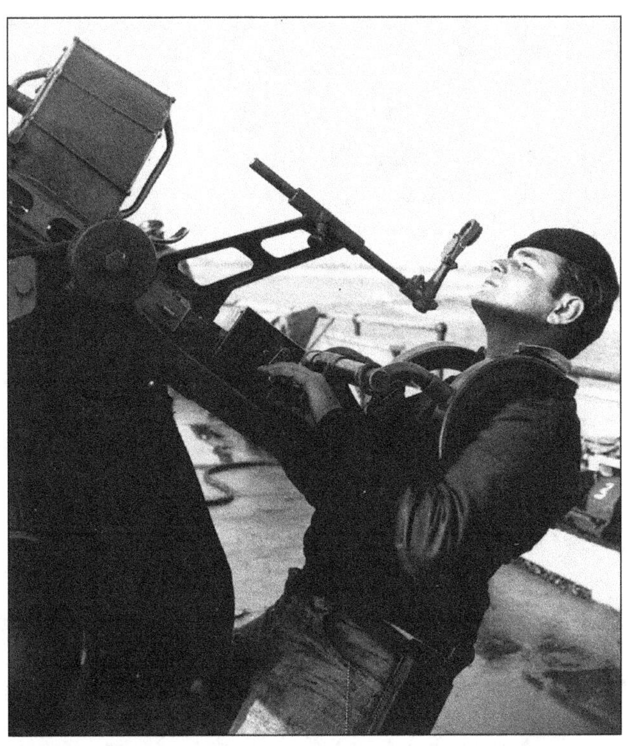

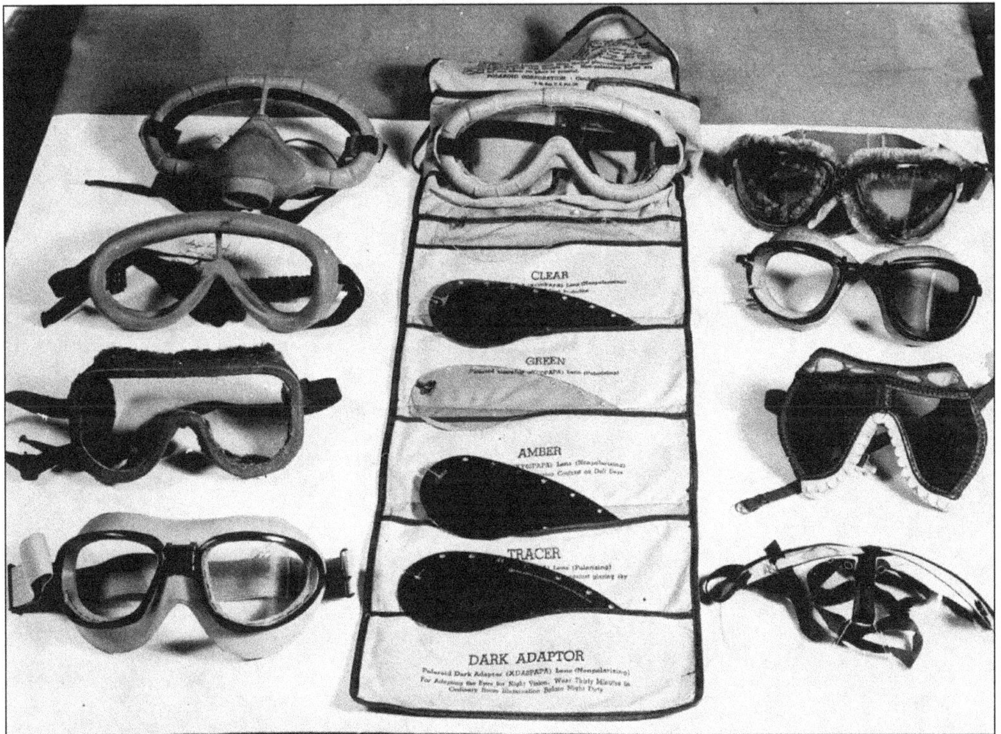

Polaroid produced aviation, fog-free, all-purpose, and dark adapter goggles for the army and the navy.

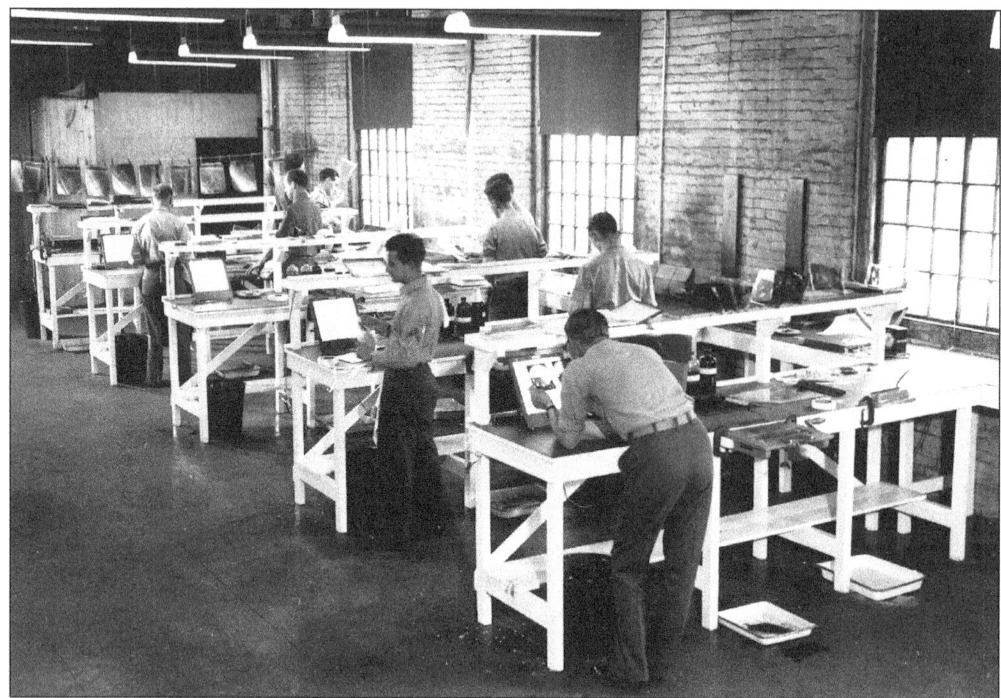

Edwin Land announced his invention of the Vectograph three-dimensional still-photography system in 1940. Polaroid Vectograph systems provided a kind of stereoscopic image that proved especially useful for aerial reconnaissance surveys during the war. In this photograph from 1943, soldiers and sailors learn how to process and make Vectograph stills at the Polaroid War School.

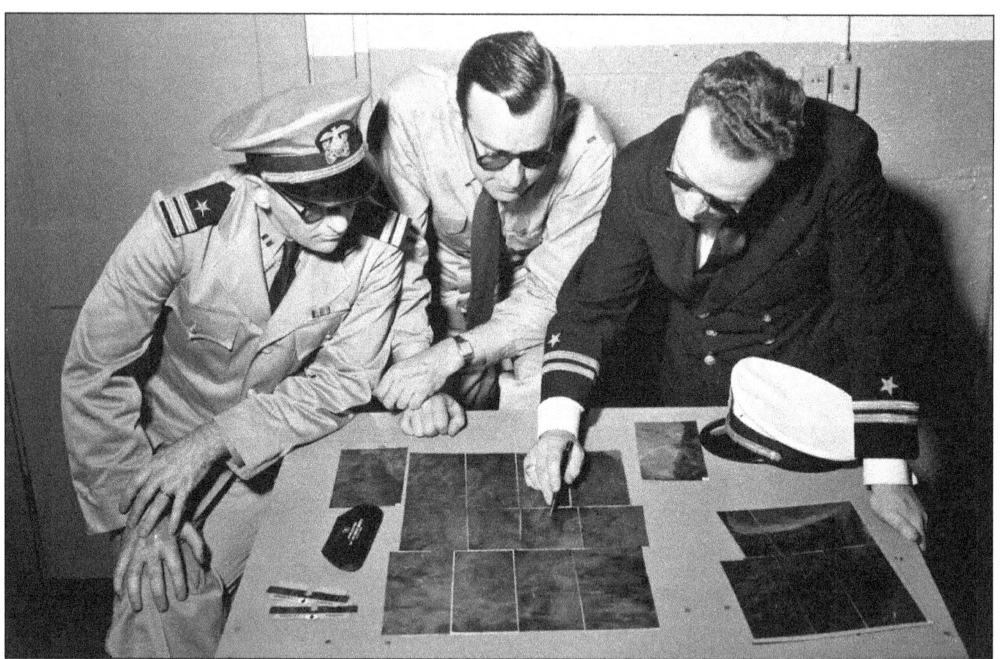

Navy officers examine Vectograph stills on a table.

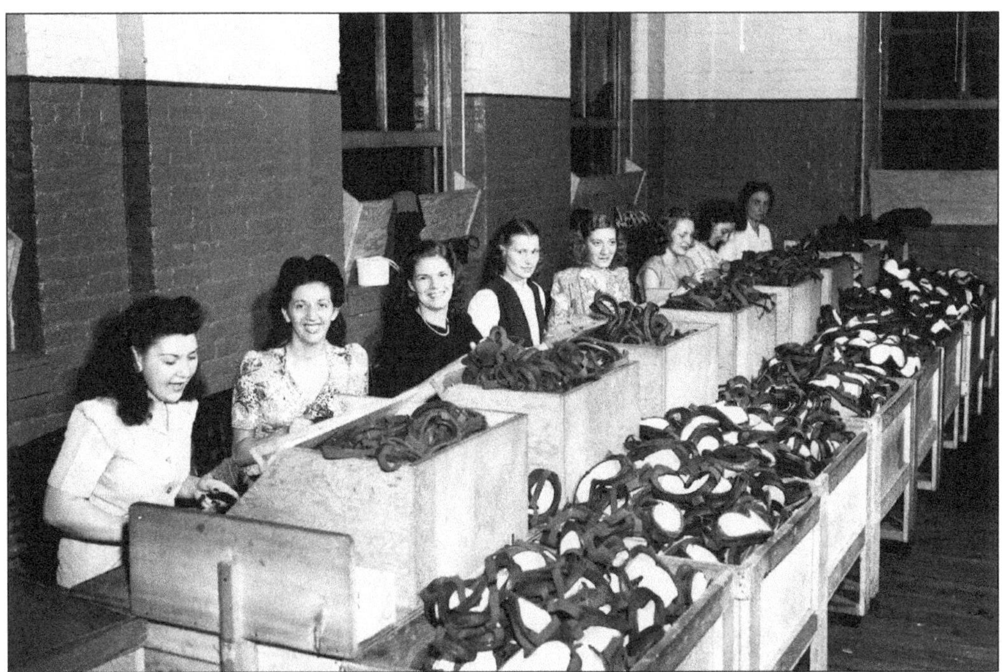

Women assemble goggles at a Polaroid subcontractor, Markay Products, in New York City.

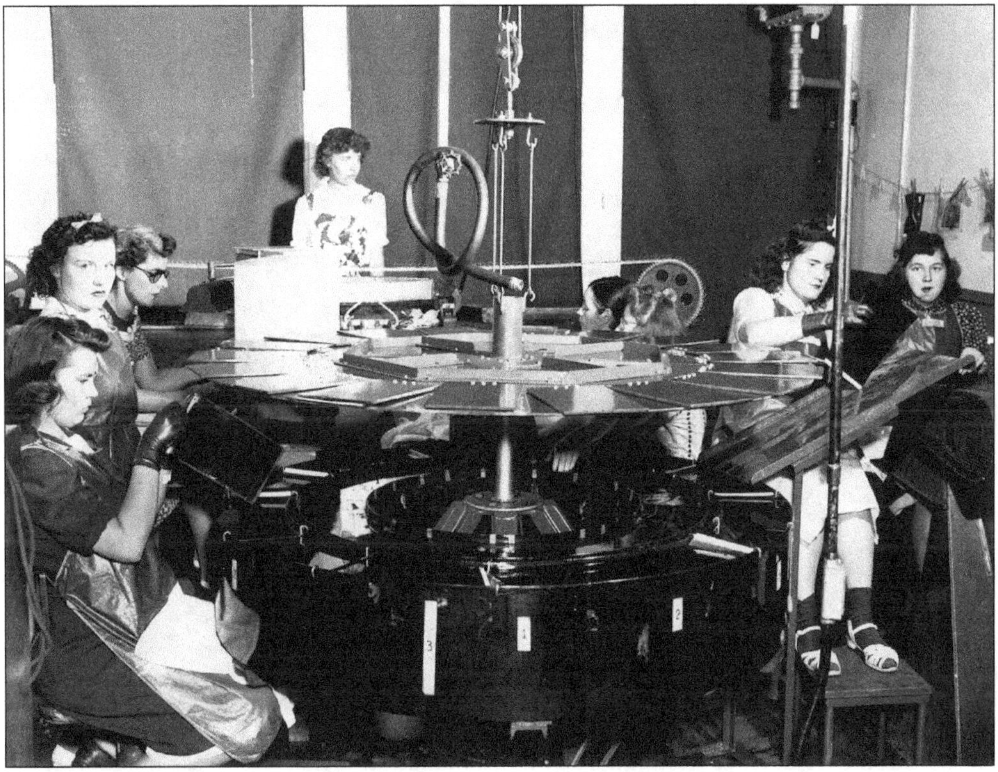

This is an Inko-fix machine for Vecto Publishing, photographed in September 1943.

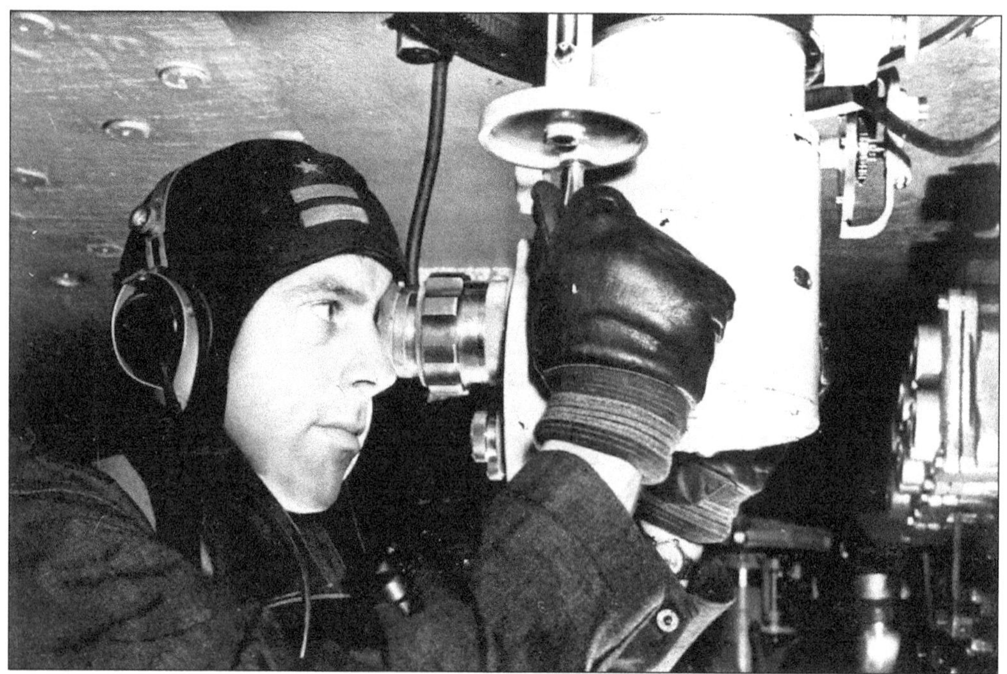

This man is using a Polaroid range finder periscope on a U. S. warship in 1943.

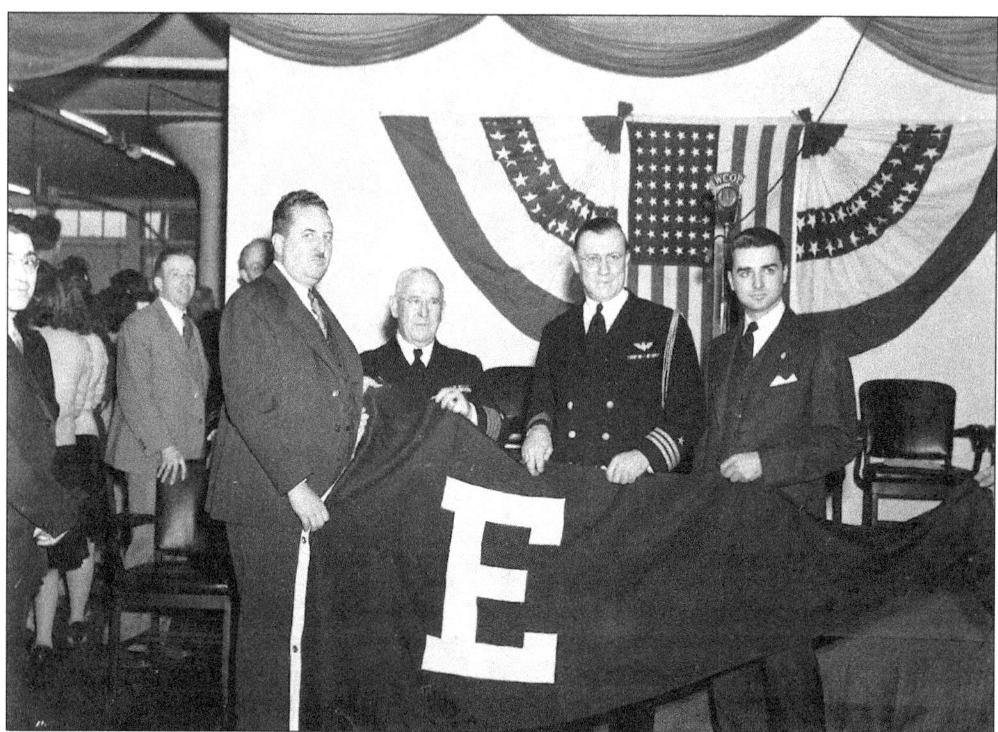

For its quality and output, Polaroid was presented with the Army-Navy E Award in 1942. Notice the WCOP microphone behind Edwin Land, indicating that the occasion was probably broadcast live to Boston radio audiences.

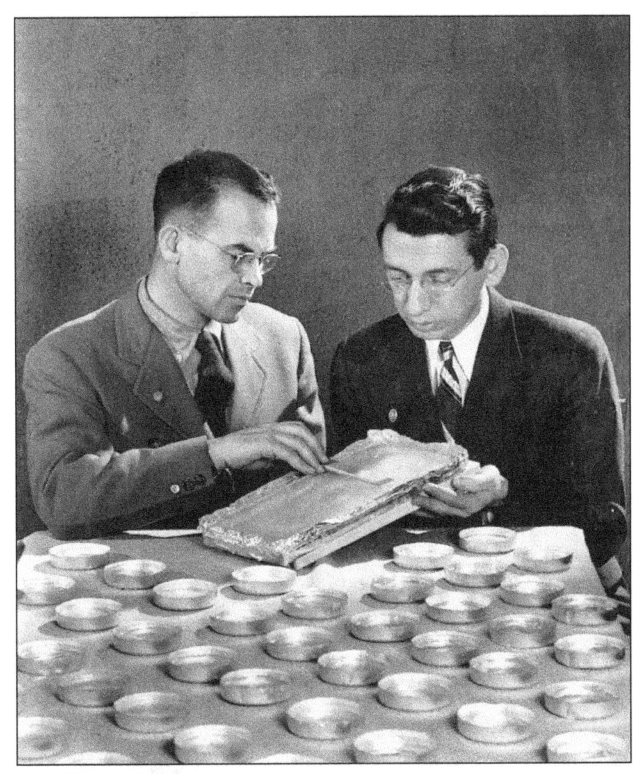

Dr. Cutler D. West and Dr. Frederick J. Binda of Polaroid are shown here in 1945. They are measuring large sodium nitrate crystals produced by their new invention for manufacturing synthetic optical crystals larger than those found in nature. Sodium nitrate crystals have optical properties similar to calcite, a natural crystal used in highly specialized precision optical equipment. The large crystals are formed by floating mica on molten sodium nitrate in aluminum pans like those on the table.

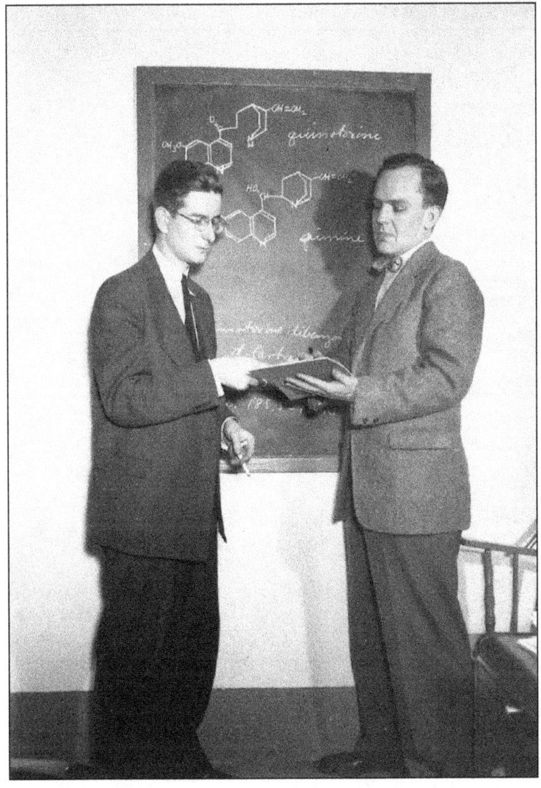

In April 1944, Polaroid's research laboratory announced the solution of a classic problem in organic chemistry, the total synthesis of quinine. This photograph records one of the company's great wartime triumphs. Quinine, a malaria remedy, was in short supply during much of the war. Twenty-seven-year-old chemists Dr. Robert B. Woodward of Harvard and Dr. William E. Doering of Columbia University were working for Polaroid at the time they discovered a way to manufacture synthetic quinine. The synthesis required 14 months of research and later contributed to Woodward's winning of a Nobel Prize.

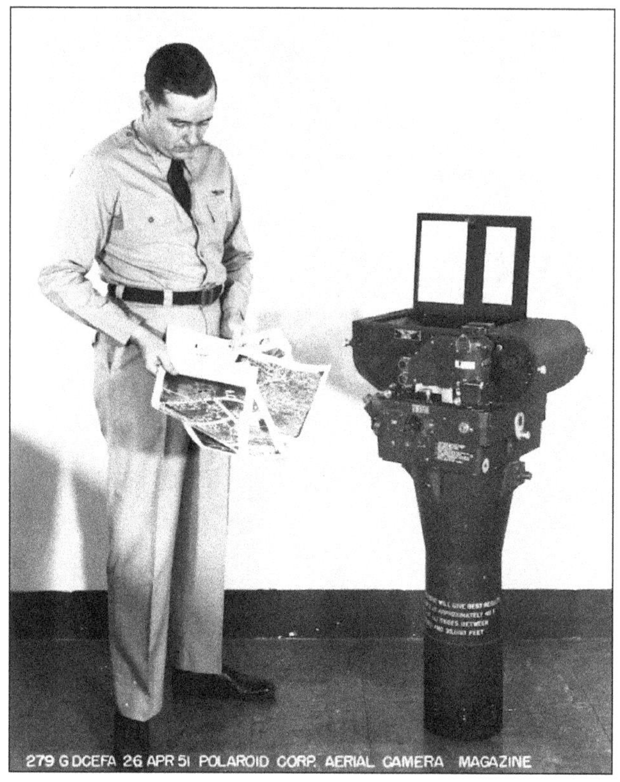

There is more to this picture than meets the eye. Nominally, it is a photograph of a Polaroid aerial camera from 1951. But this was only one part of a long procession of products used in aerial reconnaissance starting during World War II with Vectograph systems. In fact, the key research work done by Land and many of his inner circle throughout the cold war led directly to development of the famous U-2 spy plane and the surveillance satellite programs that followed.

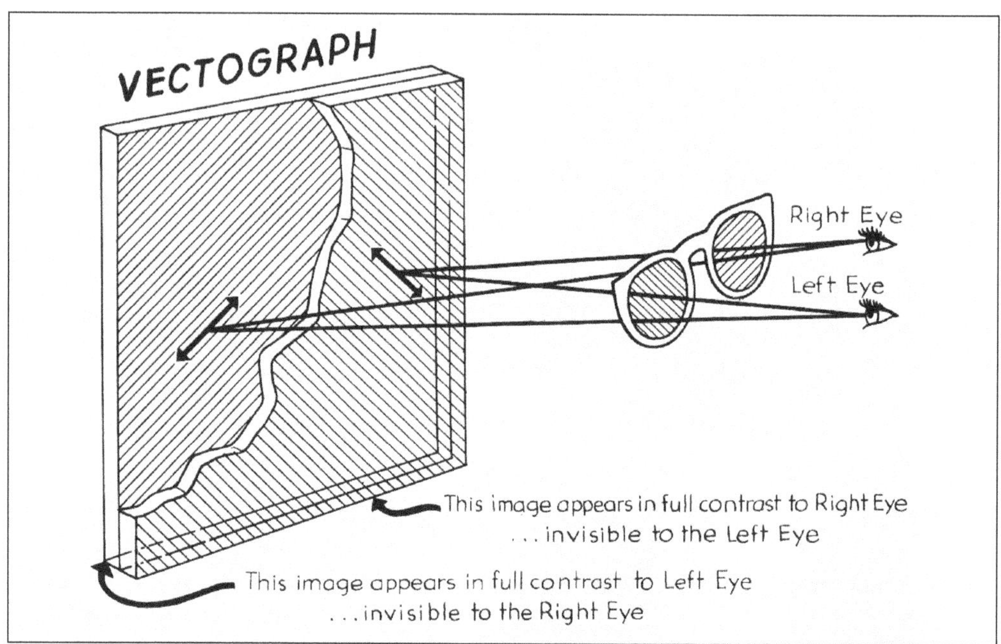

This diagram illustrates the way in which a 3-D Vectograph works. The Vectograph film has an image on each of its two sides. The images are polarized in different directions, at 90-degree angles to each other. Polaroid 3-D viewing spectacles have their polarizing lenses similarly arranged.

Lieutenant Commander Quackenbuch is shown here viewing a Polaroid Vectograph.

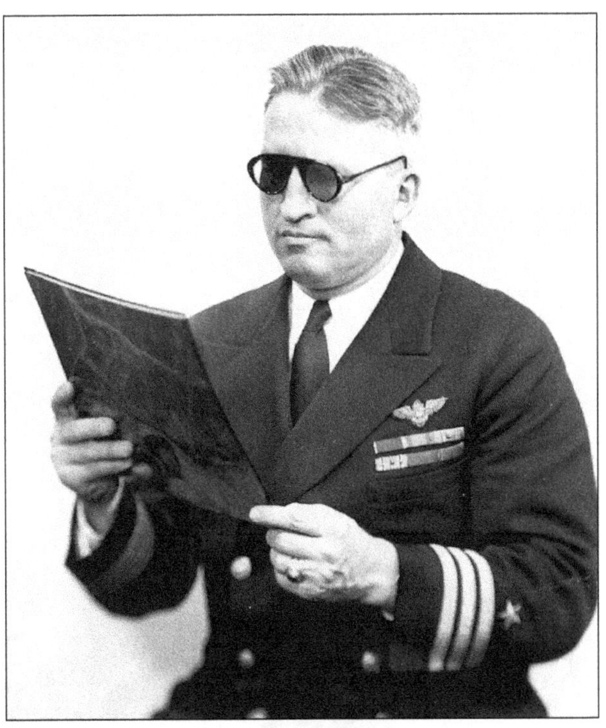

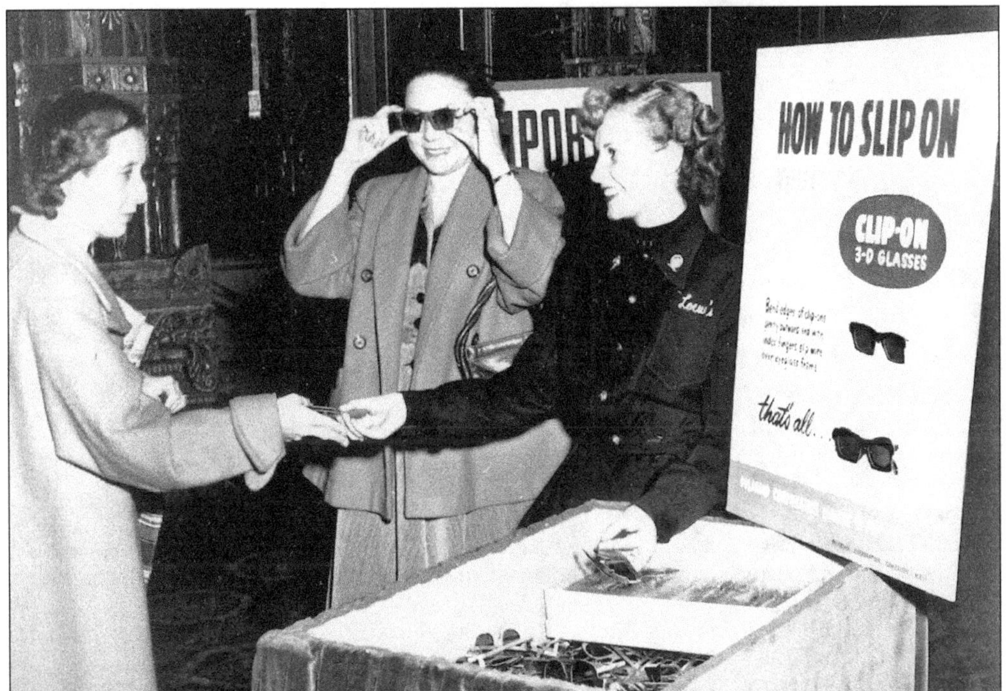

These clip-on 3-D glasses, part of the system for viewing 3-D movies, seemed to promise great opportunities for Polaroid, which had pioneered the technology. The first 3-D Hollywood movie, *Bwana Devil,* premiered in 1952. The audience wore Polaroid 3-D glasses while the film was projected through polarizing filters.

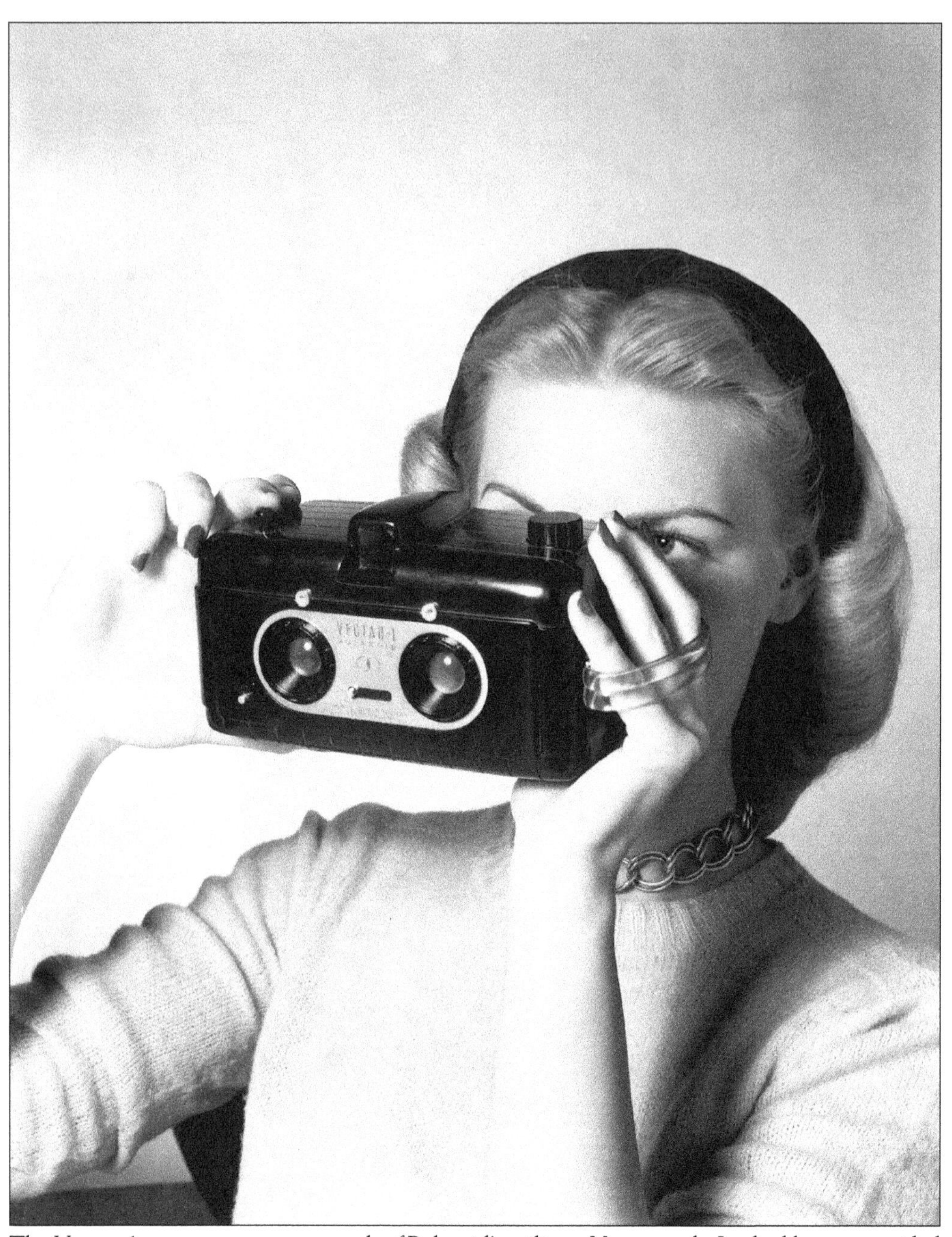

The Vectar-1 was a postwar outgrowth of Polaroid's military Vectograph. Its dual lenses provided stereo photography.

Four

Polaroid People

As Polaroid grew, it absorbed the talents and energies of more and more people, initially in the Cambridge area and later in other communities. While the core of the company was its talented chemists and optical scientists, over time, the company ended up employing people in innumerable job categories. Between the mid-1930s and the early 1950s, Polaroid's phenomenal growth shaped the future of the company.

For most people in the community, Polaroid was an employer of choice with a good reputation and strong prospects for those seeking advancement. Clearly, too, the company fostered a strong spirit of camaraderie. Employees took part in the activities of clubs such as the Peers Club, enjoyed company outings, had sport teams, played in orchestras, and invited speakers such as Ansel Adams to enlighten the Camera Club.

Edwin Land, who respected results above all else, made the company a place of opportunities for people not widely represented in the workforce at the time. In particular, women played an important role at Polaroid from the earliest years. Among the best known were Eudoxia Muller and Meroë Morse, but over the years, many women were recruited from colleges such as Smith College (with the help of Land's friend, Prof. Clarence Kennedy).

As a progressive manager, Land supported teamwork and individual responsibility among the employees and promoted programs and policies for their growth. Polaroid's pioneering management policies—such as profit sharing, job rotation, education reimbursement, day-care programs, and internal job posting and training—set precedents for American and Japanese companies.

In the 1960s, in response to the civil rights movement and social unrest in the Boston area, Land took steps to further open opportunities to African Americans, helping to make Polaroid one of the most diverse companies in the region. By 1977, the workforce in Polaroid's U.S. facilities included 14 percent African Americans and 31 percent women.

In a paper presented at the Mellon Institute in 1963, Edwin Land wrote, "The second great product of industry is the rewarding working life."

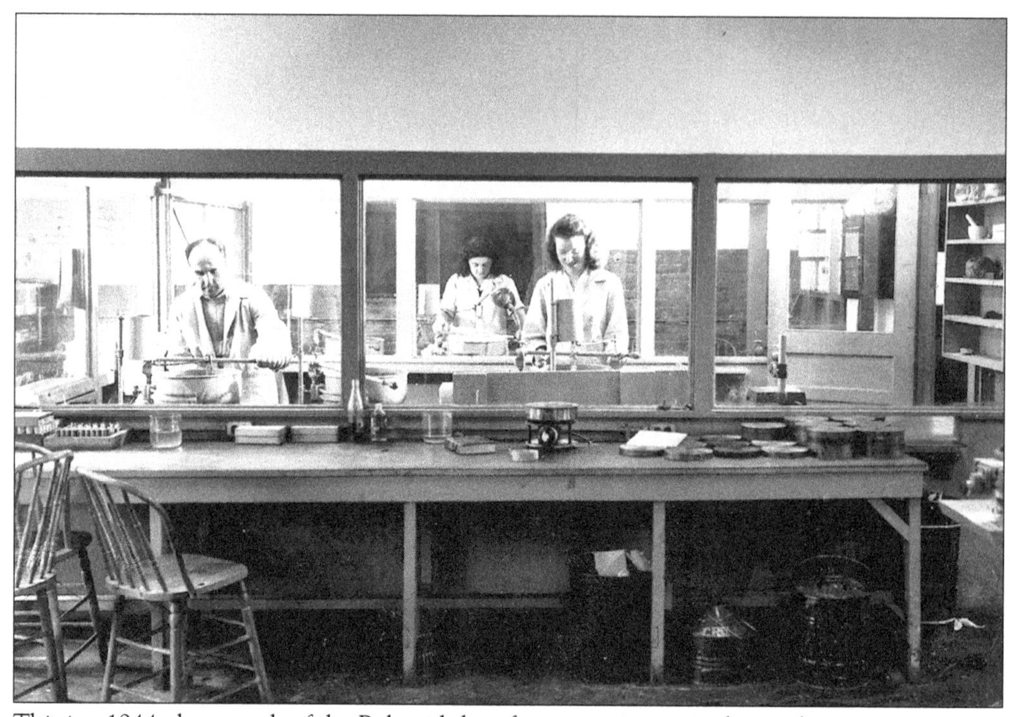

This is a 1944 photograph of the Polaroid shop for processing optical crystals.

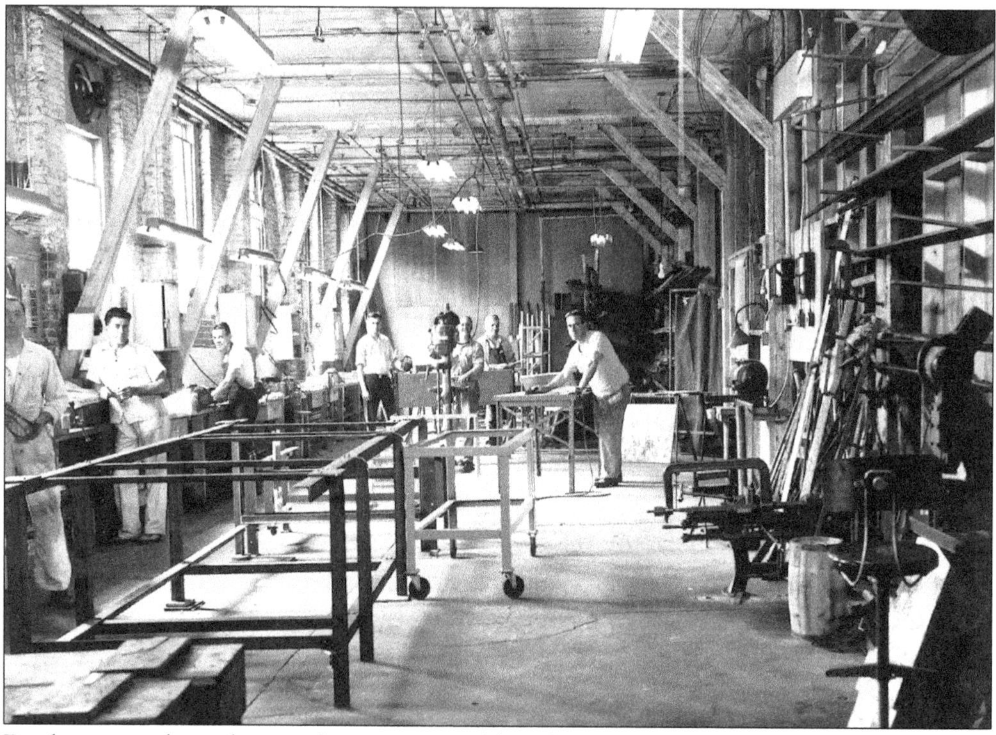

Employees are shown here in the company welding shop in 1943.

A lab worker contemplates her next move in this photograph of the crystal shop.

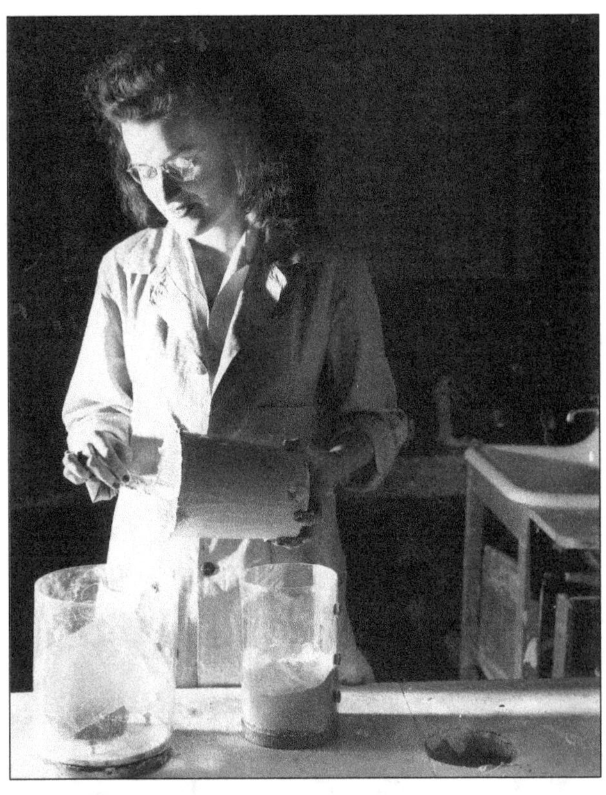

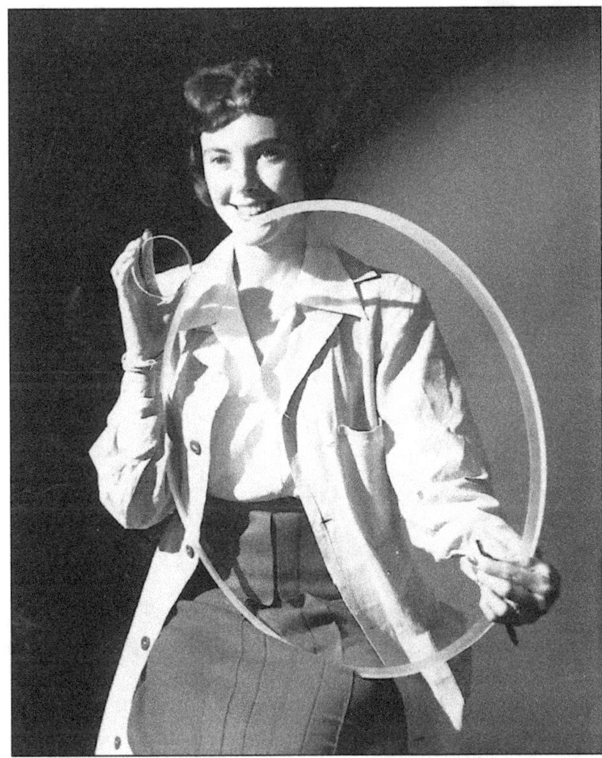

An employee is holding a large and a small optical corrector plate in a photograph dated 1950.

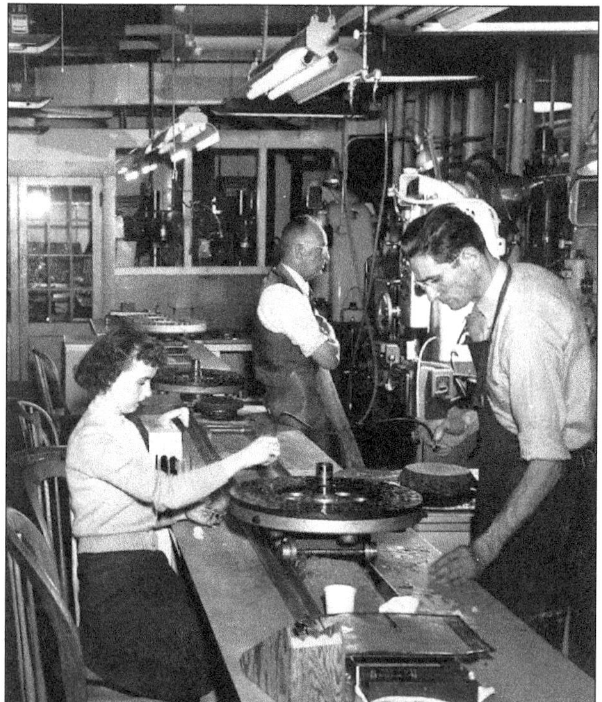

A note on this photograph reads, "Frank Cooke's Glass Optical Department." The department, at 12 Ames Street in Cambridge, was established in 1942.

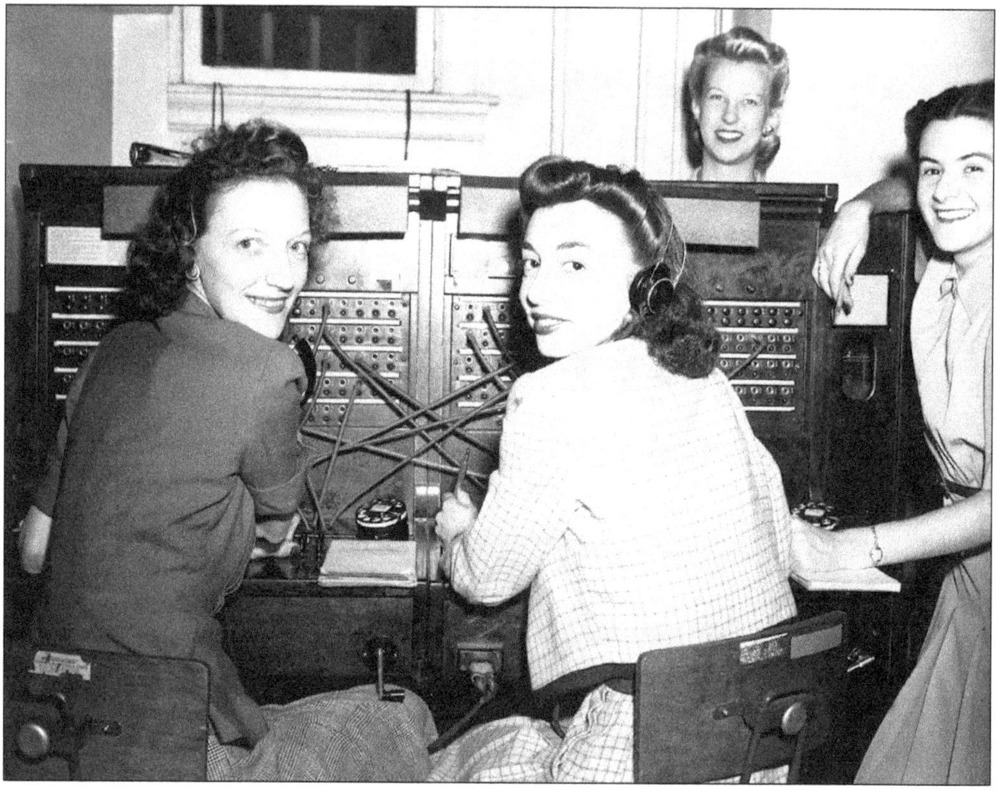

Seen in June 1945 are telephone operators at the Massachusetts Avenue building in Cambridge.

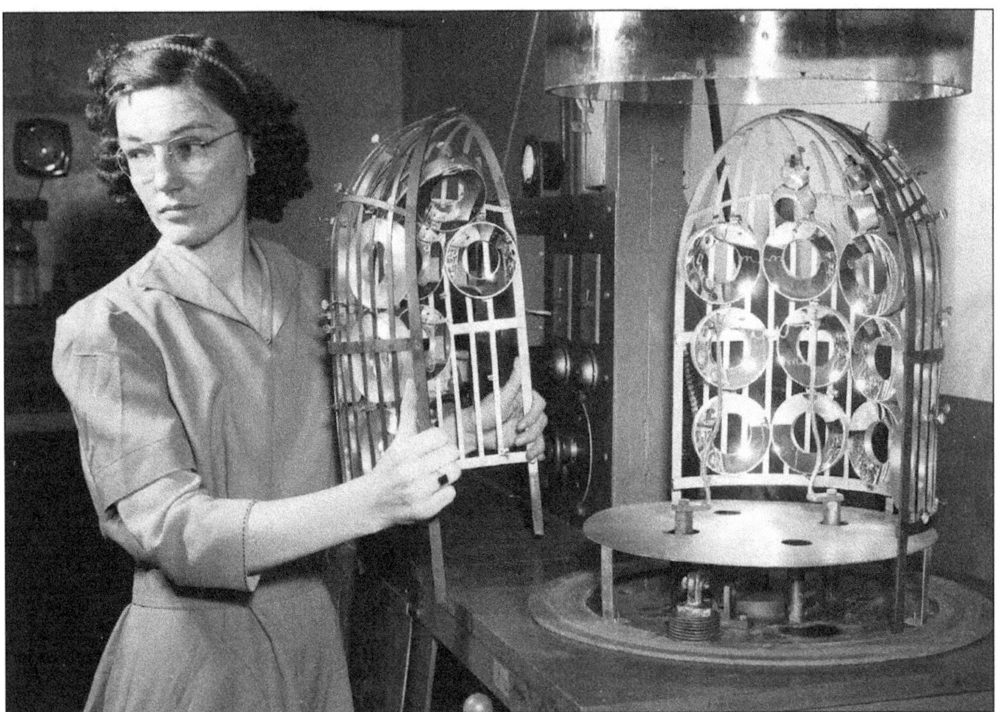

Plastic optics, shown here in processing, were a challenging product given the state of the art in polymer chemistry in 1944. Despite the difficulties, Polaroid was successful and retained a leadership position in the field for years.

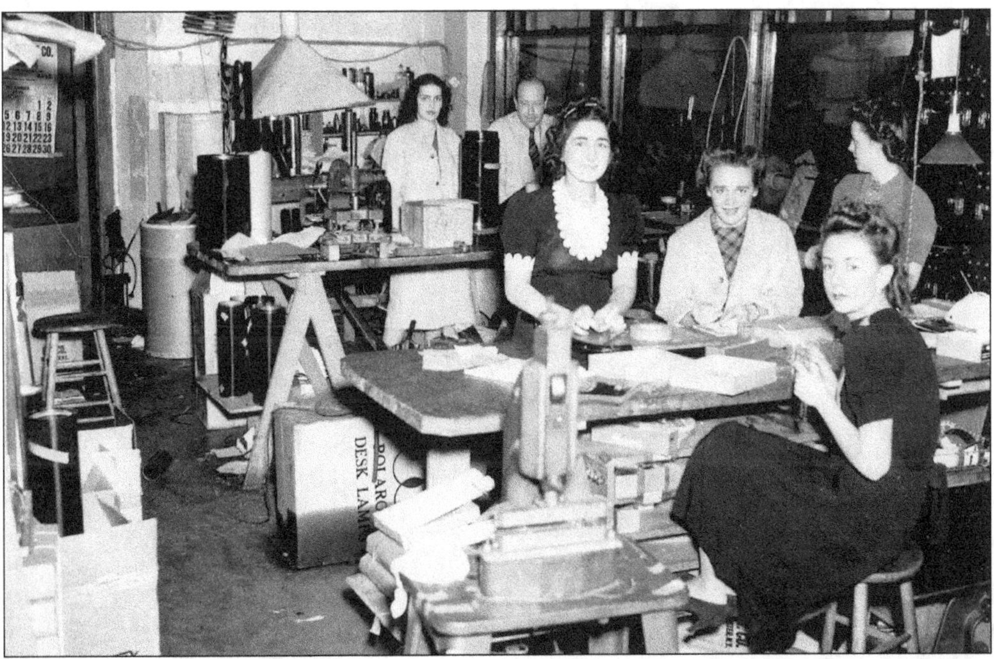

This 1939 image shows "Mrs. Sheperd's Laminating Room" at Polaroid's facility on Columbus Avenue in Boston.

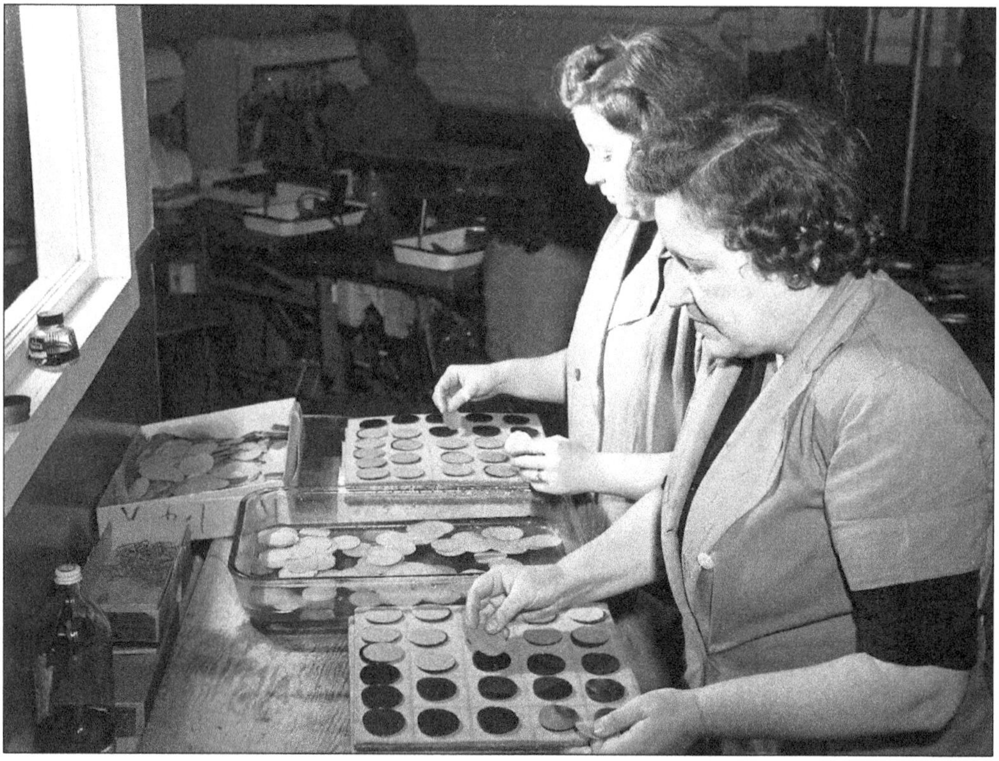

A packaging operation for Polaroid filters is shown in this image from 1945.

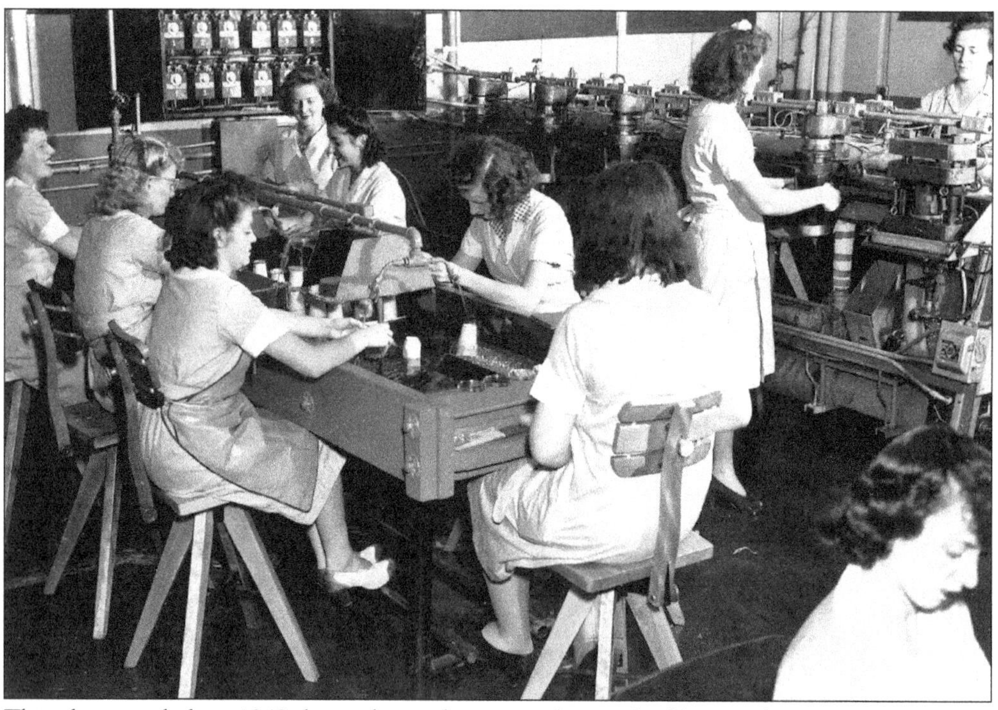

This photograph from 1943 shows the quality-control room for filter production.

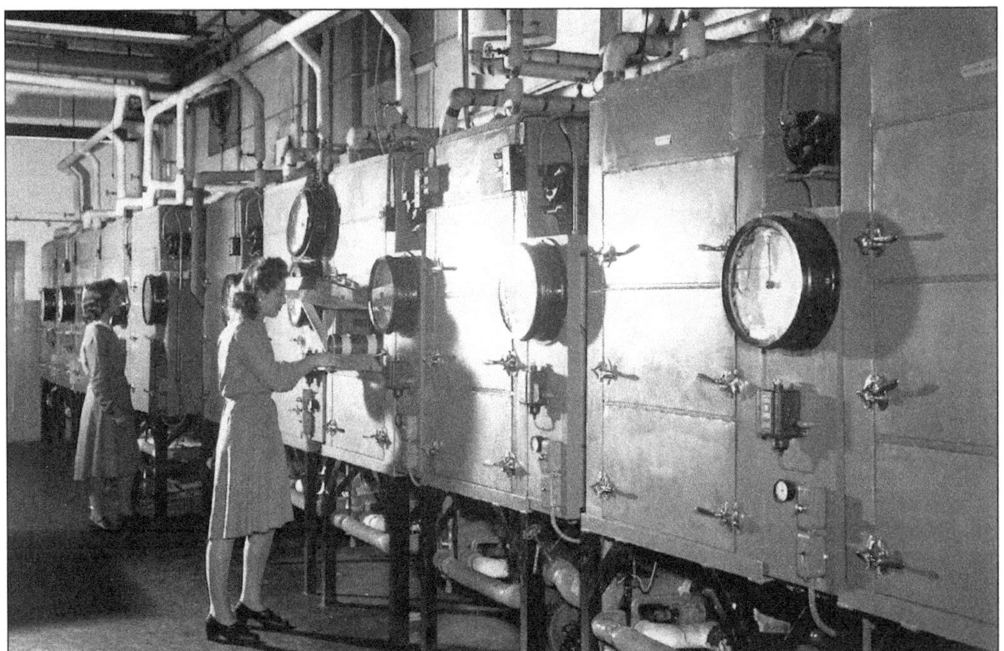

These are the curing ovens in the plastic optics area in 1944. Employees are placing a batch of optical parts into one of the oven doors.

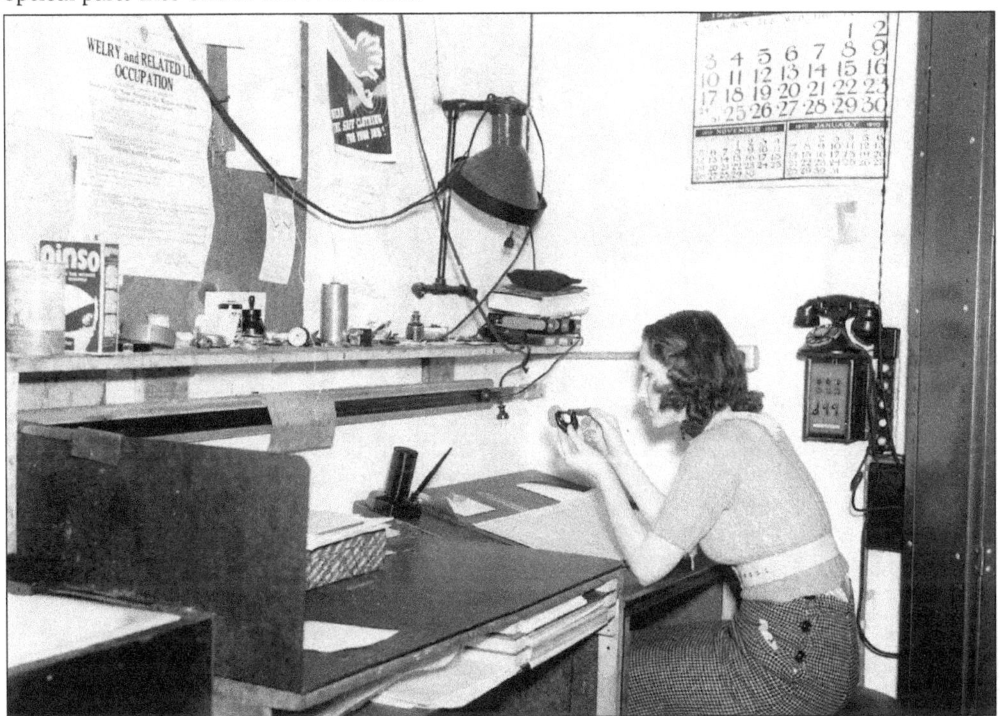

From its inception, the company employed a wide range of talents and significant numbers of women. In this view from 1939, an employee uses a micrometer to measure the thickness of material at the Columbus Avenue facility. A poster on the wall advises, "Wear the safe clothing for your job."

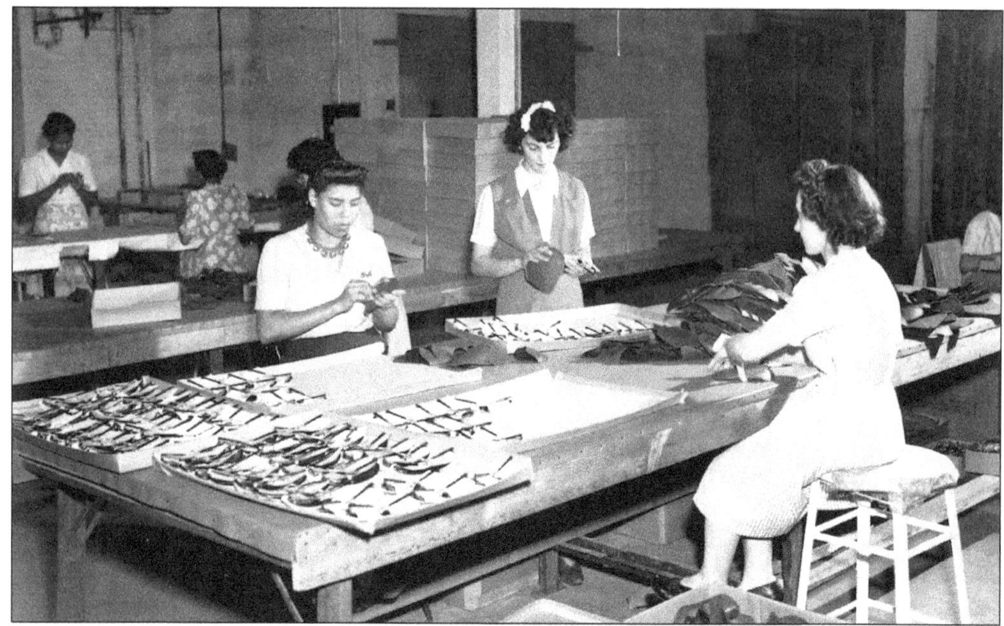

In this 1945 photograph, workers are assembling and packaging goggles at one of Polaroid's wartime subcontractors, Mutual Sunset Lamp, in Trenton, New Jersey.

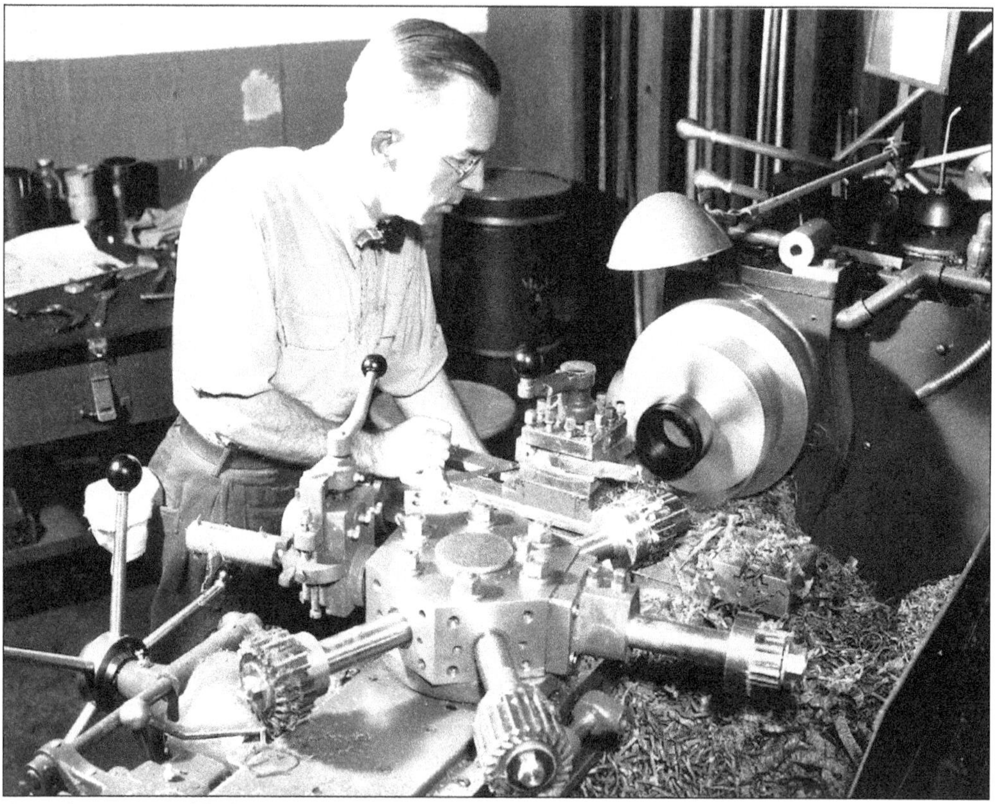

A worker responsible for instrument production operates a turret lathe.

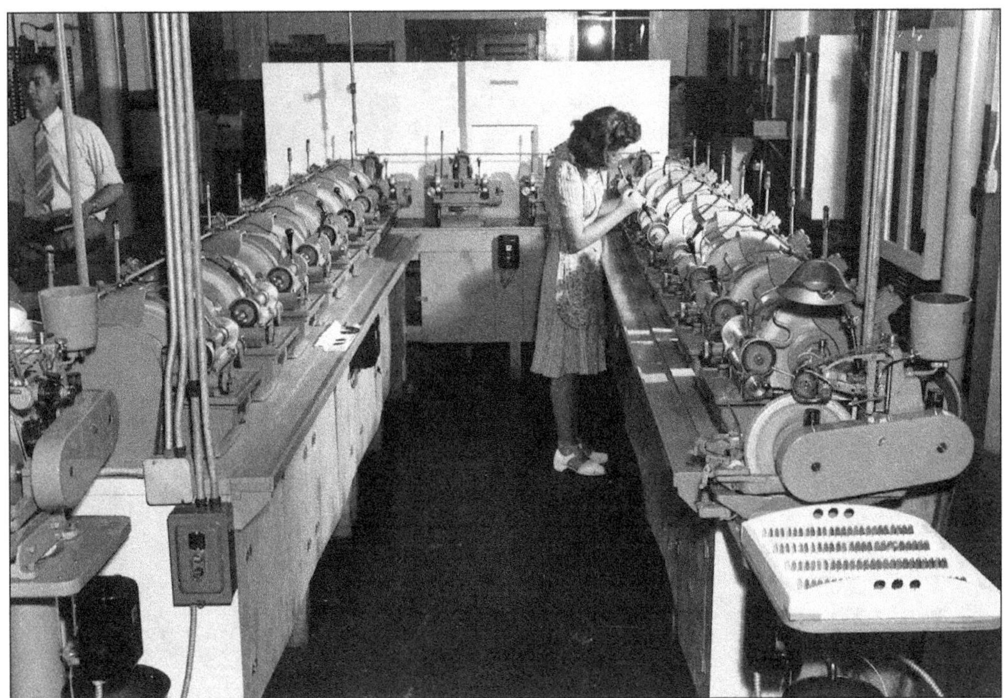
This view of the glass optics shop, on Ames Street in Cambridge, shows the equipment operator working with a grinding machine in 1943.

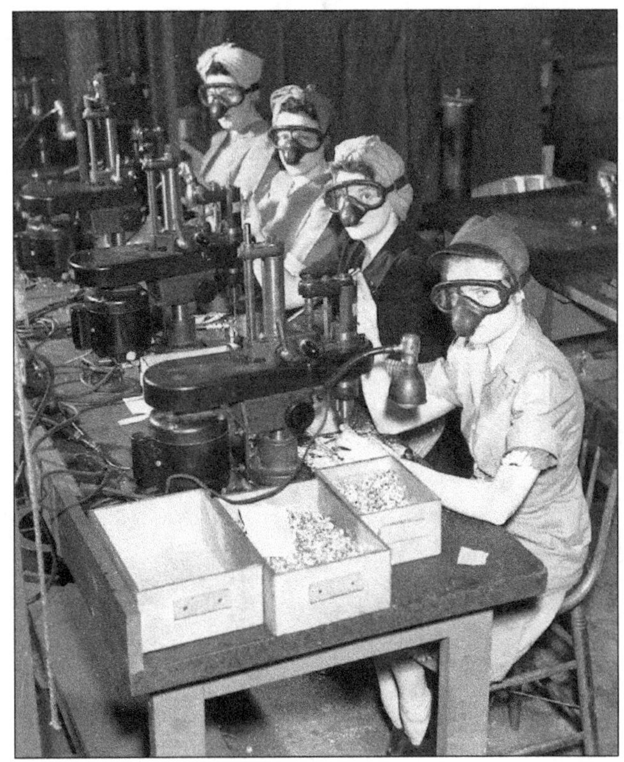
Employees in one of the company's machine shops are wearing Polaroid fog-free goggles. The photograph dates from 1945.

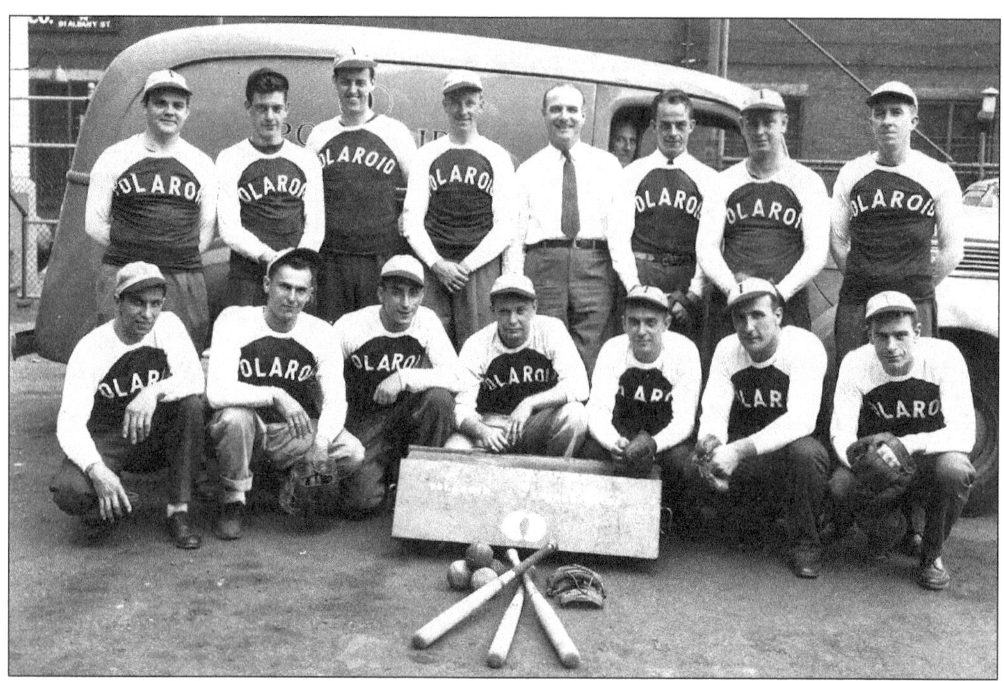

A Polaroid baseball team poses in front of a company truck near Albany Street in Cambridge.

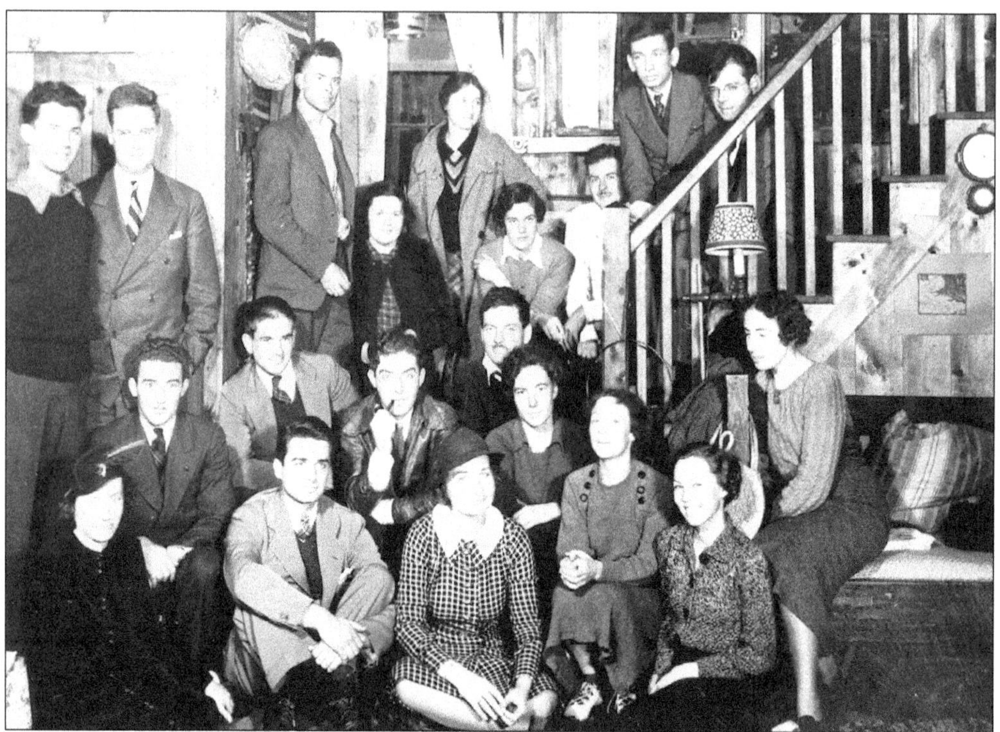

Edwin Land sits in the front row of this 1935 employee gathering, described as the first company outing, held in Wrentham, Massachusetts. The small start-up company soon became a major employer in Massachusetts. By 1977, Polaroid had 20,000 employees worldwide.

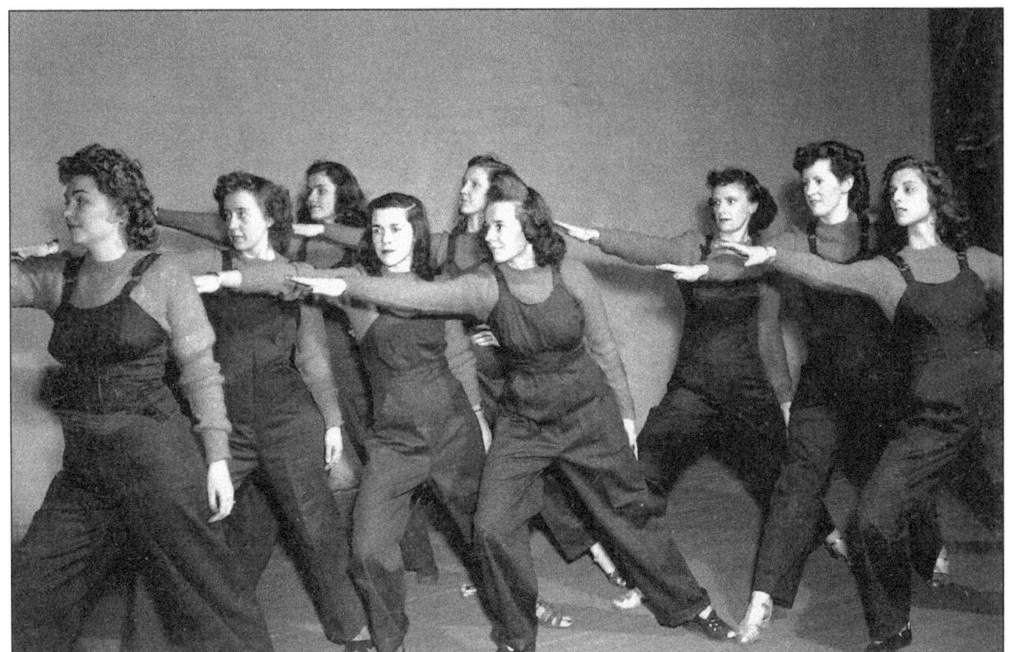

This January 1945 image is labeled "Polaroid 'Peers Club' Revue." The Peers Club was a social organization for employees that organized picnics, dances, and even musical groups.

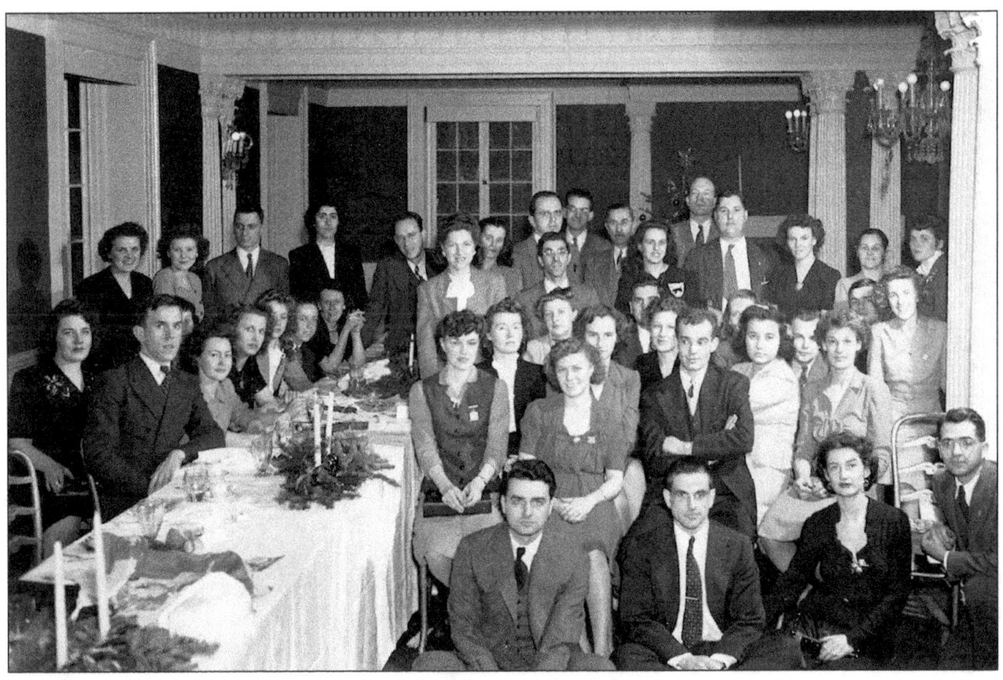

At Polaroid's Christmas party in 1944, Land sits in the front row.

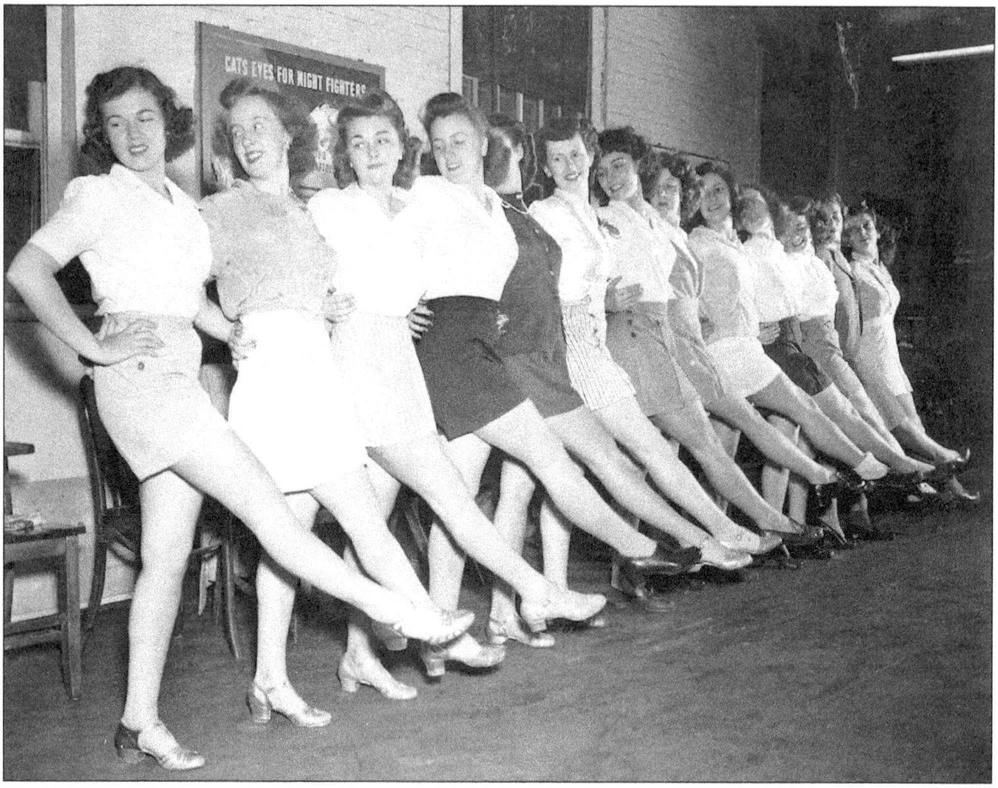

The Polaroid Revue Chorus performs in front of a poster extolling the need to produce "Cat's Eyes for Night Fighters."

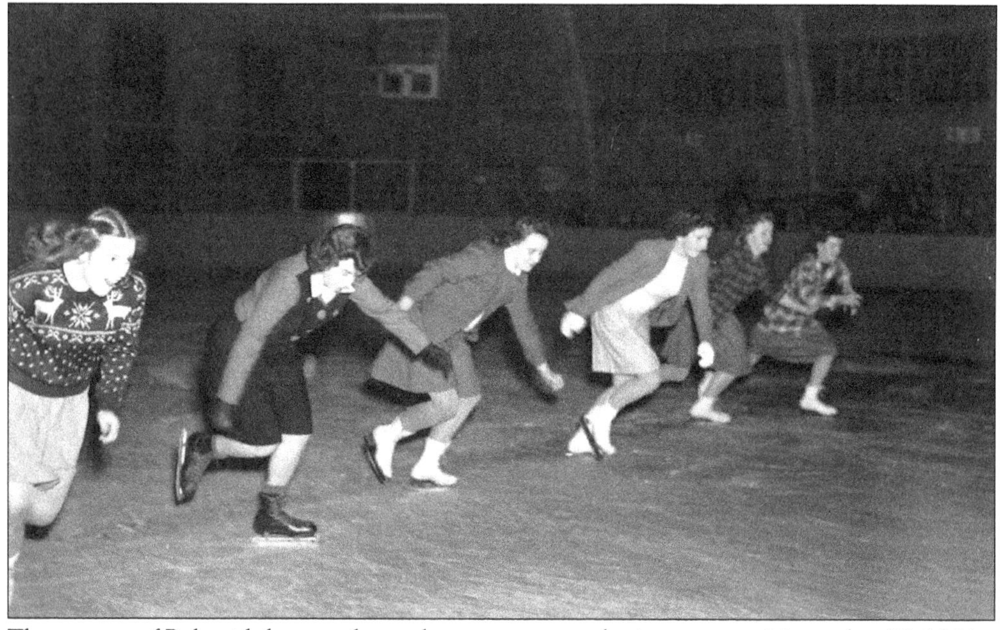

The women of Polaroid skate exuberantly at a company skating party on November 20, 1944.

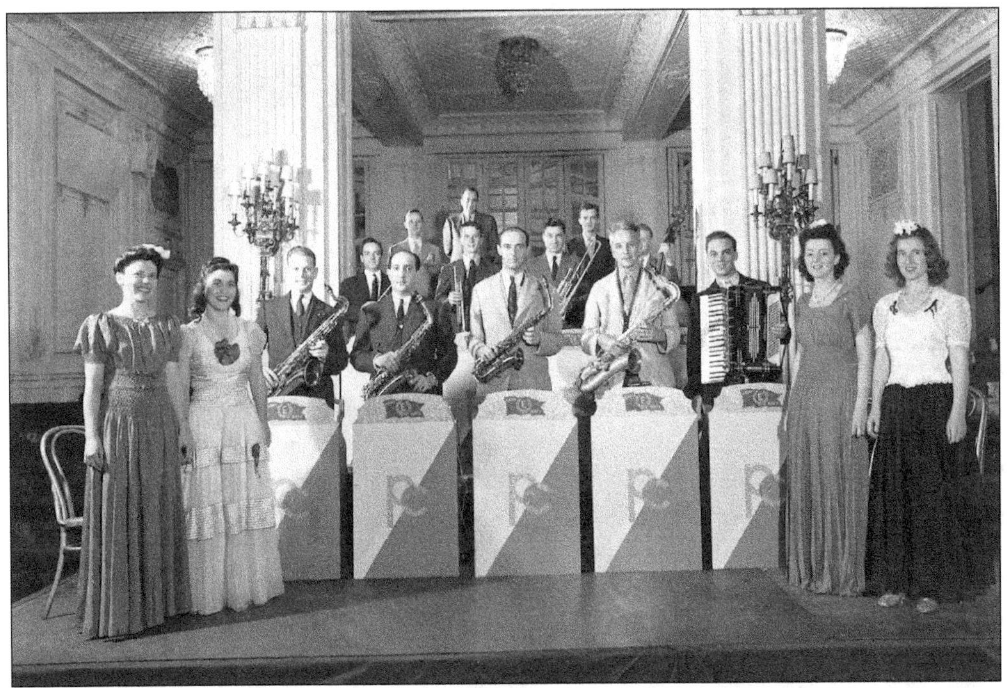

The Polaroid band, yet another employee organization, is shown around 1943. The Peers Club logo (PC), styled to match the corporate logo, can be seen along with a miniature representation of the Army-Navy E Award.

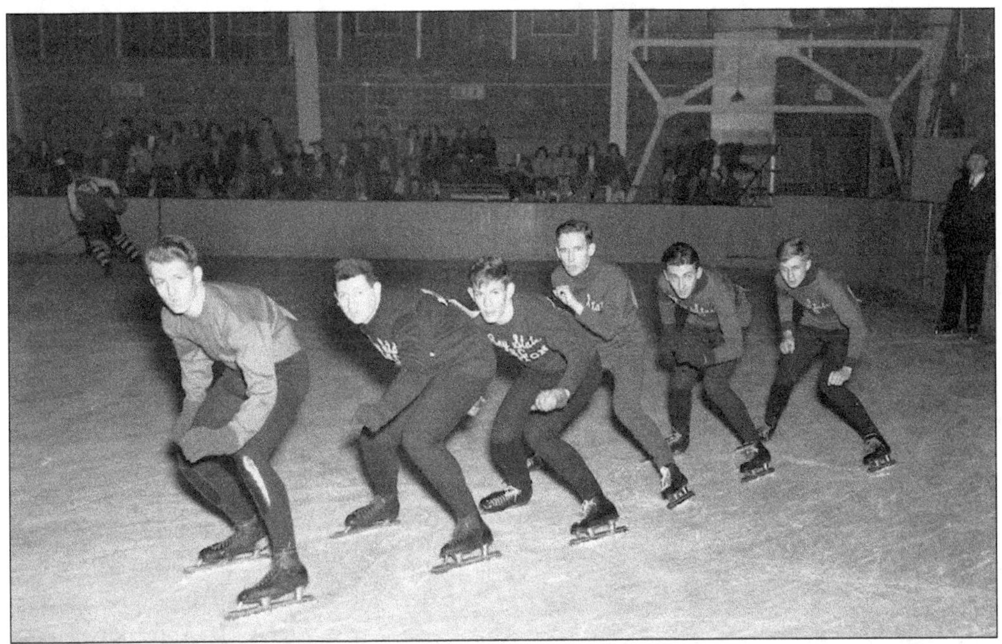

The men of Polaroid also appear to be having a good time at the company skating party. By this stage of the war, men were a rarity in civilian life and were badly needed to fill out the ranks of the armed forces, particularly the army. Polaroid rehired many of its veterans after the war.

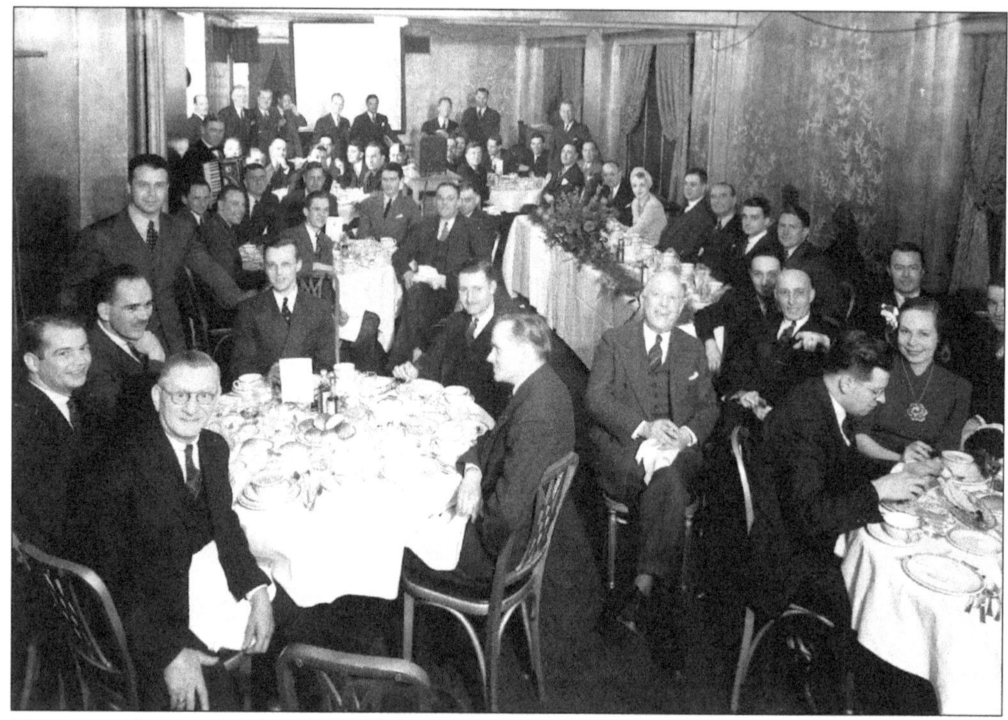

This spirited prewar gathering, on March 29, 1940, is a celebration for the production of the millionth pair of Polaroid sunglasses. Land is visible at the long table on the right.

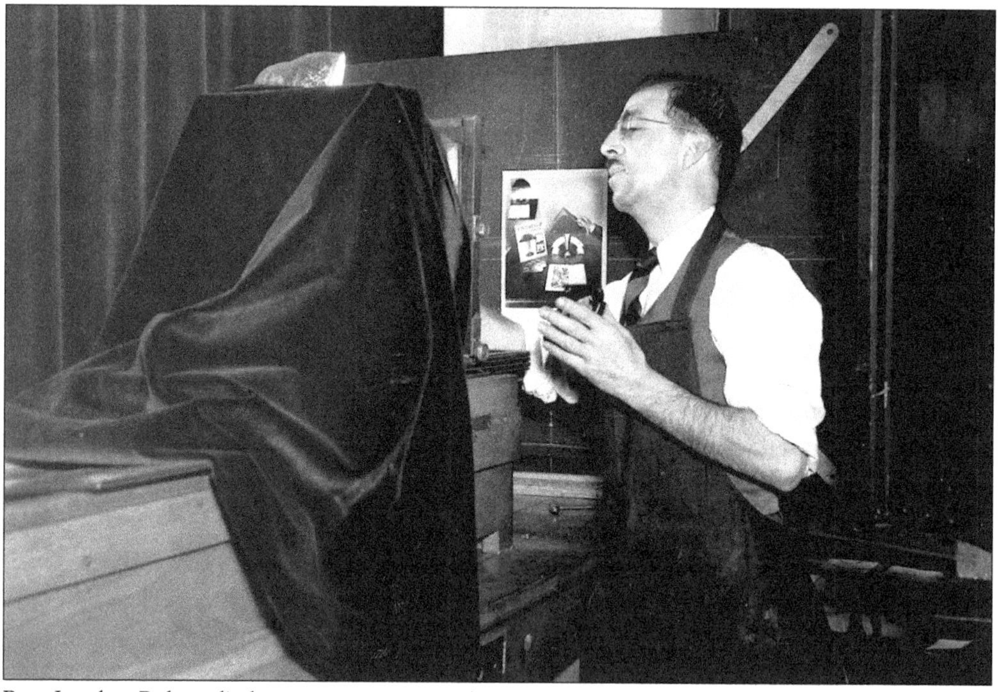

Roy Jacoby, Polaroid's longtime company photographer, is himself the subject of this image from 1940.

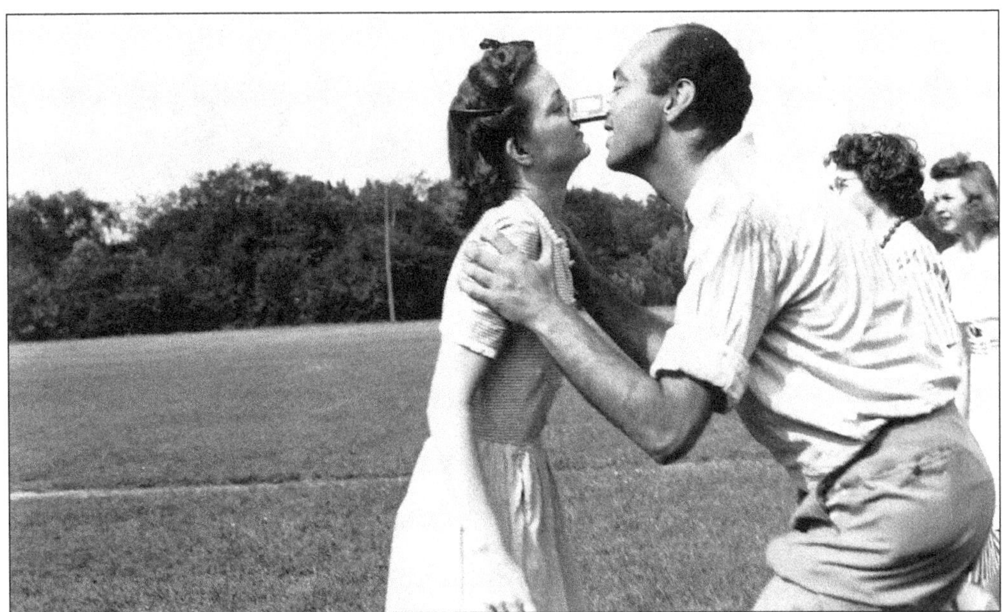

Spirited hijinks are the order of the day at this 1943 company outing. A group photograph taken this day reveals that the small Cambridge company had grown to include hundreds of employees.

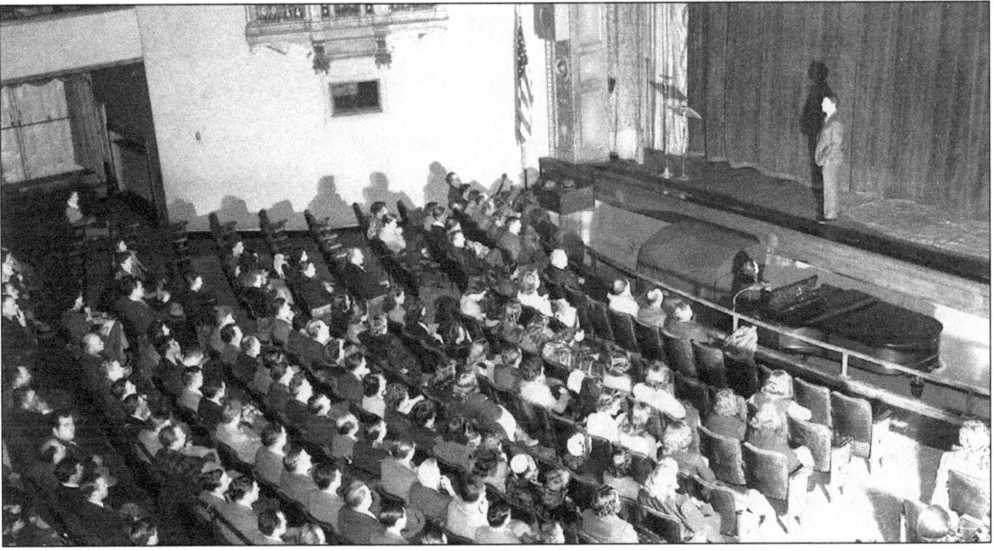

Land is on stage at the Harvard Square Theater in this view of the 1945 Polaroid Christmas party. The company was in the midst of a transition from its frenetic wartime growth (sales had risen from just over $1 million in 1941 to nearly $17 million in 1945) toward the instant photography future that Land was already envisioning. Teasing his audience at a similar event the next year, Land showed part of the popular film *The Horn Blows at Midnight*, in which an angel's passport photograph develops instantly. "Now you know what 'SX-70' is," he told them. Most of the employees had to wait in suspense for another year to find out more. SX-70 was the research code name for the instant photographic developing process, a name revived in 1972 for the next-generation instant camera.

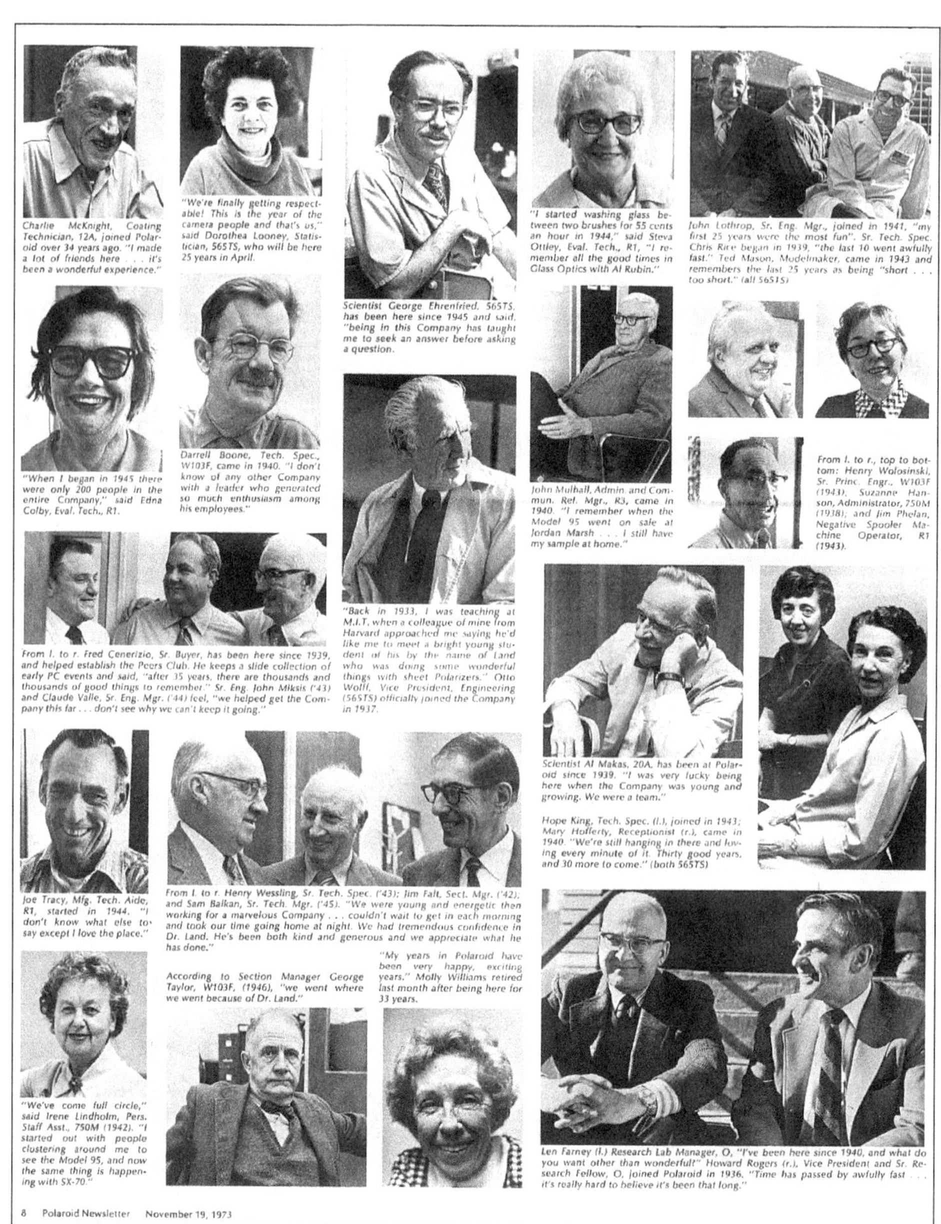

Charlie McKnight, Coating Technician, 12A, joined Polaroid over 34 years ago. "I made a lot of friends here . . . it's been a wonderful experience."

"We're finally getting respectable! This is the year of the camera people and that's us," said Dorothea Looney, Statistician, 565TS, who will be here 25 years in April.

Scientist George Ehrenfried, 565TS, has been here since 1945 and said, "being in this Company has taught me to seek an answer before asking a question.

"I started washing glass between two brushes for 55 cents an hour in 1944," said Steva Ottley, Eval. Tech., R1, "I remember all the good times in Glass Optics with Al Rubin."

John Lothrop, Sr. Eng. Mgr., joined in 1941, "my first 25 years were the most fun". Sr. Tech. Spec. Chris Rice began in 1939, "the last 10 went awfully fast." Ted Mason, Modelmaker, came in 1943 and remembers the last 25 years as being "short . . . too short." (all 565TS)

"When I began in 1945 there were only 200 people in the entire Company," said Edna Colby, Eval. Tech., R1.

Darrell Boone, Tech. Spec., W103F, came in 1940. "I don't know of any other Company with a leader who generated so much enthusiasm among his employees."

John Mulhall, Admin. and Commun. Rel. Mgr., R3, came in 1940. "I remember when the Model 95 went on sale at Jordan Marsh . . . I still have my sample at home."

From l. to r., top to bottom: Henry Wolosinski, Sr. Princ. Engr., W103F (1943); Suzanne Hanson, Administrator, 750M (1938); and Jim Phelan, Negative Spooler Machine Operator, R1 (1943).

From l. to r. Fred Cenerizio, Sr. Buyer, has been here since 1939, and helped establish the Peers Club. He keeps a slide collection of early PC events and said, "after 35 years, there are thousands and thousands of good things to remember." Sr. Eng. John Miksis ('43) and Claude Valle, Sr. Eng. Mgr. ('44) feel, "we helped get the Company this far . . . don't see why we can't keep it going."

"Back in 1933, I was teaching at M.I.T. when a colleague of mine from Harvard approached me saying he'd like me to meet a bright young student of his by the name of Land who was doing some wonderful things with sheet Polarizers." Otto Wolff, Vice President, Engineering (565TS) officially joined the Company in 1937.

Scientist Al Makas, 20A, has been at Polaroid since 1939. "I was very lucky being here when the Company was young and growing. We were a team."

Hope King, Tech. Spec. (l.), joined in 1943; Mary Hofferty, Receptionist (r.), came in 1940. "We're still hanging in there and loving every minute of it. Thirty good years, and 30 more to come." (both 565TS)

Joe Tracy, Mfg. Tech. Aide, R1, started in 1944. "I don't know what else to say except I love the place."

From l. to r. Henry Wessling, Sr. Tech. Spec. ('43); Jim Falt, Sect. Mgr. ('42); and Sam Balkan, Sr. Tech. Mgr. ('45). "We were young and energetic then working for a marvelous Company . . . couldn't wait to get in each morning and took our time going home at night. We had tremendous confidence in Dr. Land. He's been both kind and generous and we appreciate what he has done."

According to Section Manager George Taylor, W103F, (1946), "we went where we went because of Dr. Land."

"My years in Polaroid have been very happy, exciting years." Molly Williams retired last month after being here for 33 years.

"We've come full circle," said Irene Lindholm, Pers. Staff Asst., 750M (1942). "I started out with people clustering around me to see the Model 95, and now the same thing is happening with SX-70."

Len Farney (l.) Research Lab Manager, O, "I've been here since 1940, and what do you want other than wonderful!" Howard Rogers (r.), Vice President and Sr. Research Fellow, O, joined Polaroid in 1936. "Time has passed by awfully fast . . . it's really hard to believe it's been that long."

8 Polaroid Newsletter November 19, 1973

Polaroid celebrates the 25th anniversary of instant photography in 1973. In this November 19, 1973, issue of the Polaroid newsletter, some of the employees who had been with the company since 1948 recalled their fond memories.

Five

Instant Photography

When Edwin Land believed something could be done, nothing could dissuade him from doing it. So, when World War II ended and he was again free to think about Polaroid's future, he thought about a product for which there was as yet no clearly defined market and no competitors: instant photography.

With a core of talented scientists and researchers recruited from MIT and Harvard, Land—not for the last time—staked the company's future on a vision, and he succeeded. Born in the request of his three-year-old daughter to see a picture immediately, the idea of instant photography came to seem not only possible but compelling. By 1946, the first experiments were yielding promising results, and a year later a public demonstration of instant photography at the Optical Society of America sealed Land's reputation as a modern-day wizard.

Within a year, the first Polaroid instant camera (Model 95) went on sale, setting the company on a path to growth that sustained it for decades to come.

Despite the triumphs, however, there were challenges and dark moments. For instance, the first generation of instant film prints began to curl months after use, necessitating a large consumer refund program. But Land, with a steady hand on the helm, managed to navigate through the maelstrom. Furthermore, the first-generation Polaroid film produced only sepia prints rather than black and white, which was preferred by most customers. So, once again, Land and his researchers reworked the chemistry and brought the public what it wanted.

As was the case during the war, Polaroid was again on the grow, acquiring new facilities and adding staff, this time entirely on the merits of its own products.

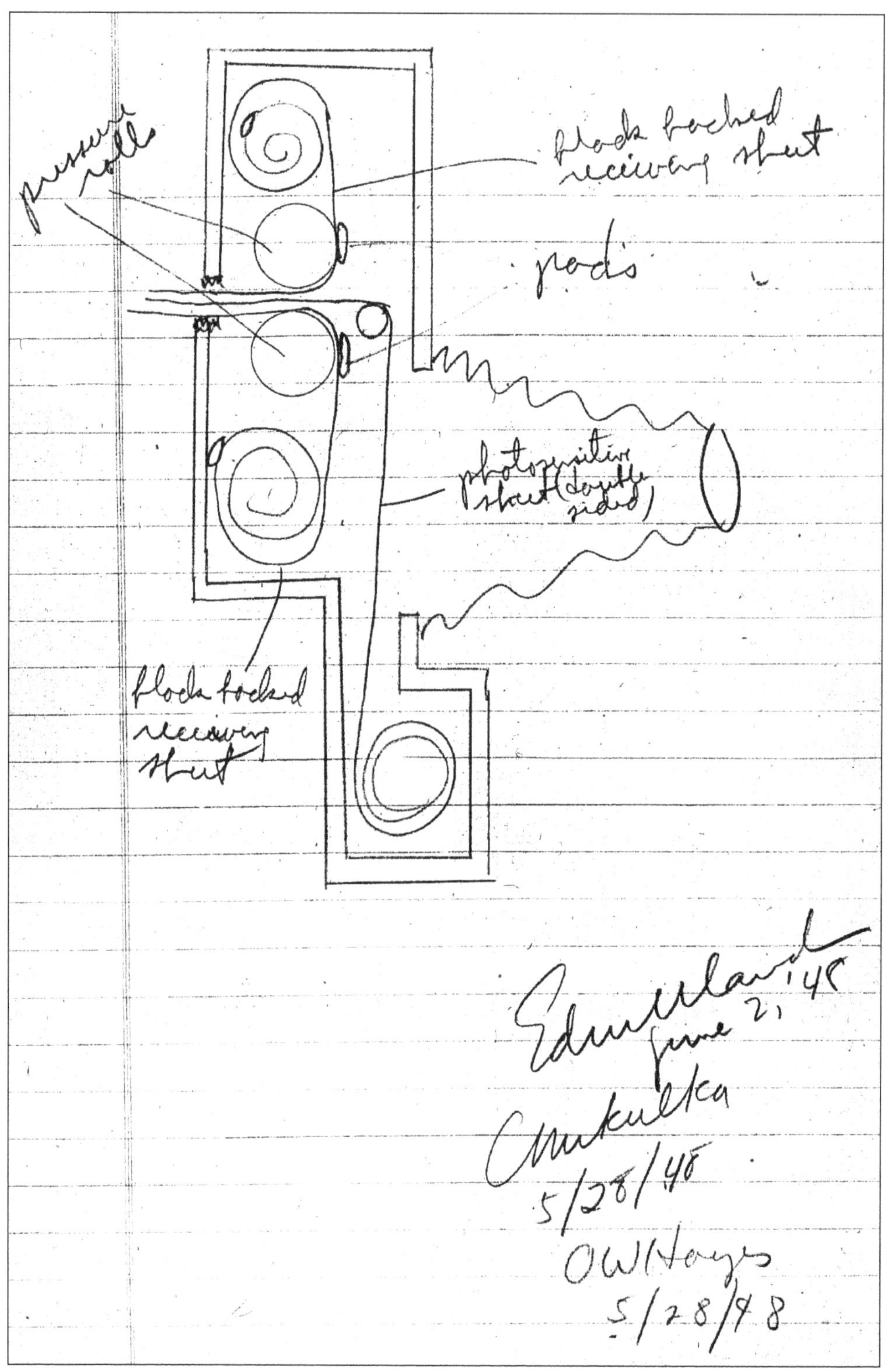

This sketch was signed by Edwin Land, as well as his patent attorney, Charles Mikulka, in June 1948.

Land looks tired but determined in this test photograph.

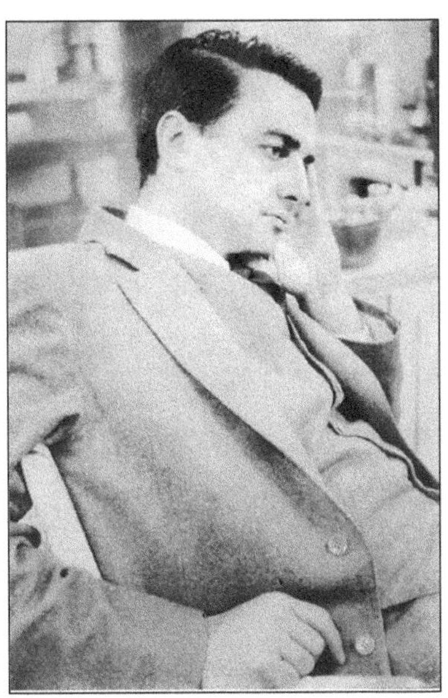

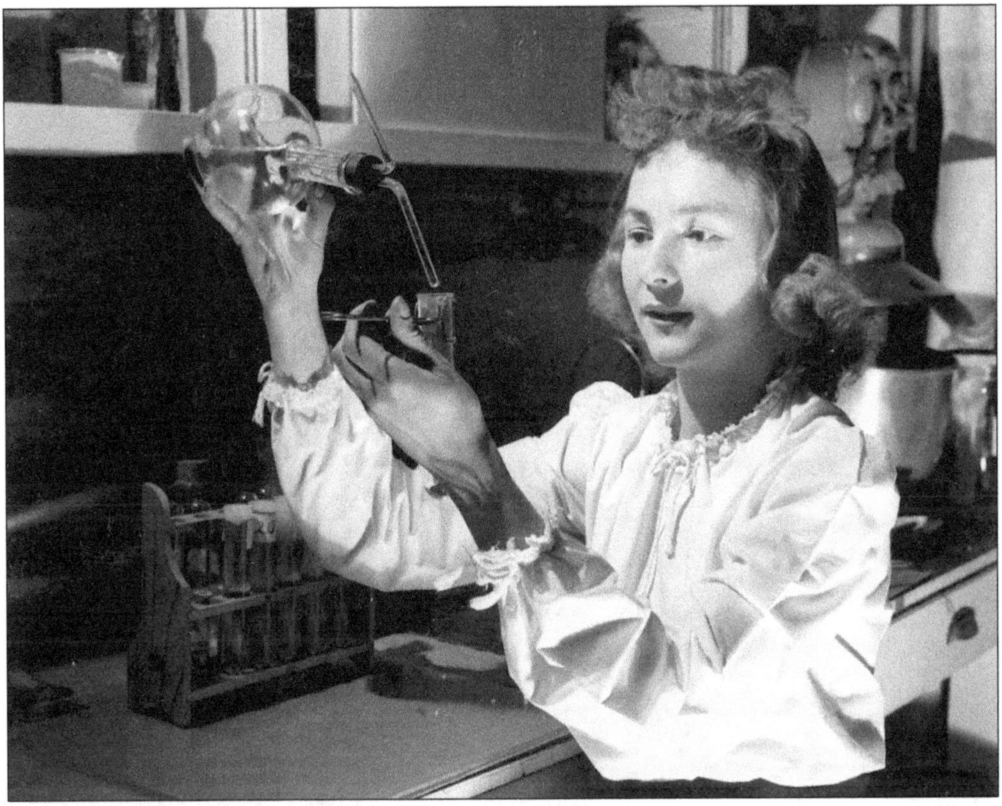

Eudoxia Muller worked on the first photographic experiment under Land's direction in 1944. Her daily laboratory report and sample pictures for the SX-70 research file was expected on Land's desk every day.

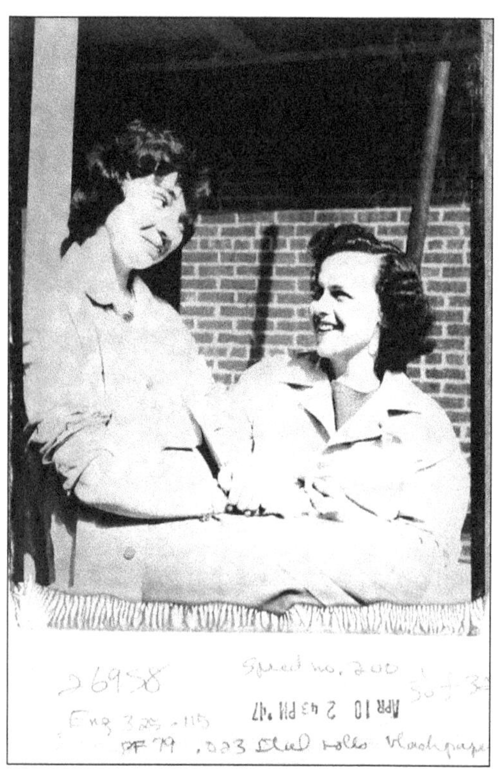

A 1947 test photograph of two lab employees reveals the date and time the photograph was taken.

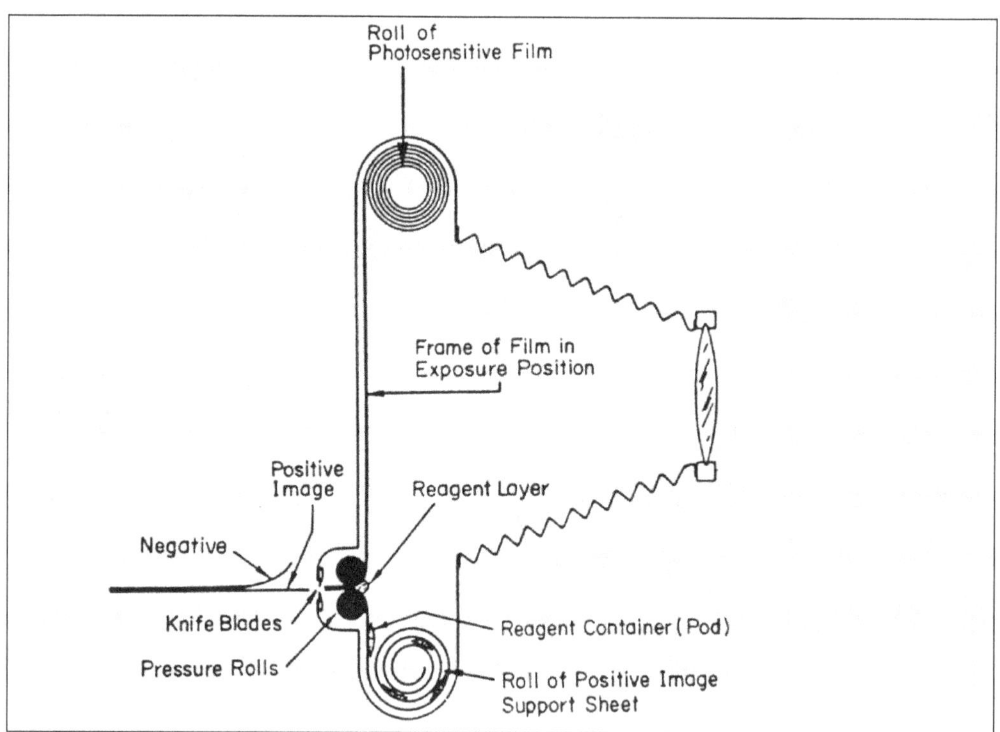

This diagram illustrates the operation of the first Polaroid instant camera, Model 95.

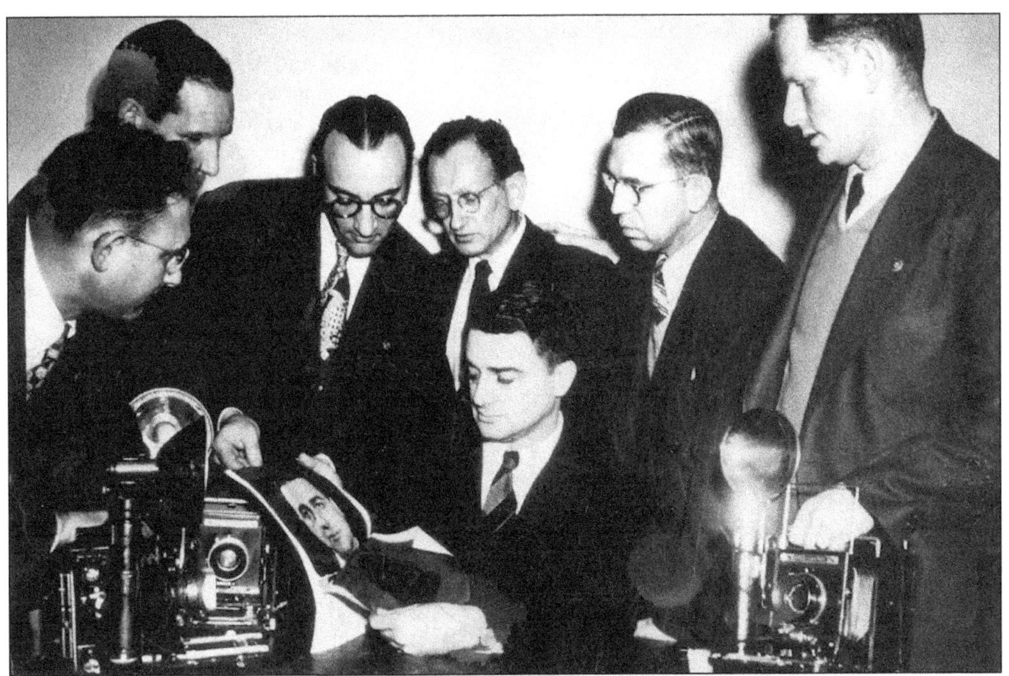

Land demonstrated the one-step photographic system at the meeting of the American Optical Society on February 21, 1947. Polaroid's instant photography was an important advancement in photography.

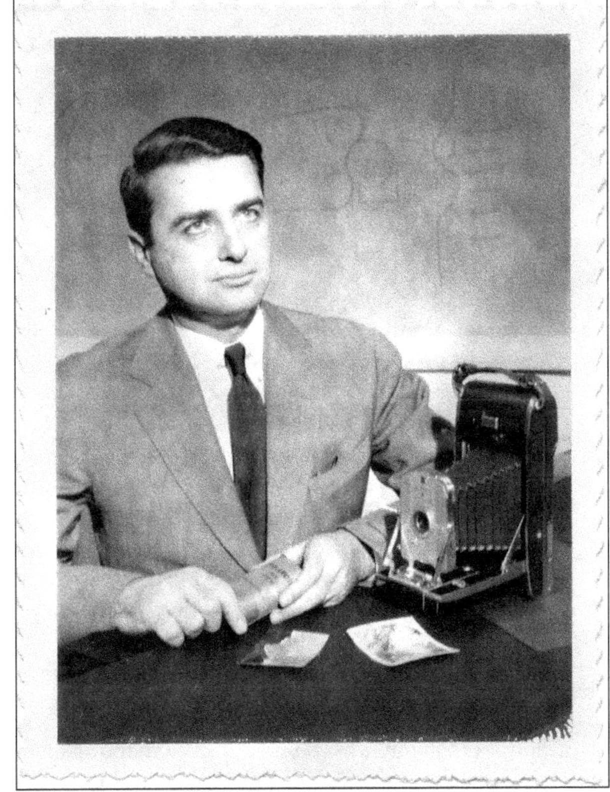

Land poses here with the Model 95 Land camera in a 1948 photograph made on Type 40 Land film. Instant photography made Land and Polaroid household names.

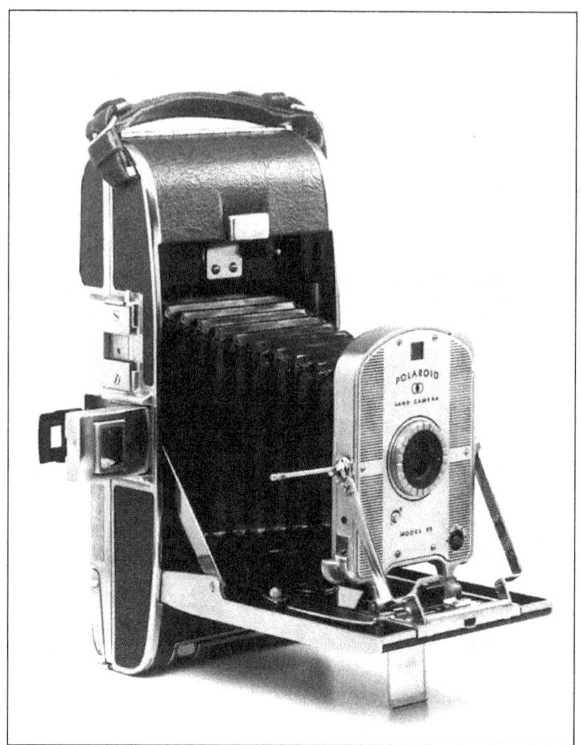

The Model 95, the first instant camera, and its successors soon became an iconic presence in 1950s America and were often seen at family events and other occasions.

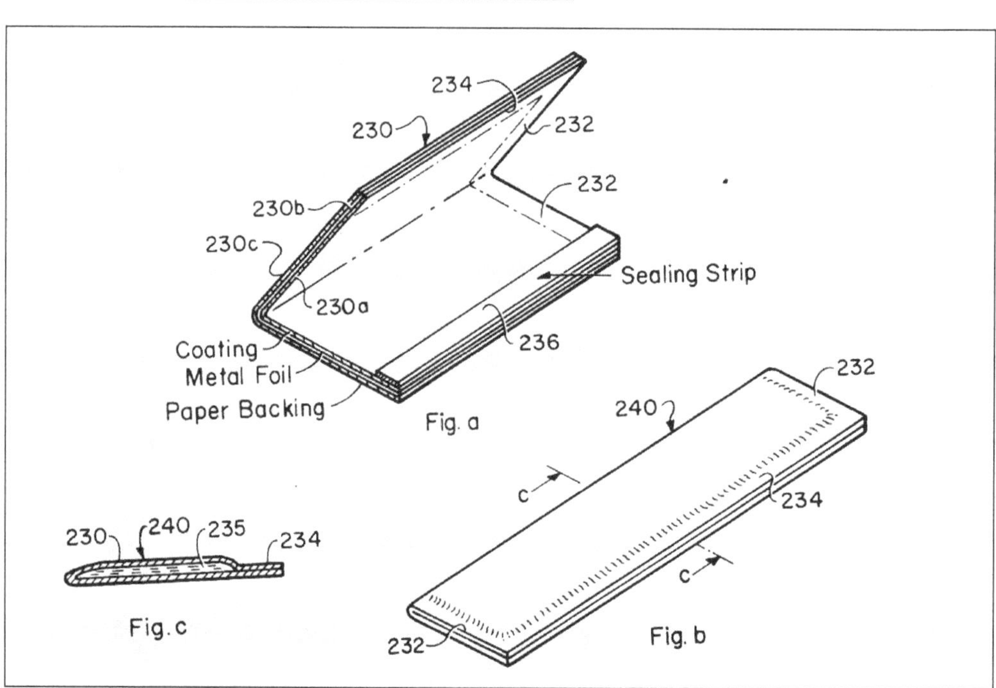

These are diagrams from the patent application for "the pod," Land's key invention for the one-step photographic system. One of the technical achievements contributing to the success of instant photography was the precise design and manufacture of reagent pods. The pods, when squeezed by rollers in the camera, provided the chemicals needed to develop the positive image.

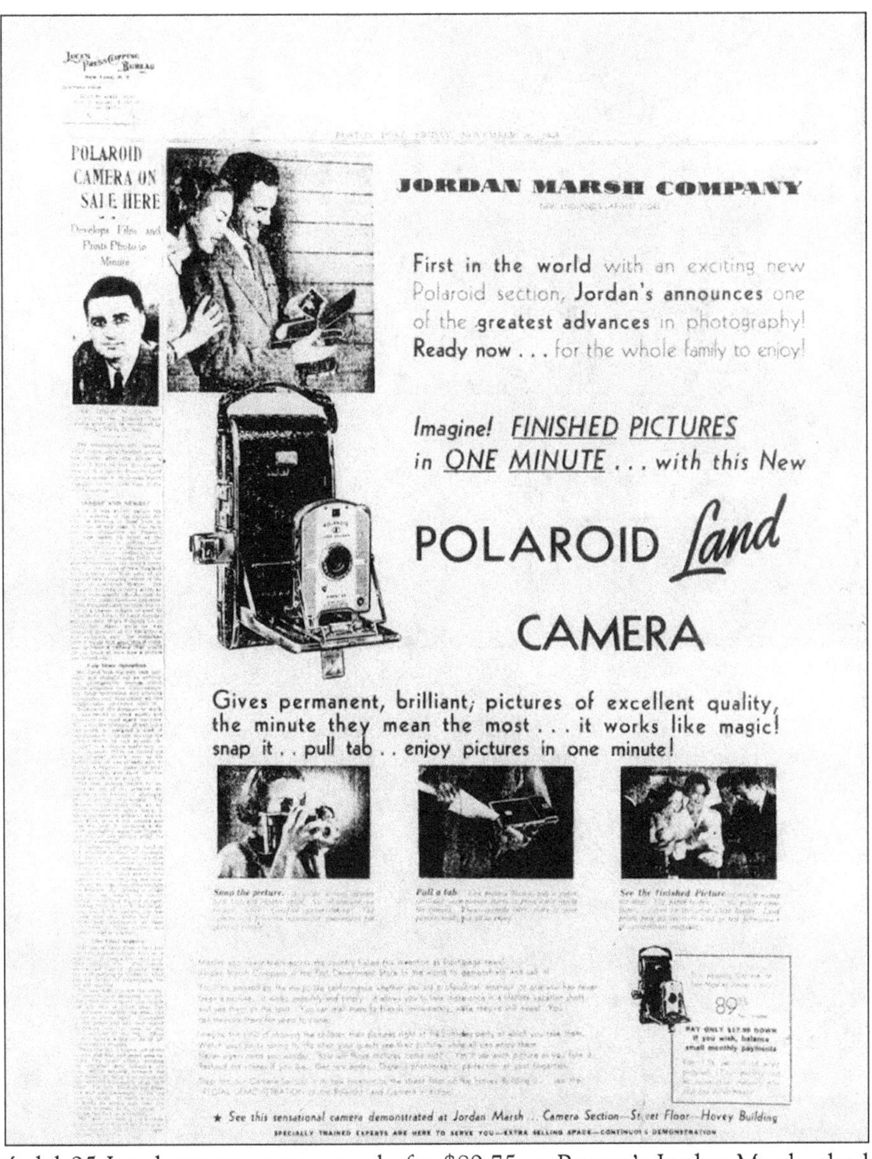

The Model 95 Land camera went on sale for $89.75 at Boston's Jordan Marsh, the largest New England retailer, in 1948. This advertisement for Jordan Marsh announces "one of the greatest advances in photography." In his quest for the consumer market, Land relied on a geographic rollout strategy to conserve money and build expectation. Boston was one of the first markets in which retailers were provided with cameras. The strategy was partly the result of Polaroid's modest size and limited ability to initially manufacture cameras in sufficient volume to meet demand.

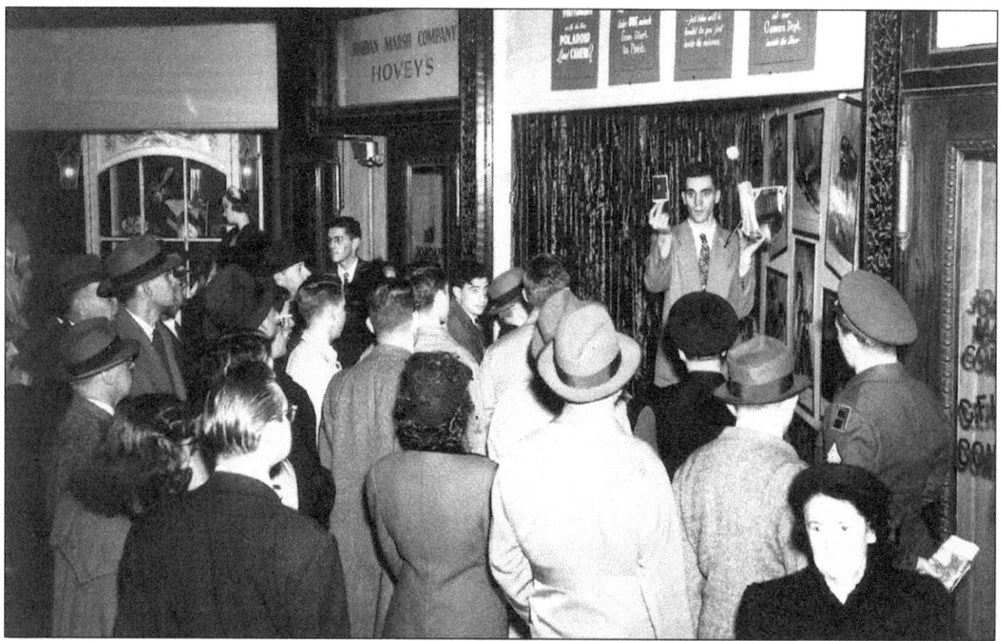

Polaroid's Land camera was first demonstrated to the public at Jordan Marsh on November 26, 1948. It became an overnight success and took America by storm. The first placard above the man demonstrating the camera at Jordan Marsh makes an offer that must have been hard to resist: "May we take your photograph with the new Polaroid Land Camera?"

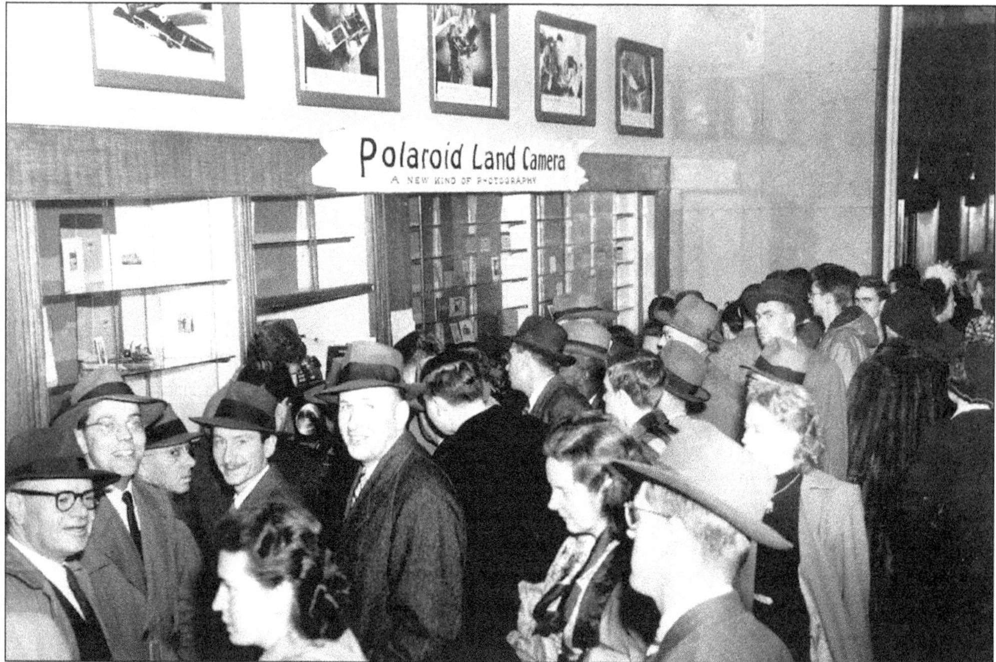

The excitement of the crowd is captured here. For a long time, Polaroid's biggest problem was simply meeting demand. The banner calls the Polaroid Land camera "a new kind of photography." The public was enchanted with this innovative product.

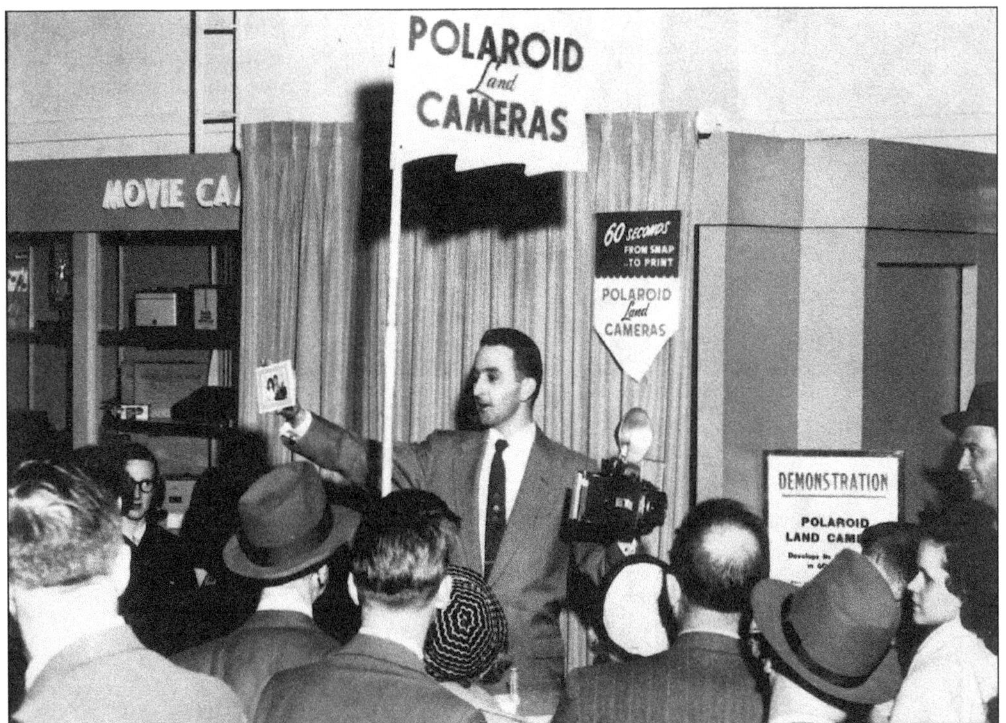

The Land camera provided excitement in an era hungry for novelty after the years of war and depression.

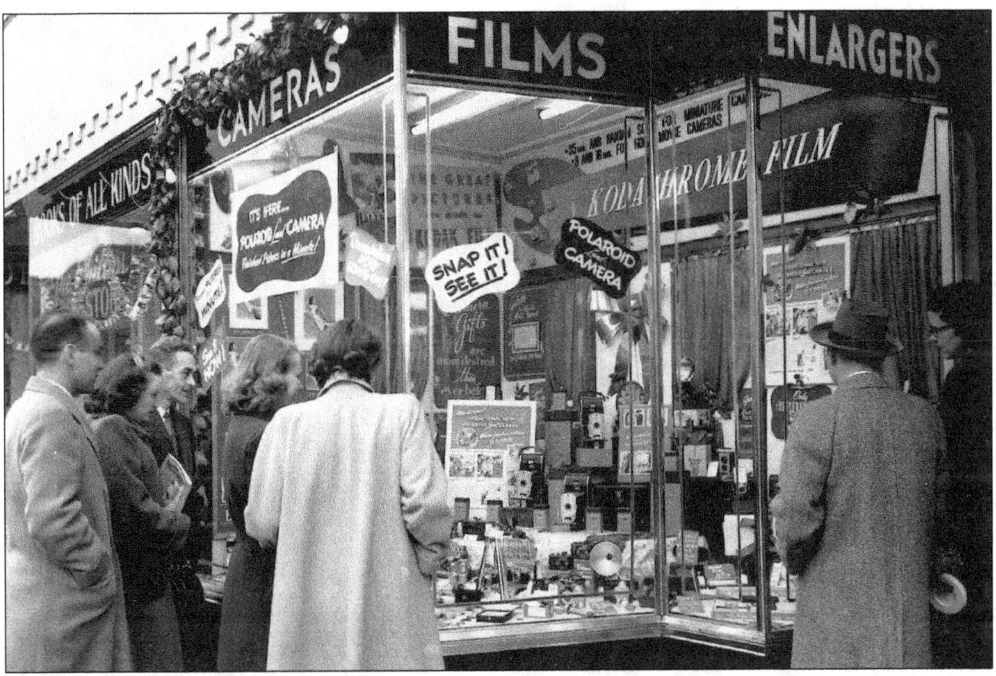

The display window at Claus Gellote, a Harvard Square photo retailer, is devoted entirely to Polaroid's Land camera in this image from December 10, 1948.

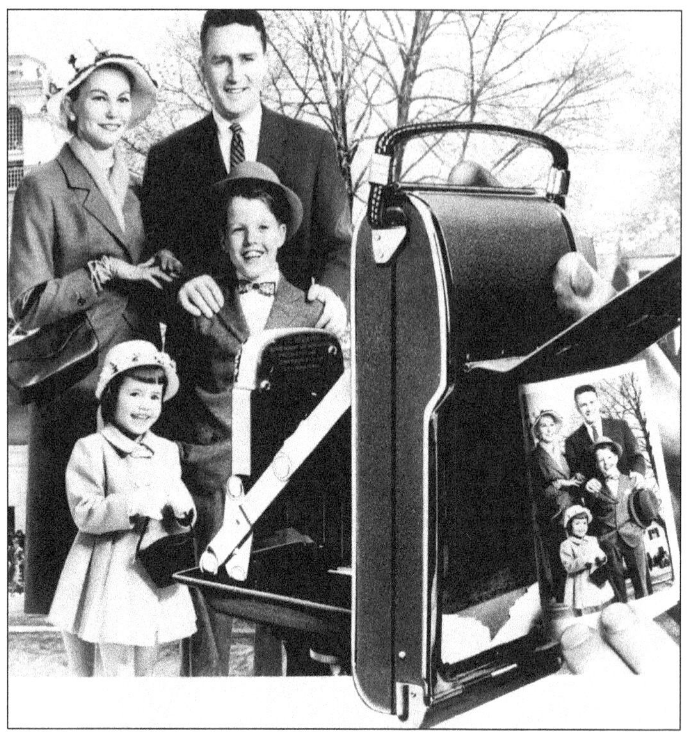

This publicity shot of a family group illustrates how quickly Polaroid's instant photography became a fixture in American life.

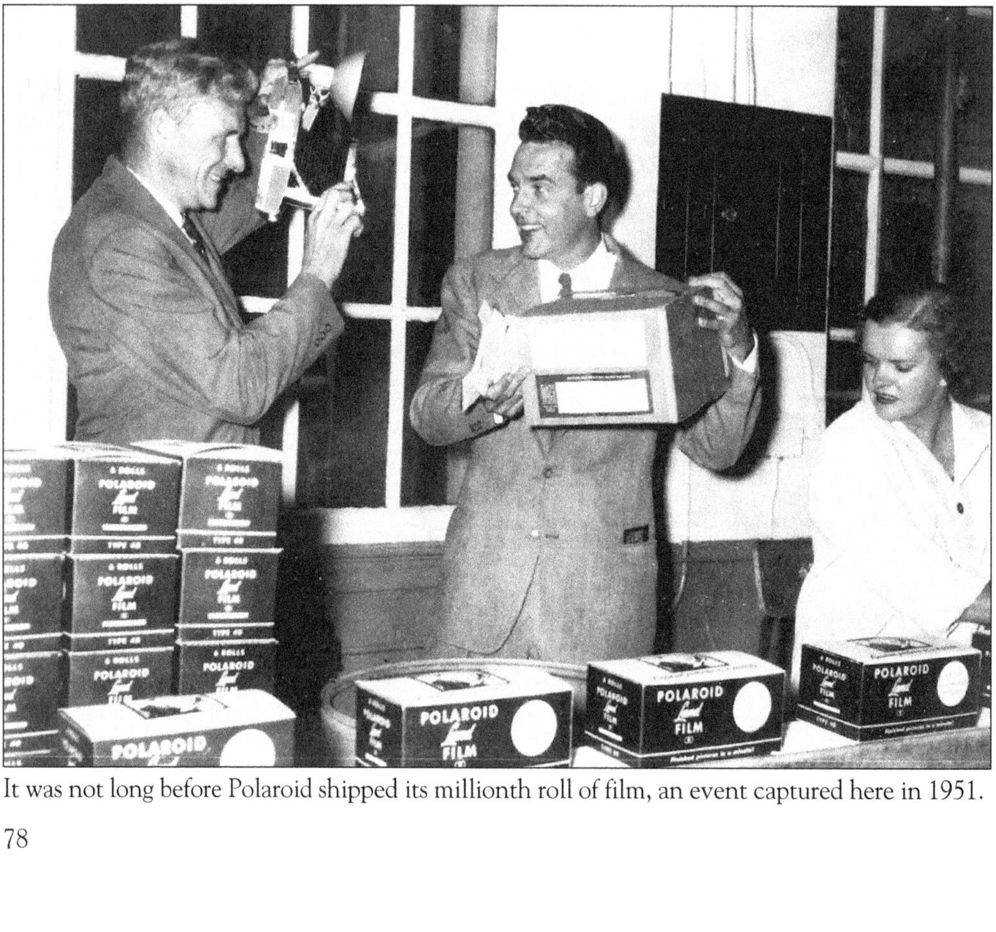

It was not long before Polaroid shipped its millionth roll of film, an event captured here in 1951.

The cover of the 1954 Polaroid annual report features the new Highlander model, which was styled by Walter Dorwin Teague.

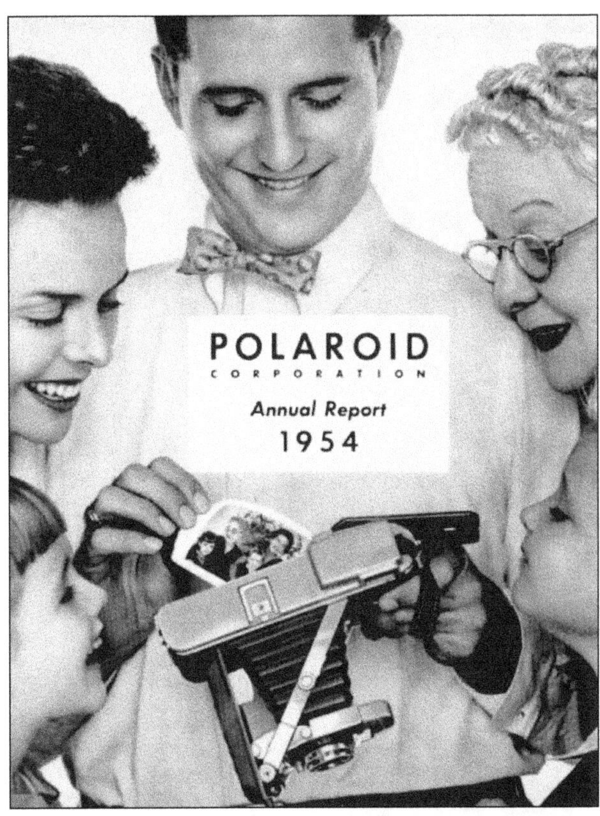

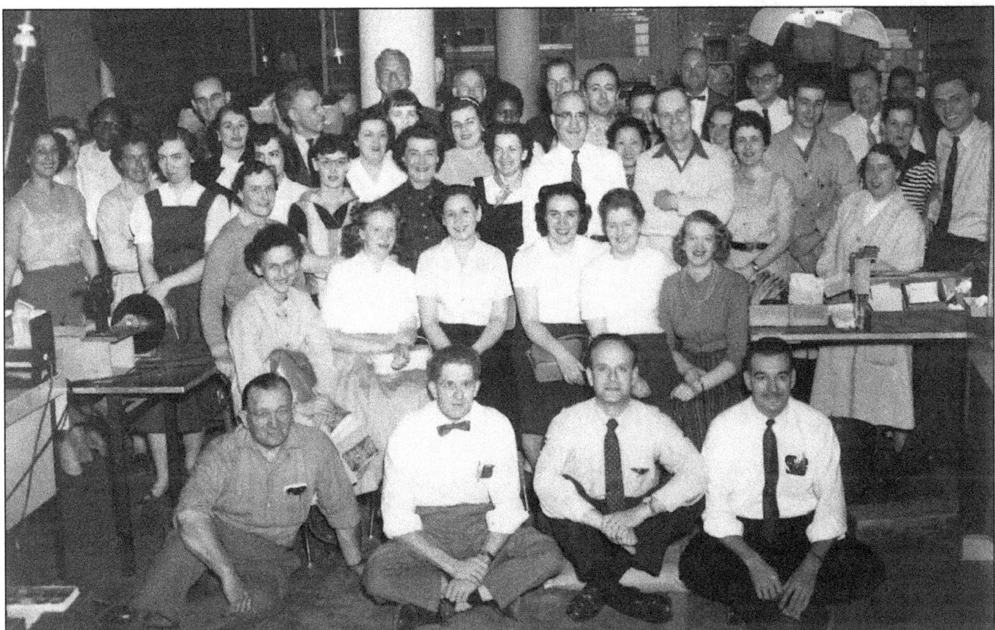

This 1952 photograph shows the staff of the photocopying department. By providing a means of duplicating favorite photographs, this service helped compensate for fact that the Polaroid process did not create negatives.

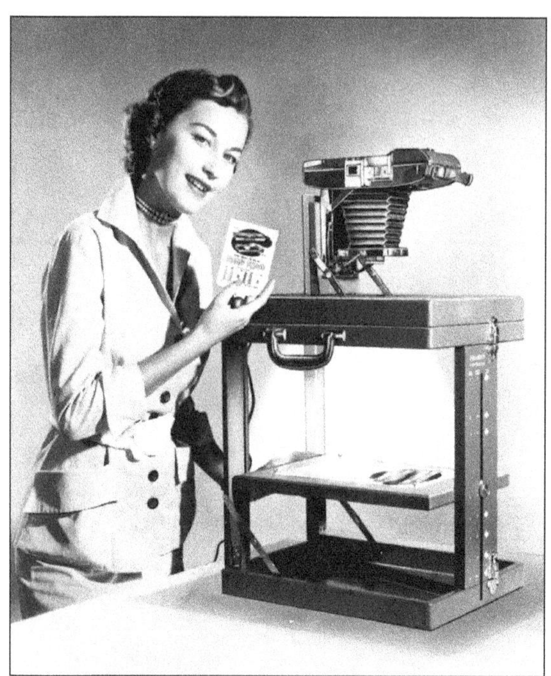

The Polaroid print copier, introduced in 1958, had an illumination and lens system for copying Polaroid prints using standard Polaroid cameras and films.

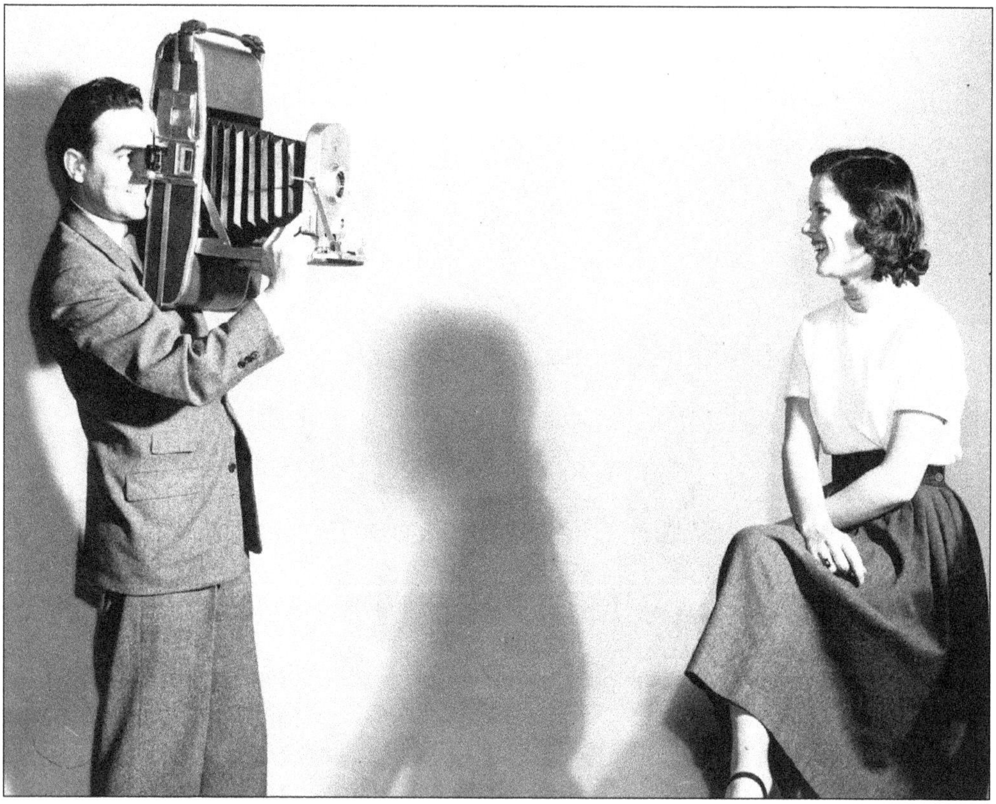

An experimental Model 95 "Jumbo" camera for producing large-format images could accommodate film up to eight by nine inches.

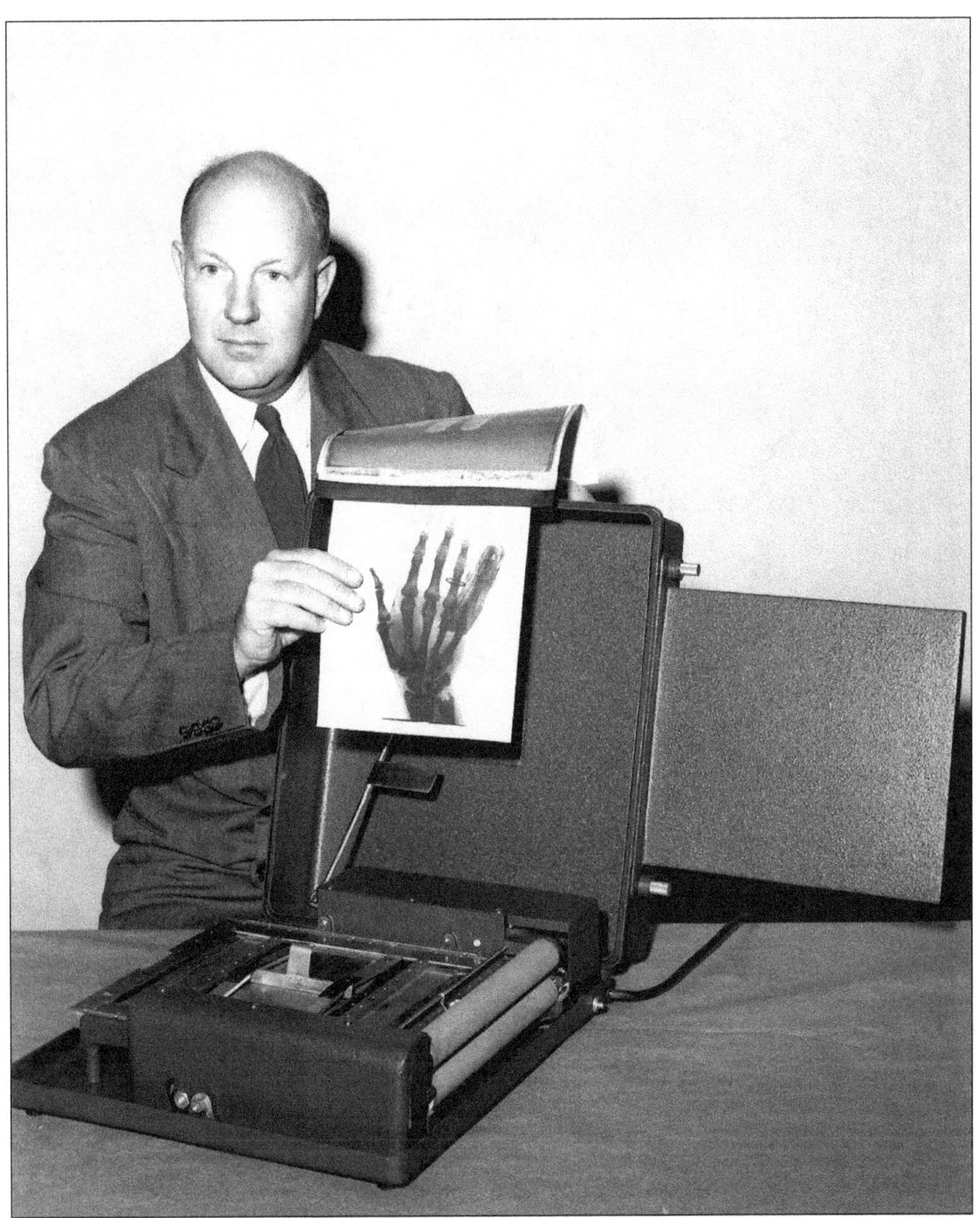

Polaroid scientist Lewis Chubb demonstrates this Picker-Polaroid X-ray machine at the American Medical Association's meeting in 1951. This system provided a new and increasingly important venue for Polaroid's instant film. Diagnosticians could now get results instantly, without having to wait for lab technicians to process film.

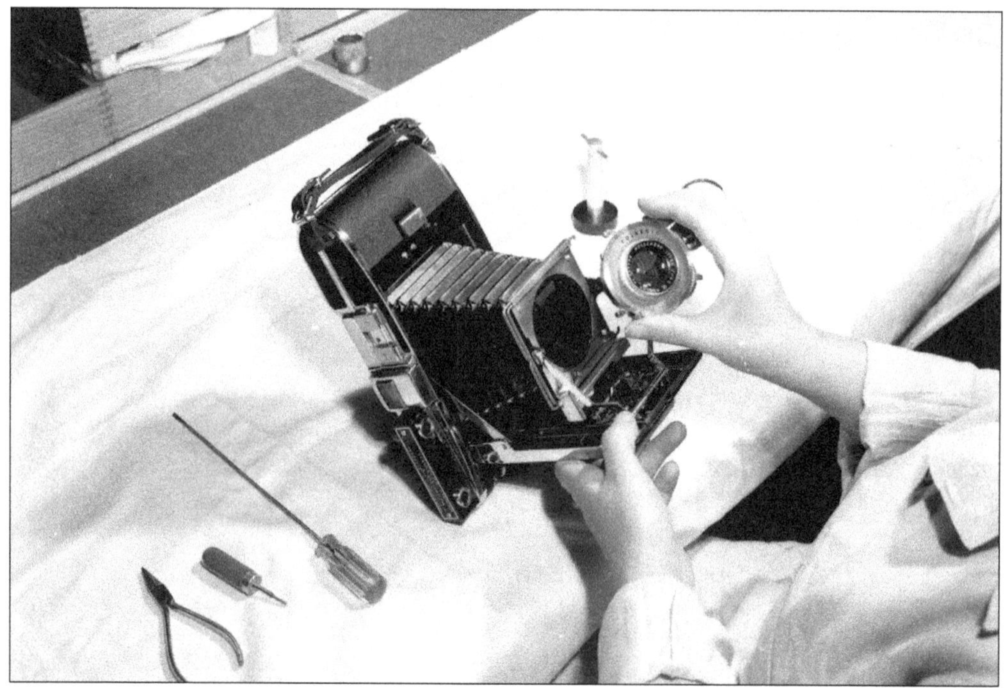

Precision assembly work on Polaroid's cameras was gradually shifted from subcontractors to in-house workers.

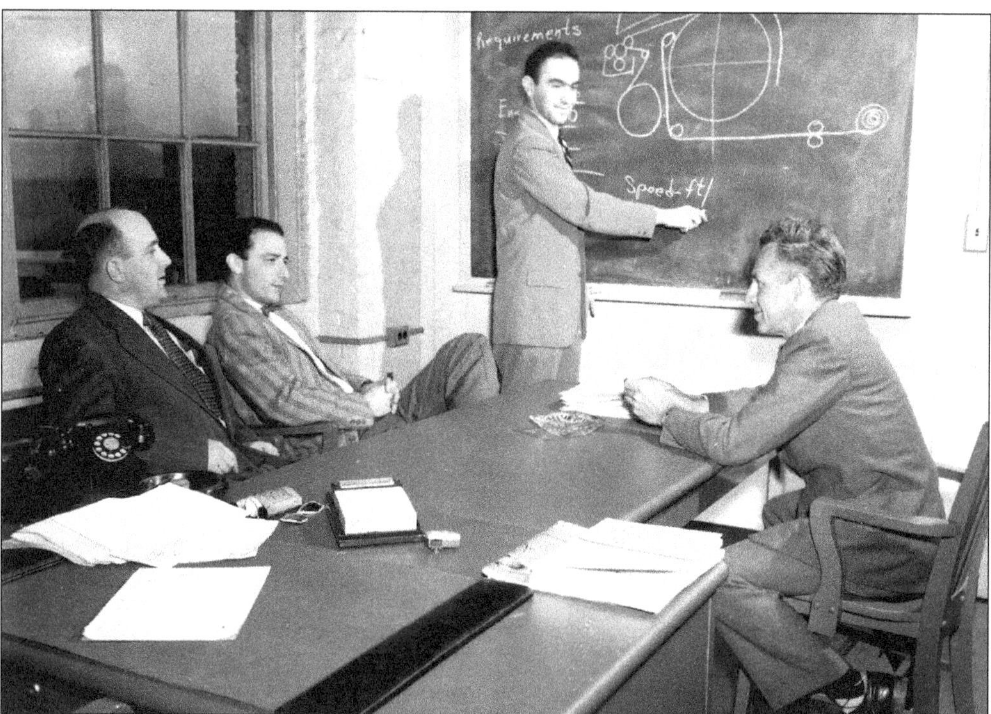

The challenges of growing the company in the early 1950s included developing and improving completely new manufacturing processes and setting up and equipping new factories. This photograph shows a meeting with David Skinner, right, vice president of manufacturing.

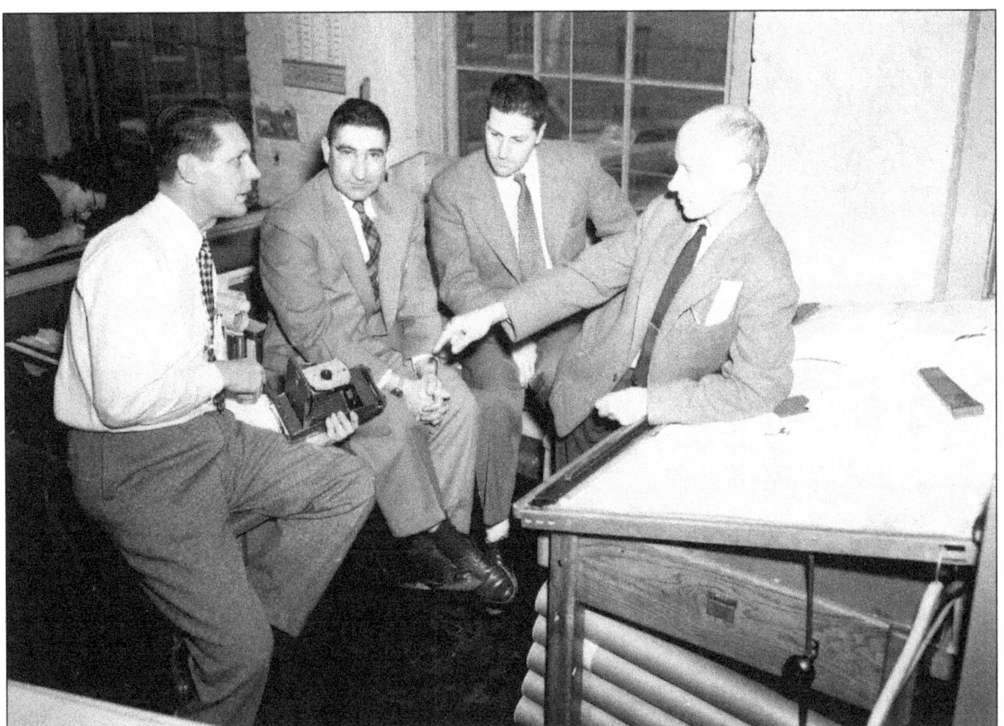

An employee leans on his drafting board. Improvements to the Pathfinder camera seem to be the point of discussion.

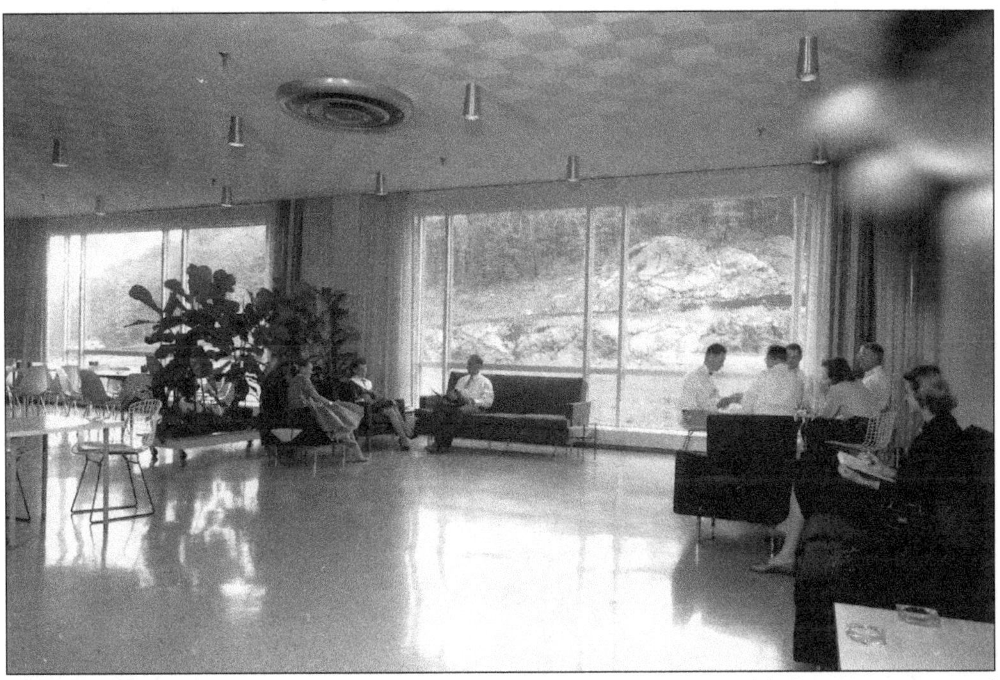

This airy cafeteria at Waltham, part of the complex built in 1957, is visible from Route 128 and remains a local landmark. Polaroid headquarters is now located in this facility.

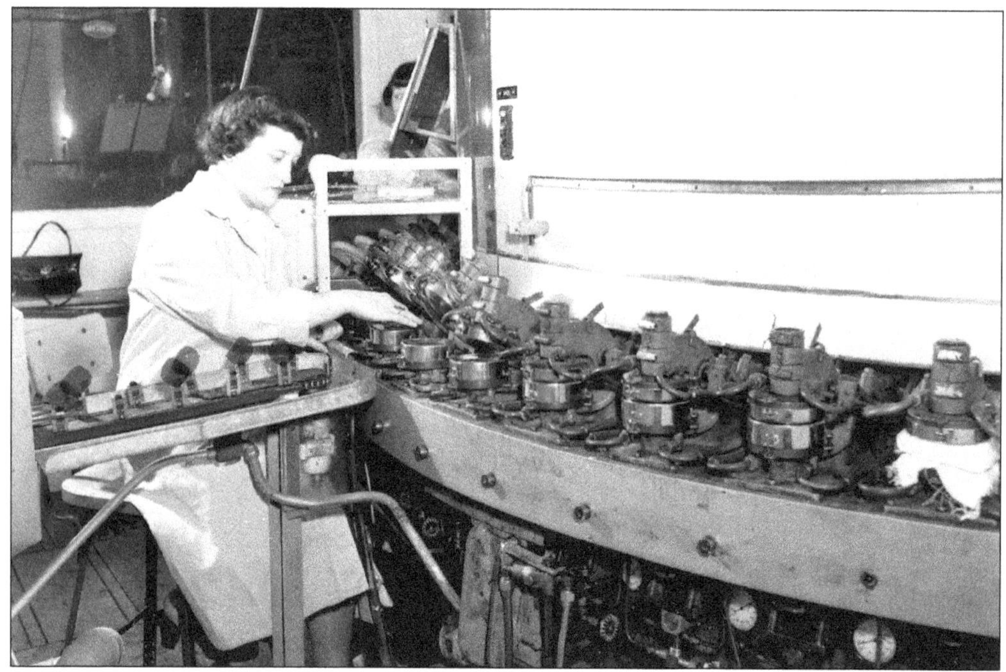

The Pathfinder camera assembly line at the Polaroid plant is shown here in a 1954 photograph.

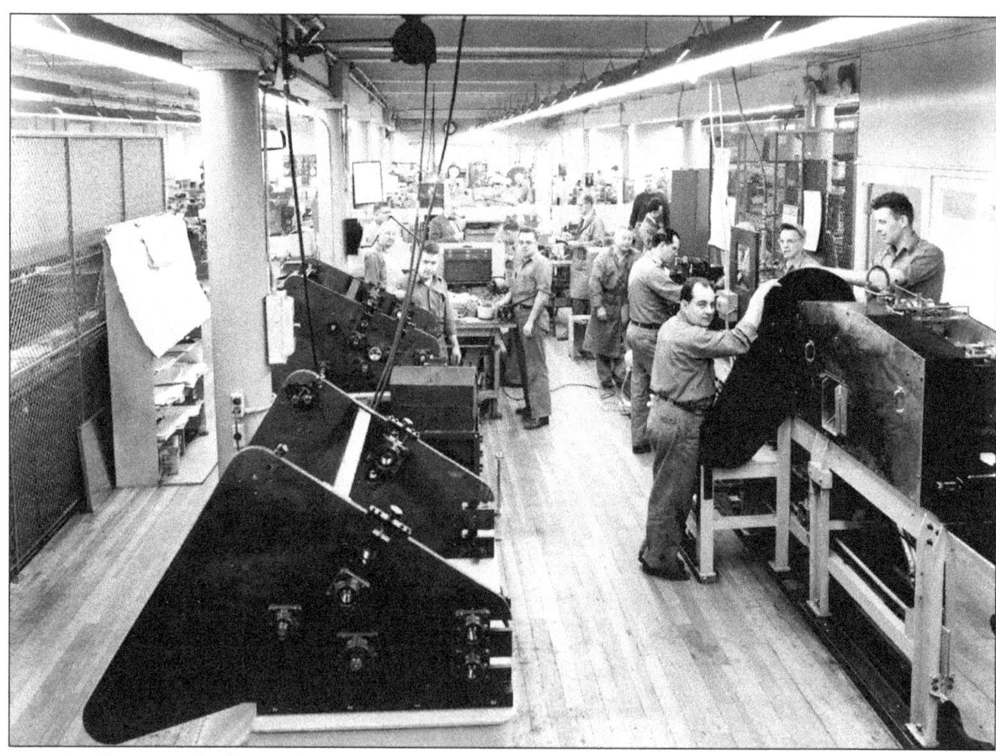

A 1953 photograph shows the machine shop at Polaroid's Albany Street facility in Cambridge.

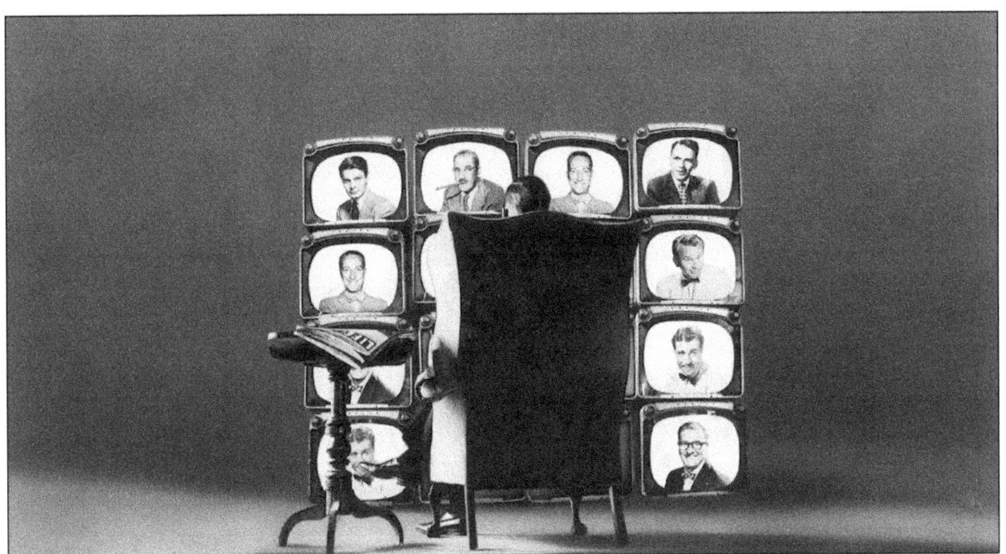

Polaroid was one of the first companies to use live television advertising. Polaroid spent a record amount on live advertising in 1957. Steve Allen, Perry Como, and Jack Parr demonstrated Polaroid cameras on their nighttime shows.

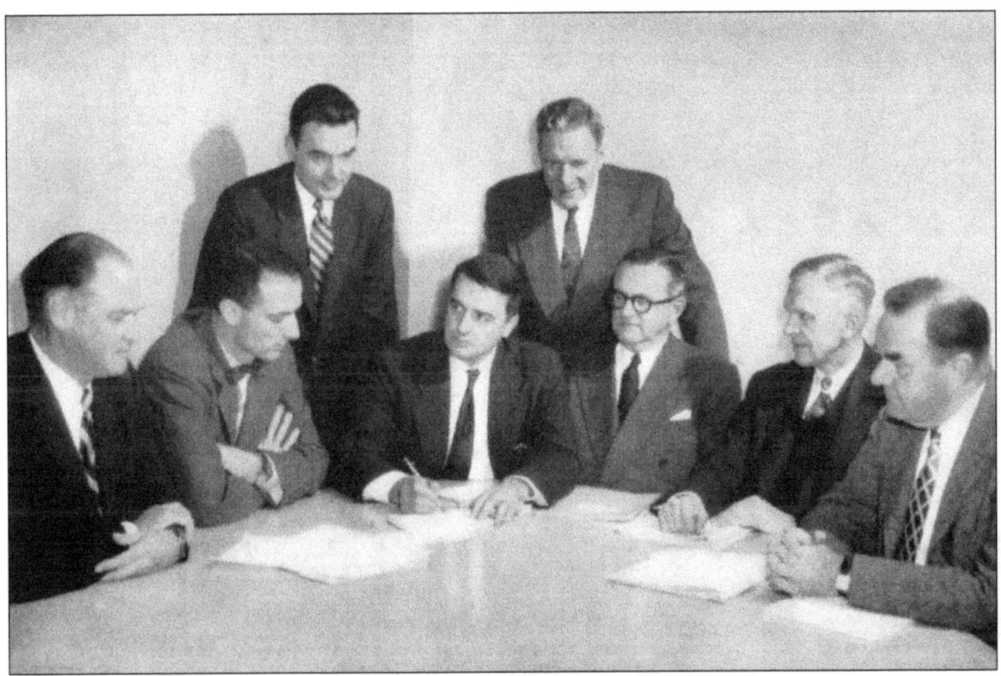

The Polaroid 1956 annual report included this photograph of Polaroid's officers. From left to right are Harold Booth, William McCune, Robert Casselman, Edwin Land, David Skinner, Julius Silver, Carlton Fuller, and Donald Brown.

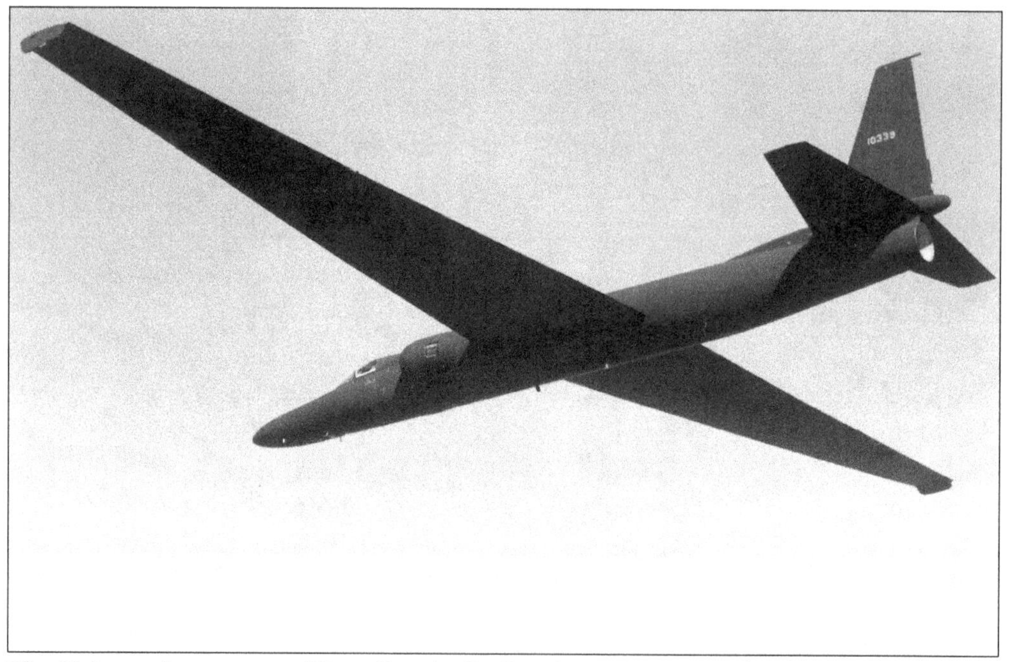

The U-2 was the creation of Pres. Dwight D. Eisenhower's science advisory committee. As a key adviser, Edwin Land played a critical role in pushing the development of the U-2 spy plane and its remarkable cameras, as well as the even more secret and more remarkable Corona spy satellites that followed. The intelligence produced by these programs altered the course of the cold war and led to a decrease in tensions and the eventual signing of arms-control agreements in the years that followed.

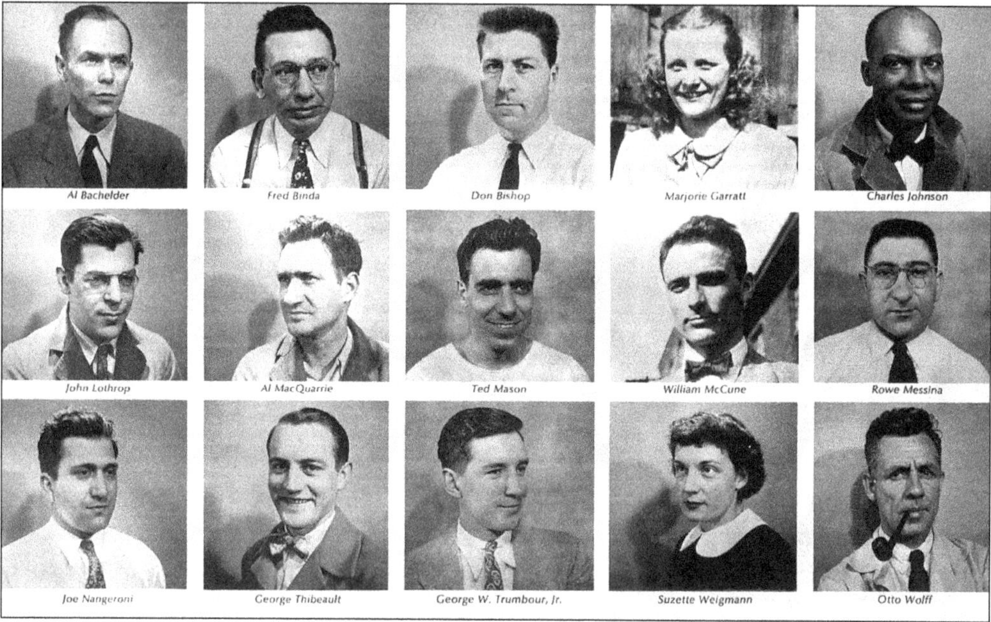

These employees (some key to the development of instant photography) were featured in the November 1973 Polaroid newsletter, which celebrated the 25th anniversary of instant photography.

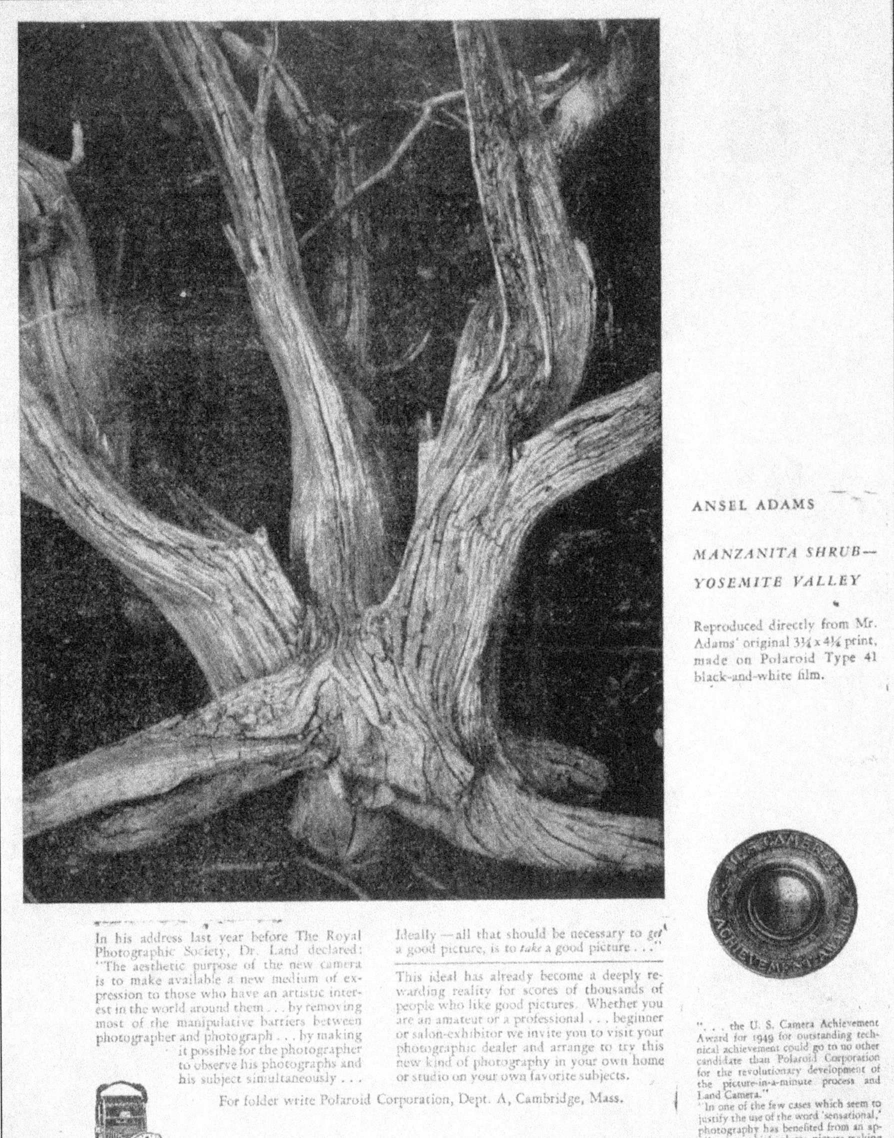

This 1949 Polaroid advertisement shows an Ansel Adams photograph, *Manzanita Shrub—Yosemite Valley*, made on Polaroid Type 41 black-and-white film. Polaroid won the U.S. Camera Achievement Award for outstanding technical achievement for "the revolutionary development of the picture-in-a-minute process and Land camera." In his 1948 address to the Royal Photographic Society, Land declared, "The aesthetic purpose of the new camera is to make available a new medium of expression to those who have an artistic interest in the world around them . . . by removing most of the manipulative barriers between photographer and photograph . . . by making it possible for the photographer to observe his photographs and his subject simultaneously. . . . Ideally—all that should be necessary to *get* a good picture, is to *take* a good picture." (Photograph by Ansel Adams. Used with permission of the Trustees of the Ansel Adams Publishing Rights Trust. All rights reserved.)

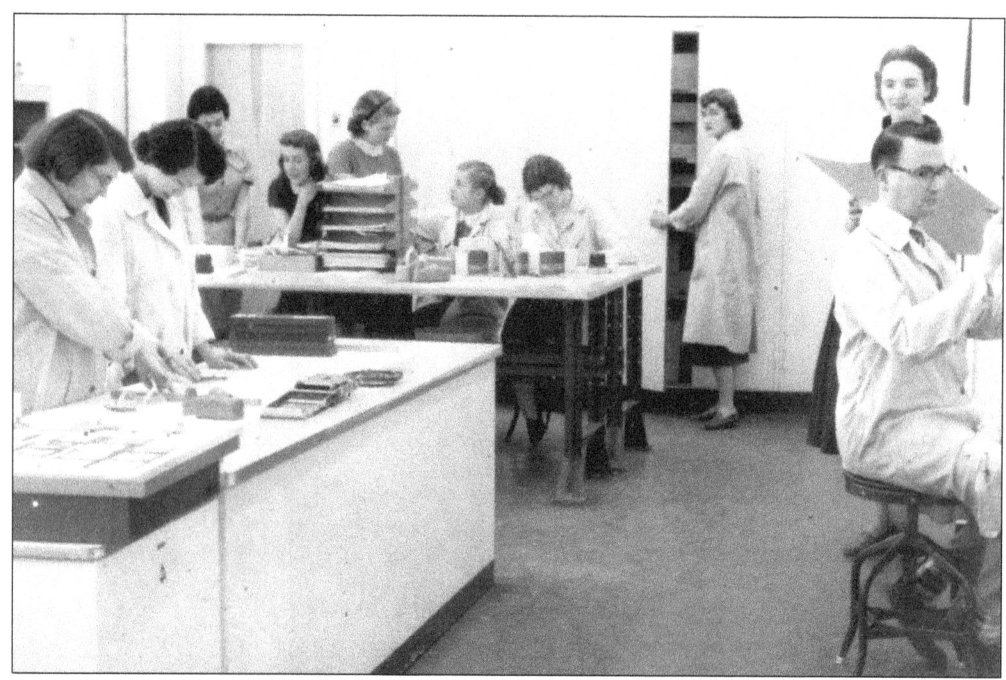

Researchers in Polaroid's black-and-white laboratory, at Osborn Street in Cambridge, are shown in this photograph. Meroë Morse is standing on the right behind the man in glasses. She was appointed manager of black-and-white photographic research in 1955.

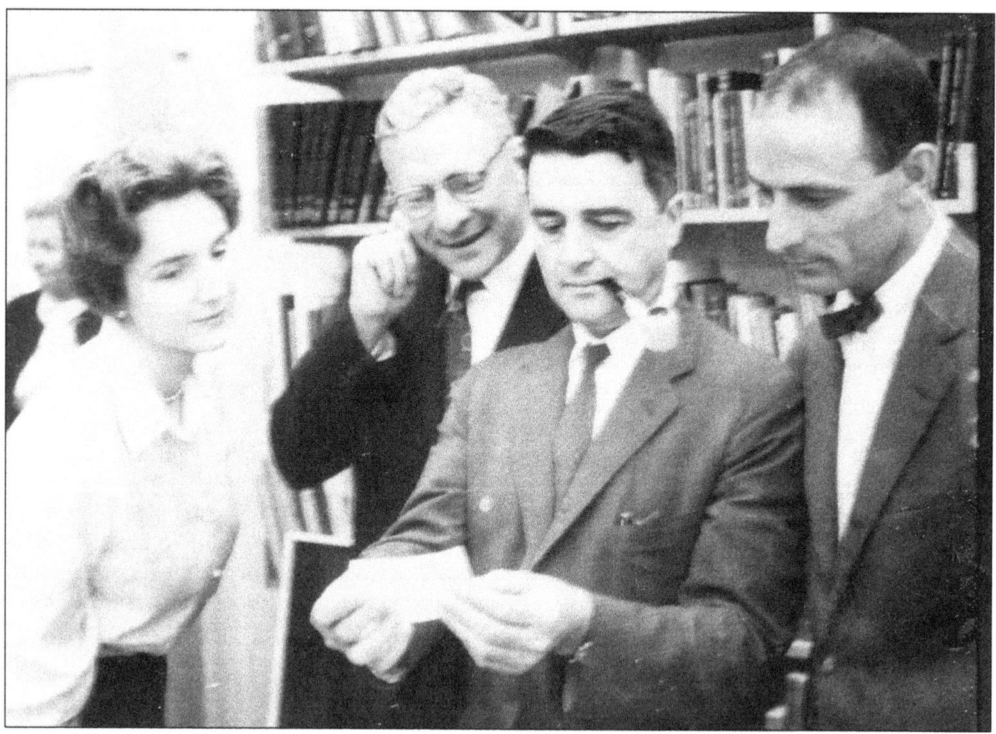

Land shows a test print to Meroë Morse, David Skinner, and William McCune, right.

Meroë Morse, with a camera and test film, is the subject of this photograph made on Type 42 Land film, the company's first panchromatic film, which was introduced in 1955.

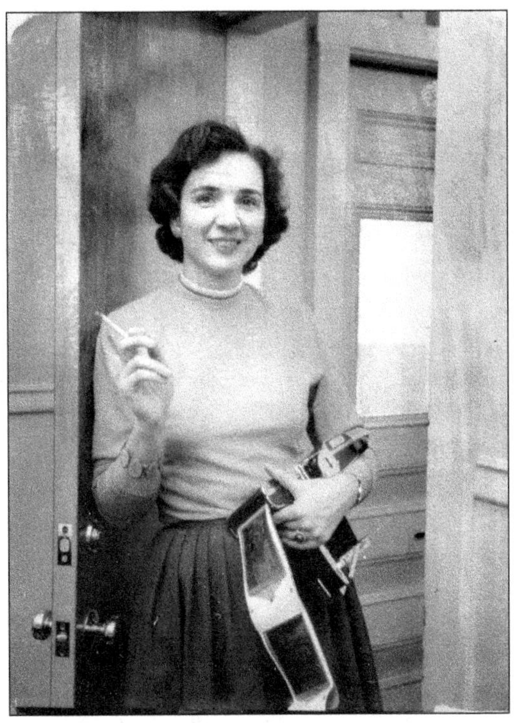

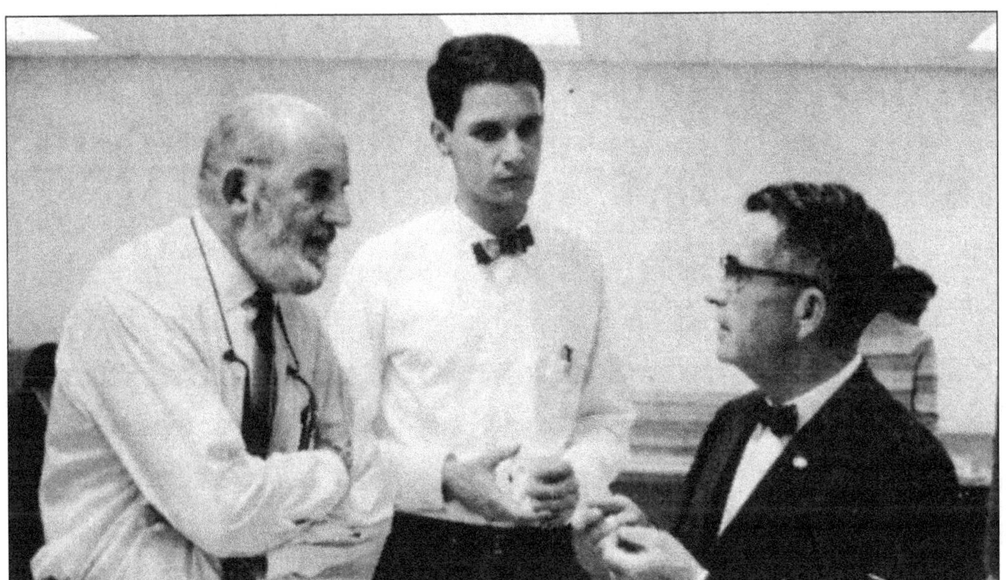

Pictured from left to right, Ansel Adams, Al Bellows (president of the Polaroid Photography Club), and Dick Kriebel continue the discussion period that followed a meeting in which Adams narrated a slide presentation on the history of black-and-white photography. This photograph was printed in the October 31, 1967, issue of the Polaroid newsletter. Kriebel had been with the company since 1936, when he organized Polaroid's first press conference, at the Waldorf Astoria Hotel.

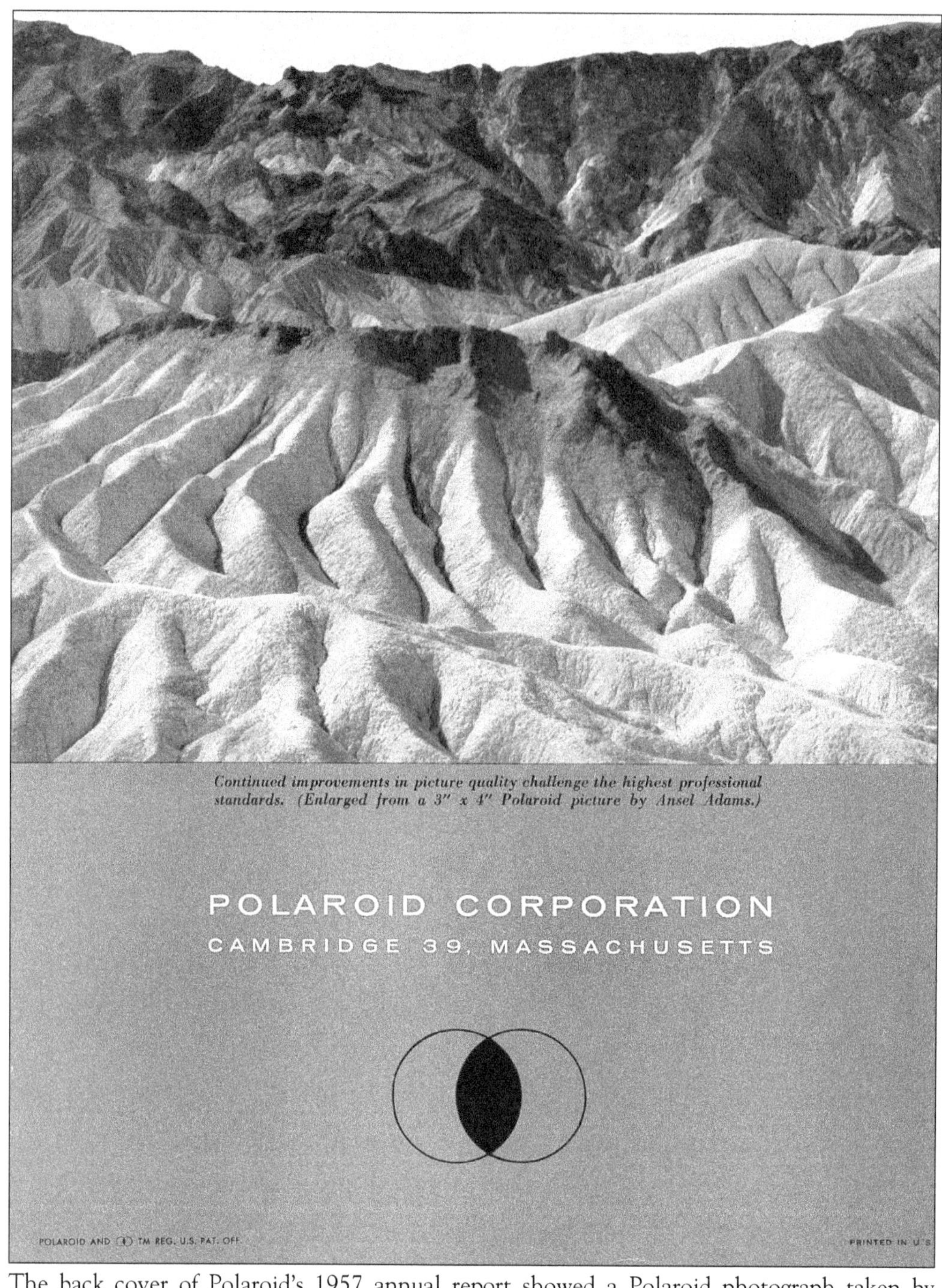

The back cover of Polaroid's 1957 annual report showed a Polaroid photograph taken by Ansel Adams. Adams, the company's longtime consultant, had a special relationship with Land and Polaroid. Land believed that the instant results would alter the way photographers approached their work and offer more opportunities to improve their results. (Photograph by Ansel Adams. Used with permission of the Trustees of the Ansel Adams Publishing Rights Trust. All rights reserved.)

Six

Thinking Ahead

With its solid patents in polarizers and in the highly successful field of instant photography, Polaroid roared through the 1950s. It produced its millionth camera in 1956, and Polaroid stock was listed on the New York Stock Exchange the very next year. Despite the frenetic pace of innovation and the challenges of managing a fast-growing company, Edwin Land was committed to serve on various presidential science advisory boards, as well as the foreign intelligence board under the Eisenhower and Kennedy administrations.

The next decade was equally dynamic for the company. In 1963, Polaroid introduced the Polaroid Model 100 Land camera, the world's first camera to use electronically controlled shutter timing for automatic exposure control. It also introduced the first instant color film (Polacolor) and, the same year, sold its five millionth camera.

To keep consumers buying, the company introduced a string of technical improvements as well as inexpensive and easy-to-operate models, such as the Swinger camera. Then, in 1966, the company made a fruitful foray into the business of serving business with its instant identification badge systems—a product that was soon widely deployed around the globe. On the strength of these innovations, Polaroid reached annual sales of $500 million in 1970.

But that was only the beginning. In a program even more ambitious than the original instant film, Land pushed ahead with a new camera, the SX-70, and a new integral film that would develop outside of the camera. This revolutionary single-lens reflex camera was introduced in 1972 and proved to be the basis for yet another round of growth. In 1974, the company estimated that a billion instant photographs were taken with its film. Two years later, the company manufactured six million cameras. In 1977, revenues reached $1 billion, and Edwin Land was awarded his 500th patent.

But change was in the winds. Land stepped down from the position of president. His role in the company was further eroded when Polavision, the company's instant movie system that Land had championed single-mindedly, failed to catch on in the market. Nevertheless, the company's technology base and breadth of product continued to expand.

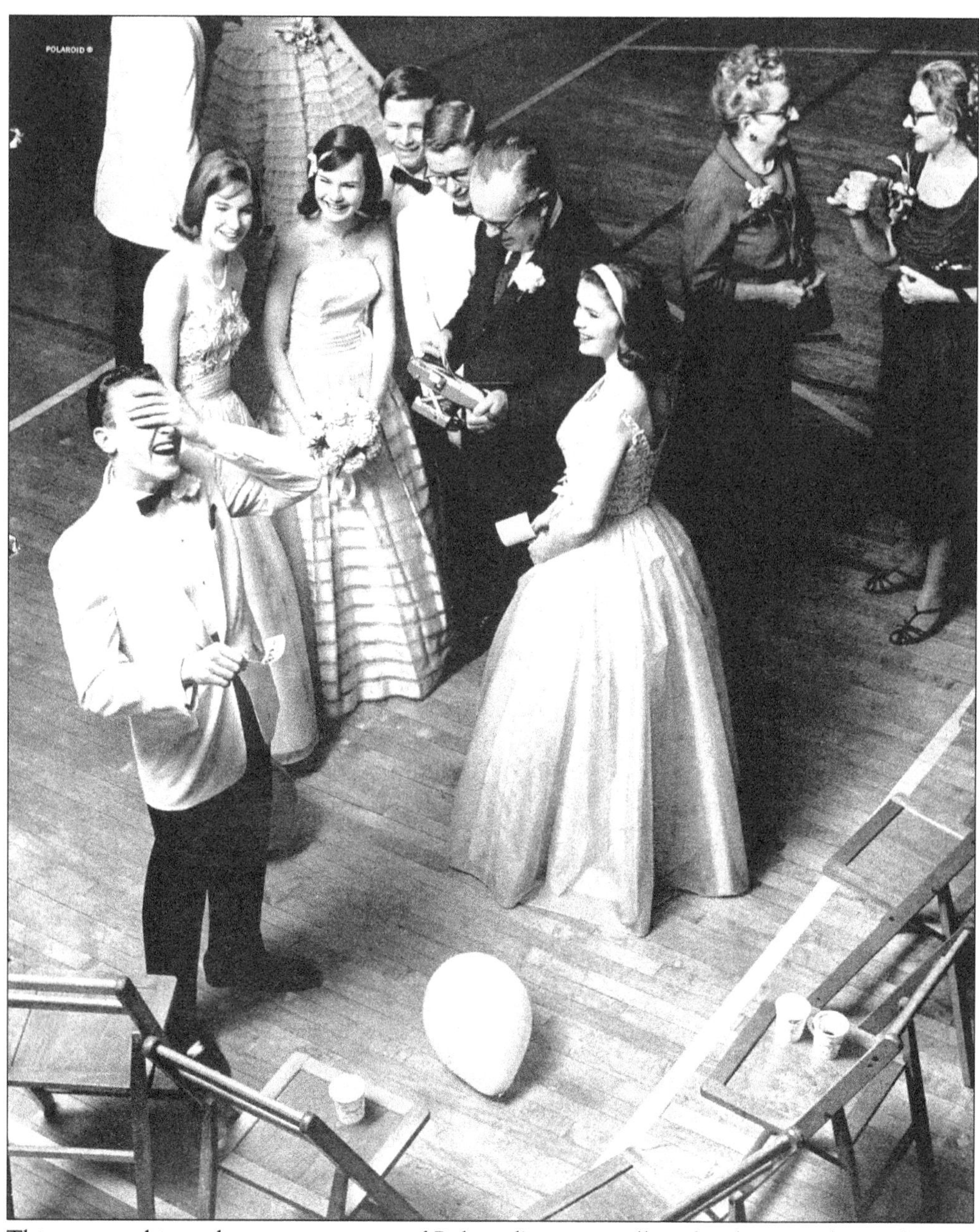

This eye-catching advertisement, part of Polaroid's continually refined approach to sales and marketing, appeared in *Life* magazine in 1962.

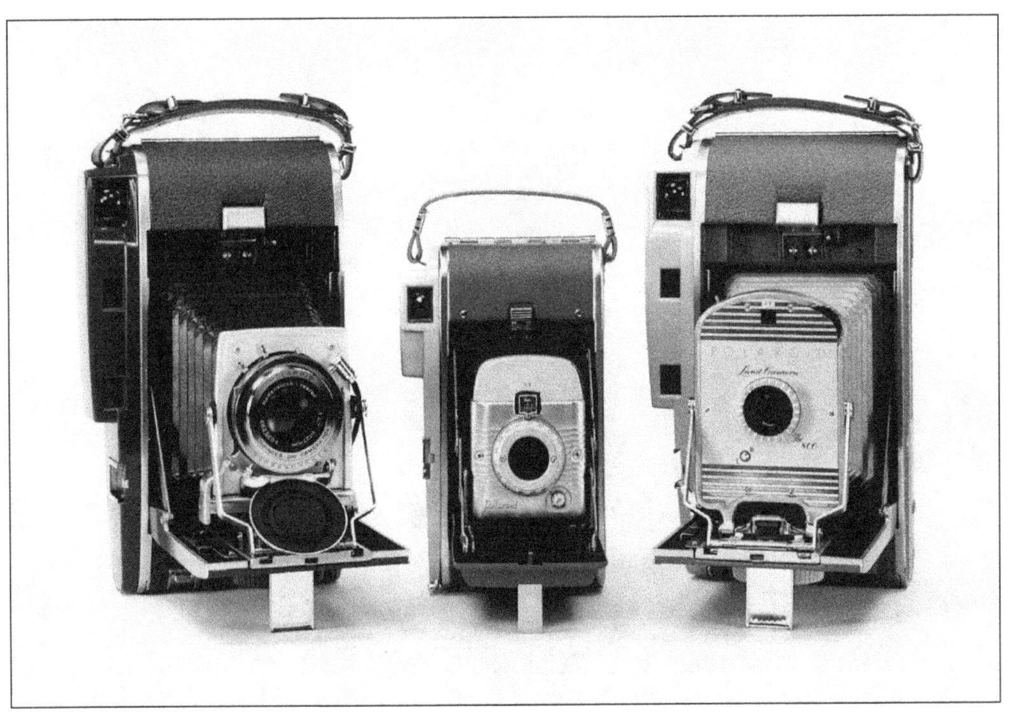

Model 110A, the Highlander Model 80A, and Model 800 cameras were all introduced in 1957.

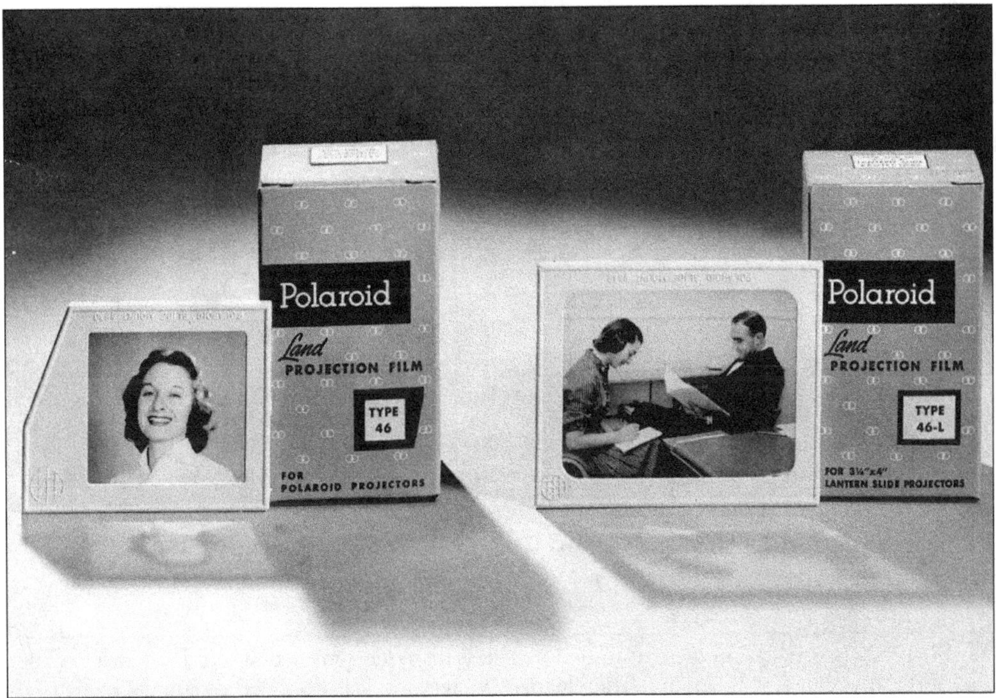

In 1957, Polaroid introduced Type 46 Land projection films. The transparencies were ready for projection in two minutes.

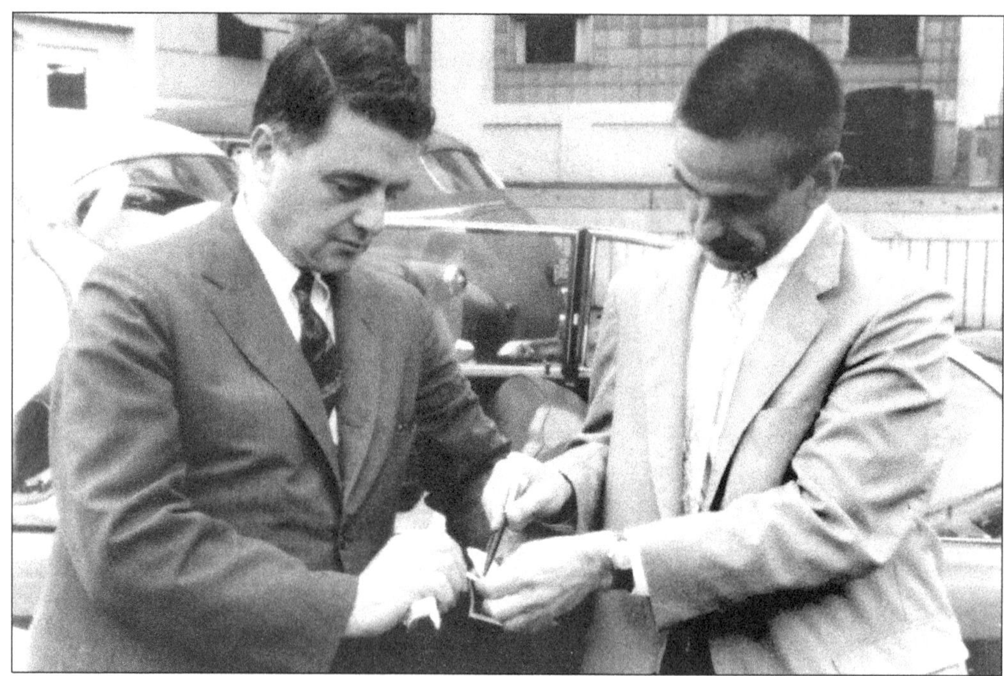

In this 1960 photograph, Land examines a test photograph outside 730 Main Street in Cambridge with colleague Howard Rogers, inventor of the Polacolor process.

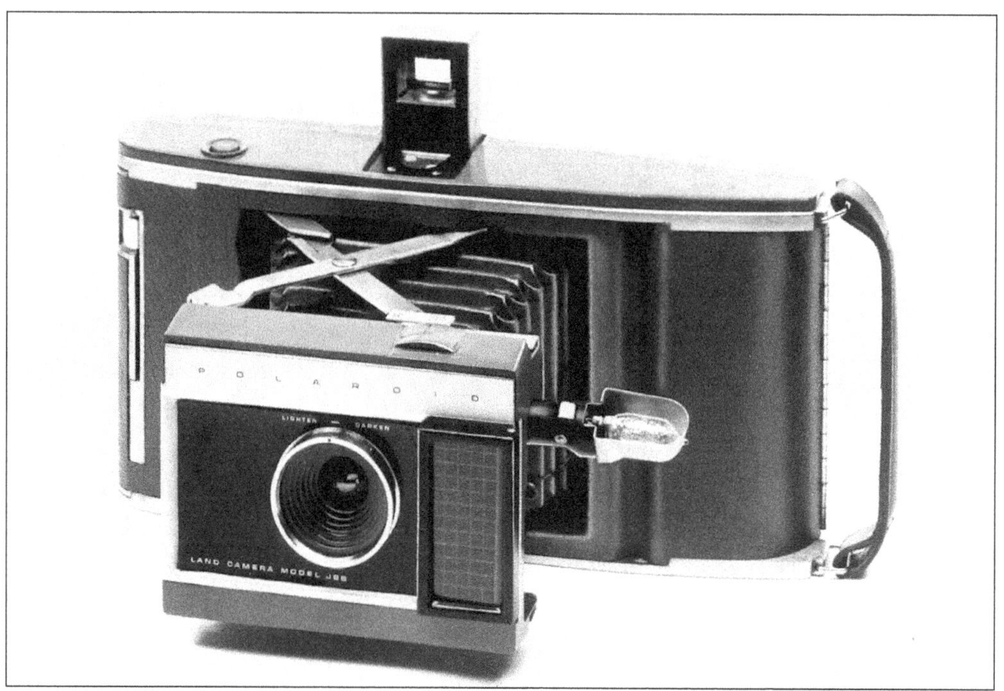

As the 1960s began, Polaroid maintained a steady introduction of new products. Model J66, one of the first cameras to include the electric eye feature, was designed by Henry Dreyfuss, a pioneer of American industrial design. He later designed the Model 100, the Swinger, and the SX-70 Land cameras.

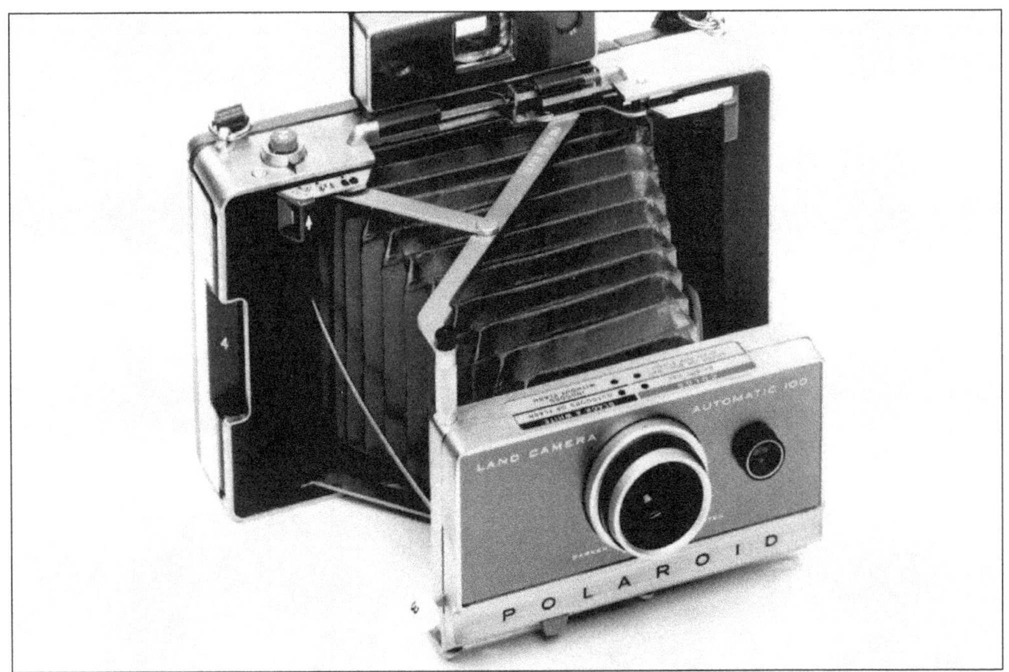

The Model 100 Land camera was the first fully automatic pack camera. Introduced in 1963, it was the first camera ever to employ a transistorized electric shutter designed by Polaroid scientists, preceding the commercial introduction of electric shutters by other manufacturers. It was designed by the renowned Henry Dreyfuss and was the first Polaroid camera to use the new pack film.

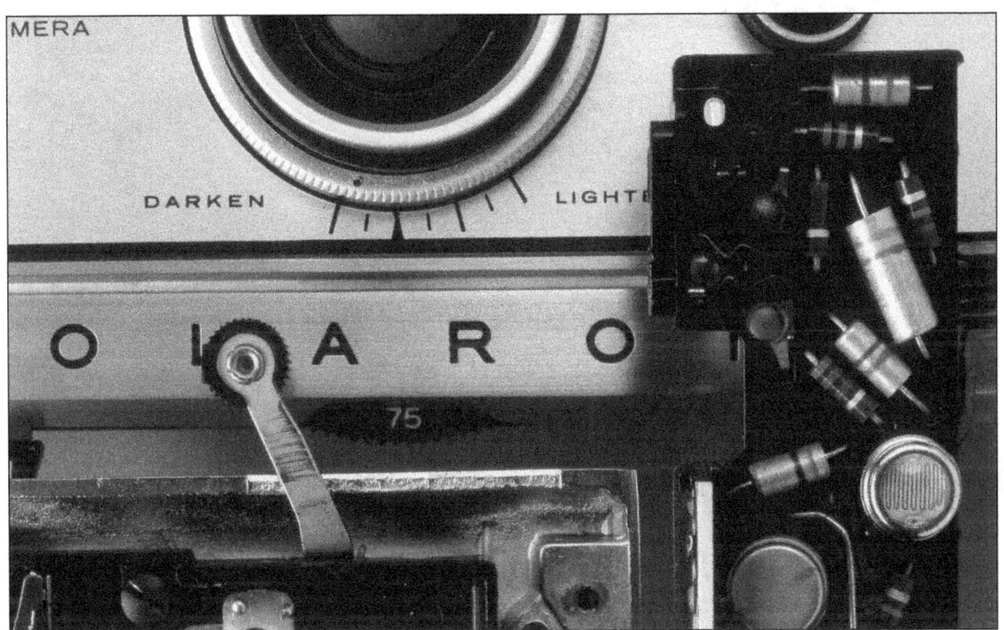

The Polaroid Model 100 Land camera was the world's first camera to use electronic shutter timing for automatic exposure control. A key to the Model 100 was this circuit with a photoelectric cell, which operated the shutter electronically.

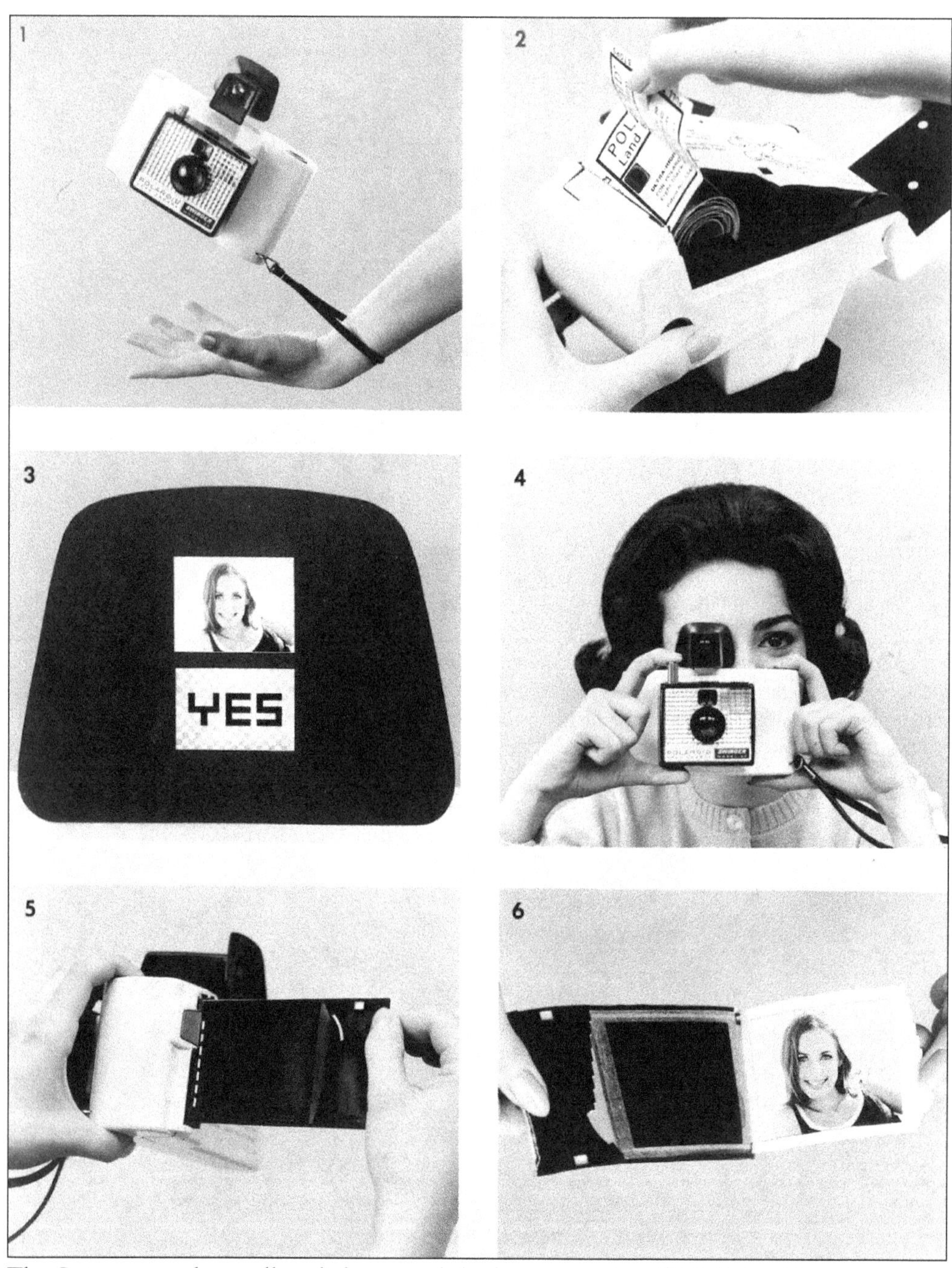

The Swinger was the smallest, lightest, and the least expensive ($20) Polaroid camera at the time of its introduction in 1965. The camera, designed by Dreyfuss, had a plastic body and single-element plastic lens. This series of images showcases the camera's operation, including the YES/NO display to indicate whether the operator had adjusted the focus.

The award-winning Swinger advertising campaign included a popular television spot with actress Ali MacGraw, swinging to the beat of the Swinger jingle.

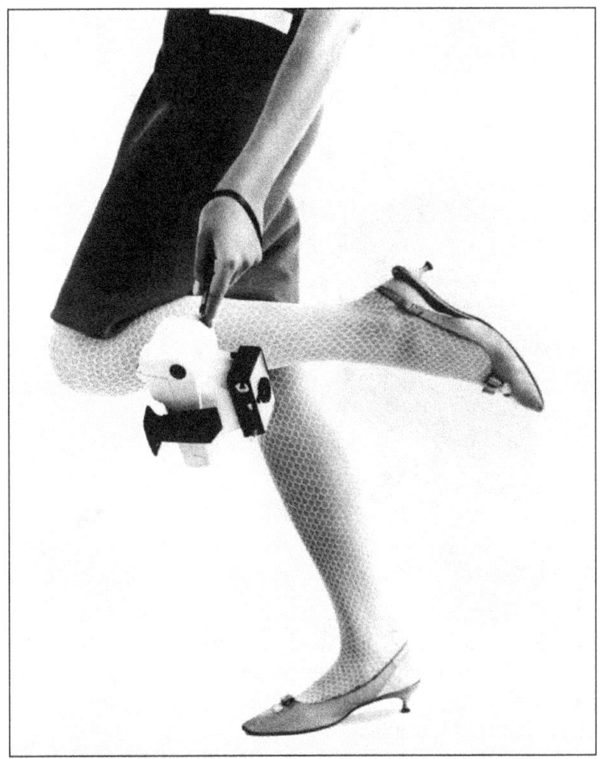

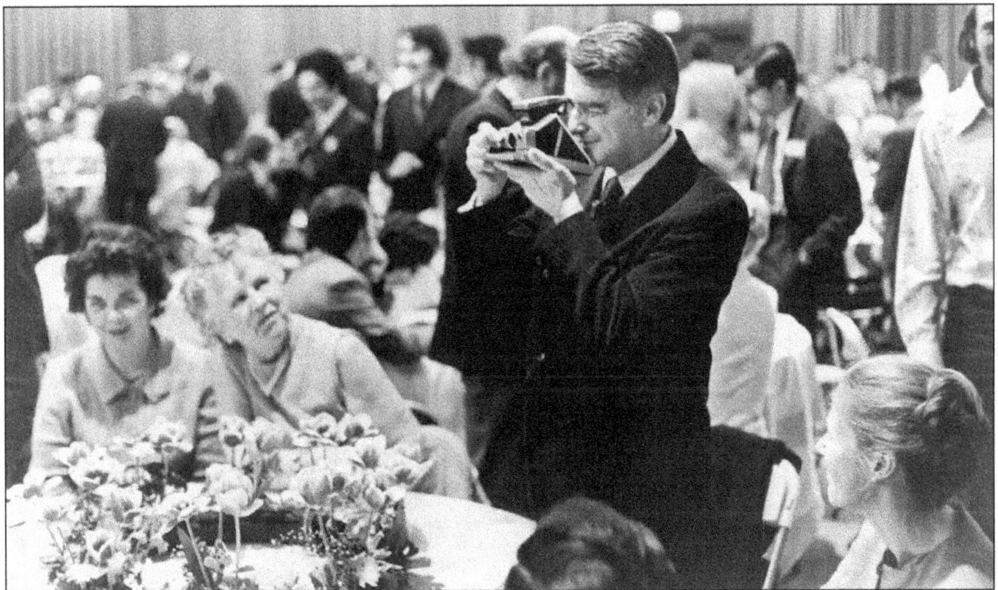

Land introduces the SX-70 Land camera at an exuberant Polaroid shareholders meeting in February 1972. Never content with the status quo, Land pushed himself and his company to the limit to introduce the next-generation camera—the SX-70, named after the original 1940s research code name for instant photography. Polaroid built three factories, a negative plant in New Bedford, a film assembly plant in Waltham, and a camera-assembly plant in Norwood to meet the demands of the market.

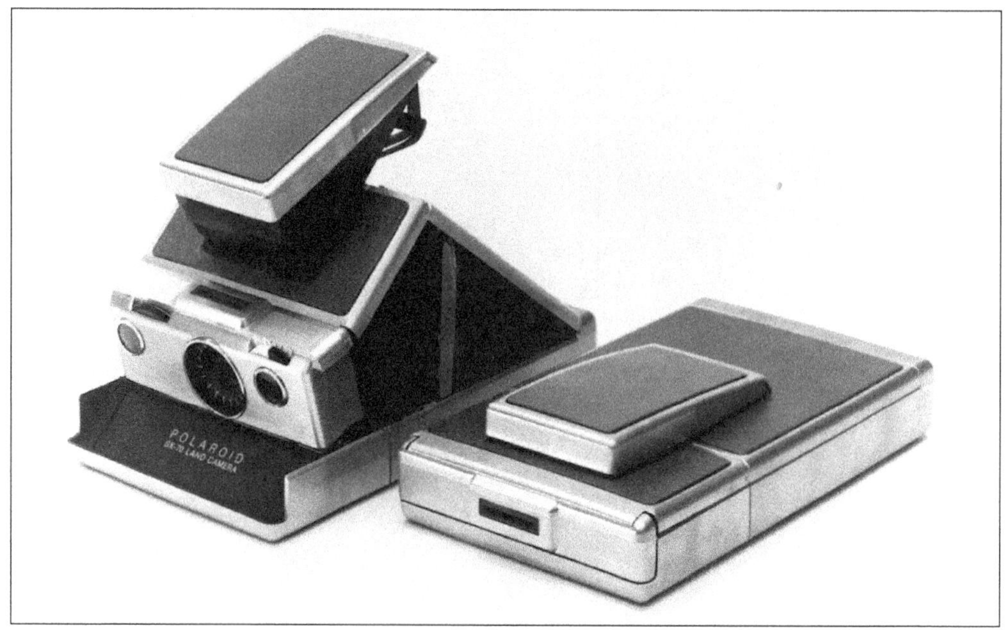

The Polaroid SX-70 embodied almost everything Land envisioned for an ideal camera. It was the first folding single-lens reflex camera to include revolutionary optics. Again, Henry Dreyfuss was commissioned to design an elegant folding camera to embody this new innovative technology.

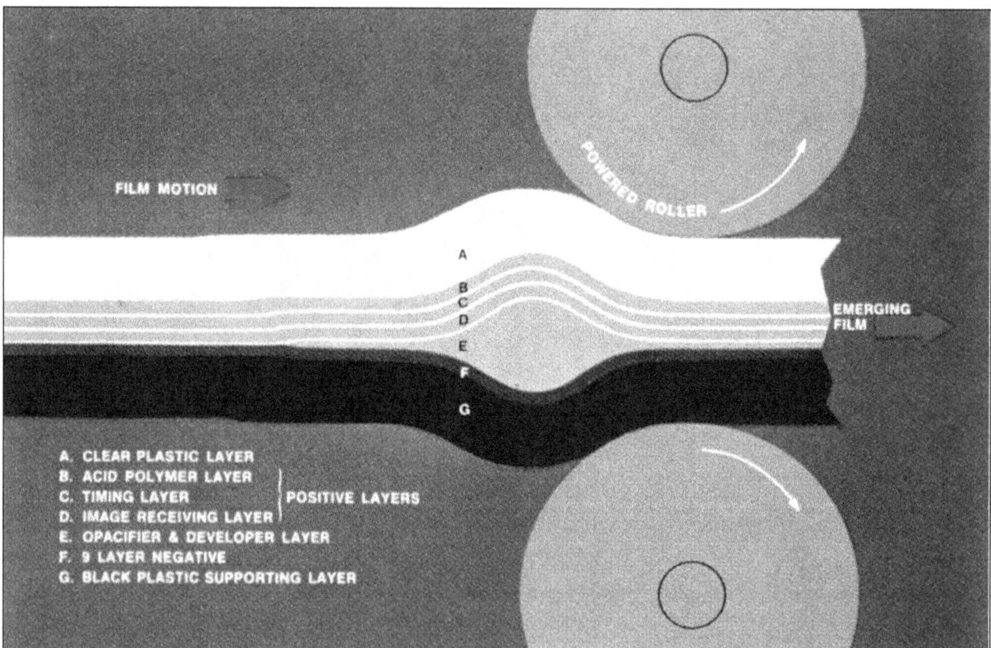

The SX-70 Land film was the first integral film that automatically self-developed in daylight. One of the greatest breakthroughs in the SX-70 system was "instant darkness," which ensured image transfer between the negative and positive while the film was ejected from the camera and into ambient light.

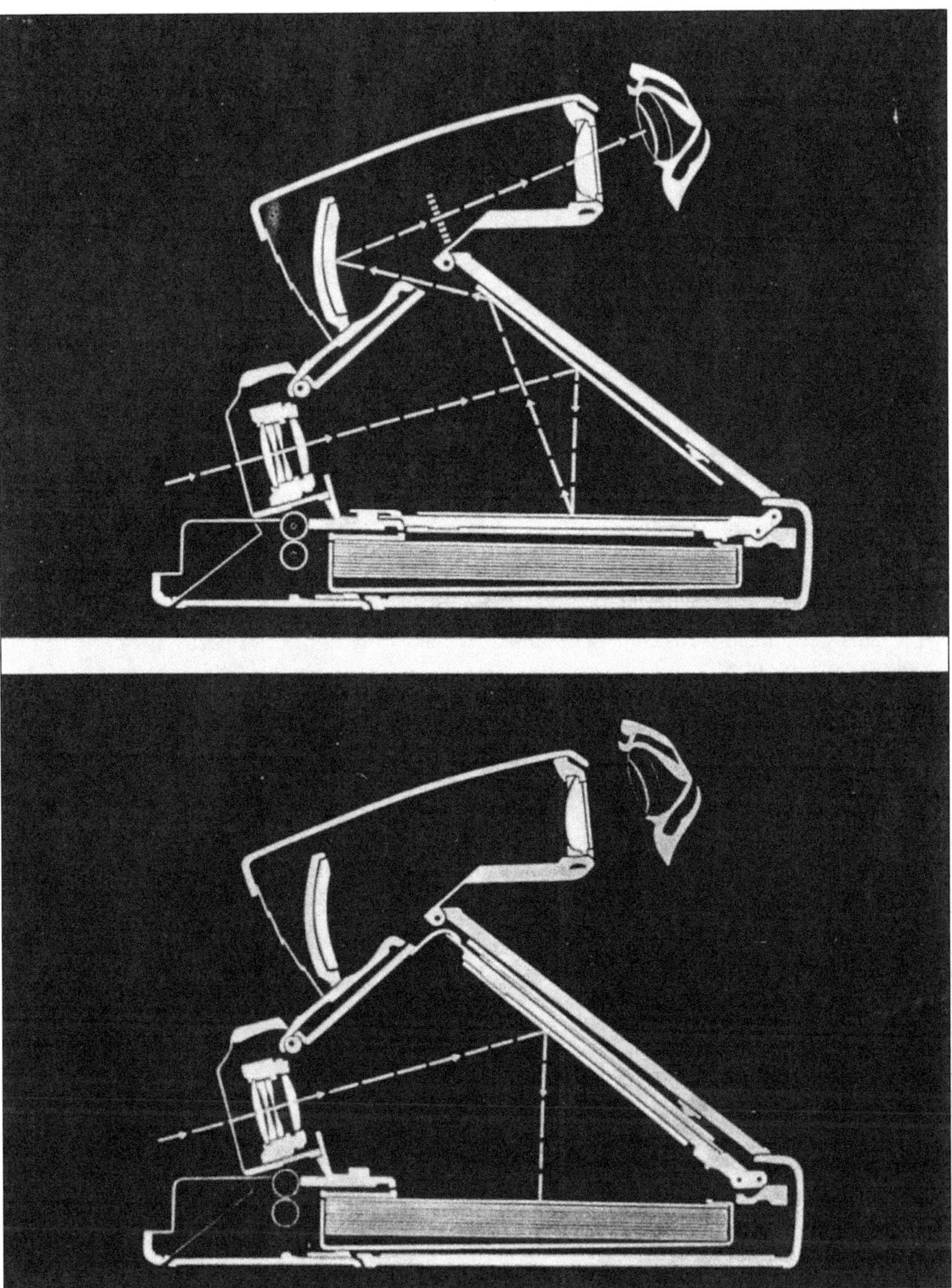

These two images show cross sections of the SX-70. The upper graphic shows the view projected through the optics to the viewfinder. A movable mirror allowed the film, at the bottom of the camera, to be exposed when the shutter was pressed. The design was a triumph made possible by optical experts such as James Baker (who also designed spy satellite cameras) and William T. Plummer. The maximum opening of the lens was f/8, and focus from 10 inches to infinity required the front lens to move about a quarter of an inch.

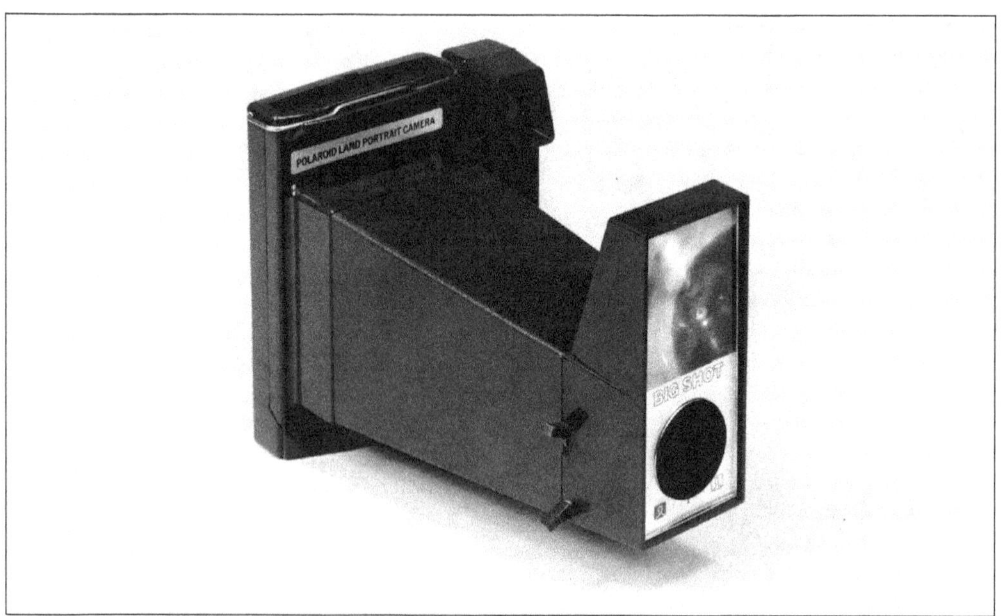

Popular with artist Andy Warhol, this unique Big Shot portrait Land camera was introduced in 1971. This was a fixed-focus camera designed to make only flash color portraits of one or two people at one distance.

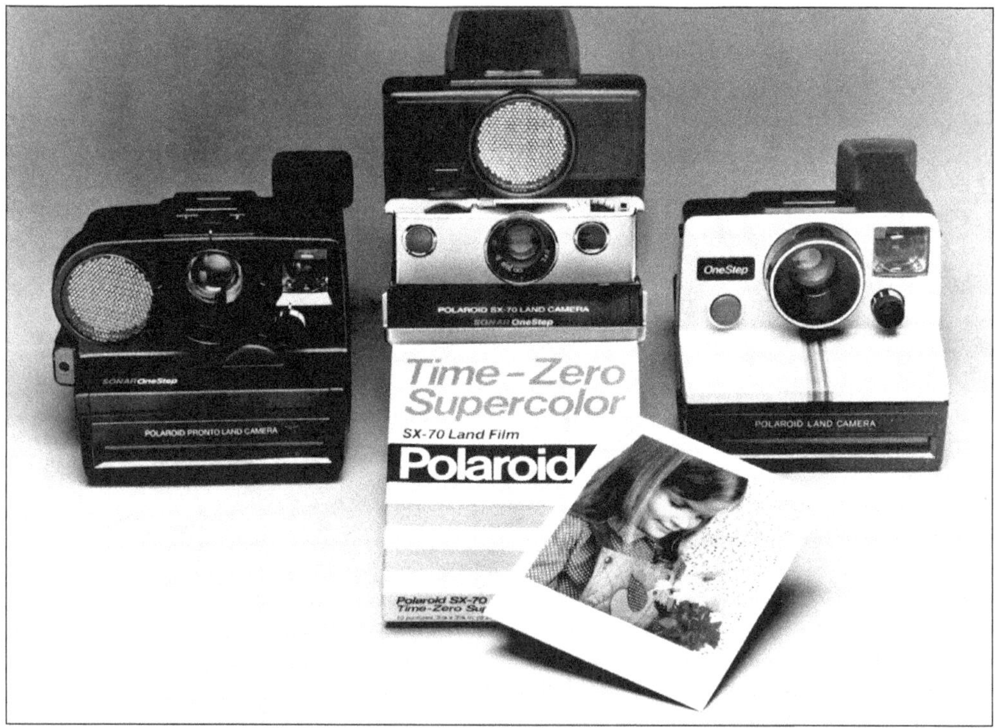

Research in sonar technology, initiated in 1963, results in the sonar auto-focus system for the SX-70 and the Pronto cameras, which were introduced in 1978. The cameras feature automatic focusing in any lighting conditions by means of an ultrasonic echoing device.

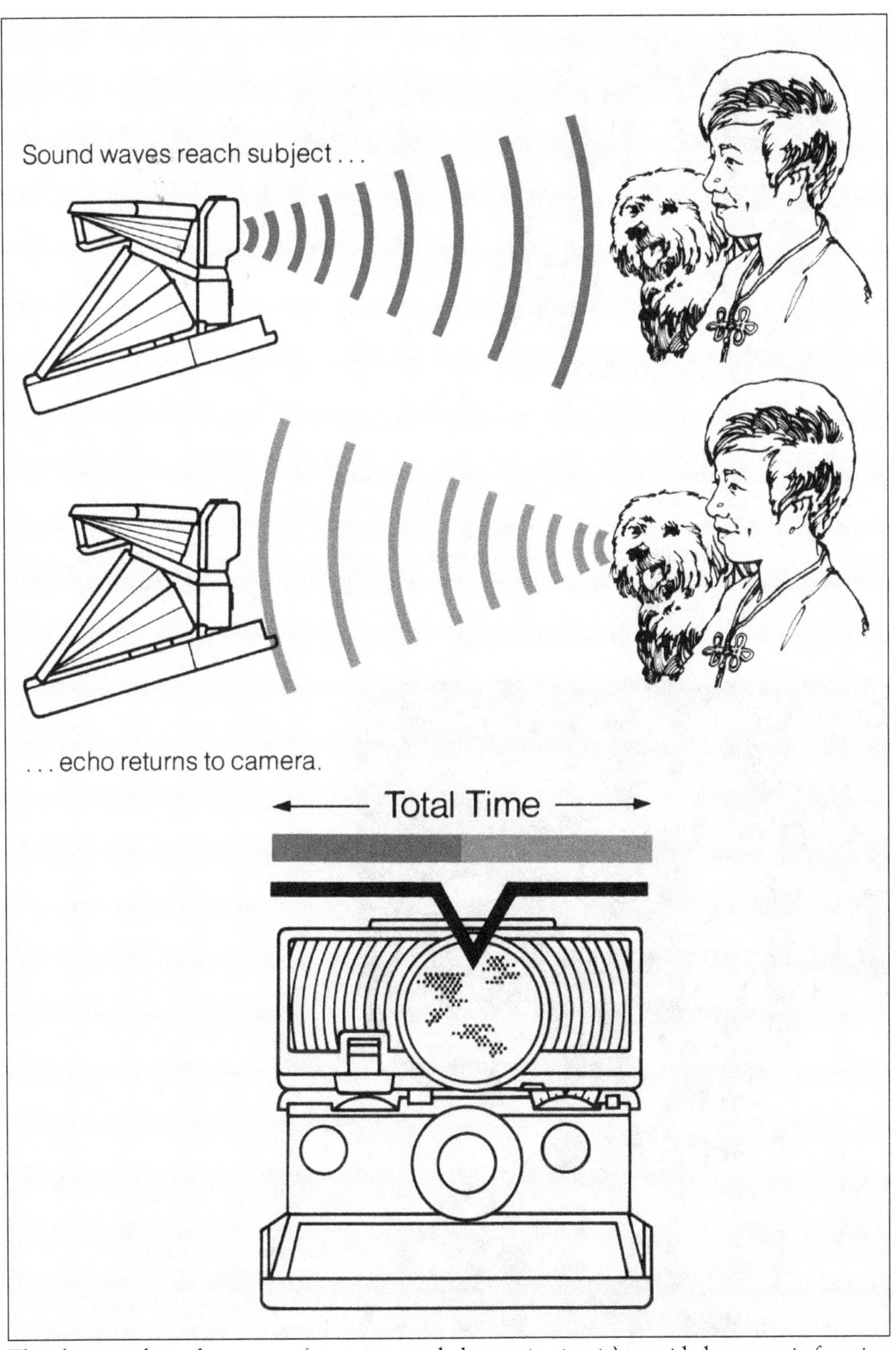

This diagram shows how sonar (a miniaturized electronic circuit) provided automatic focusing for Polaroid's cameras.

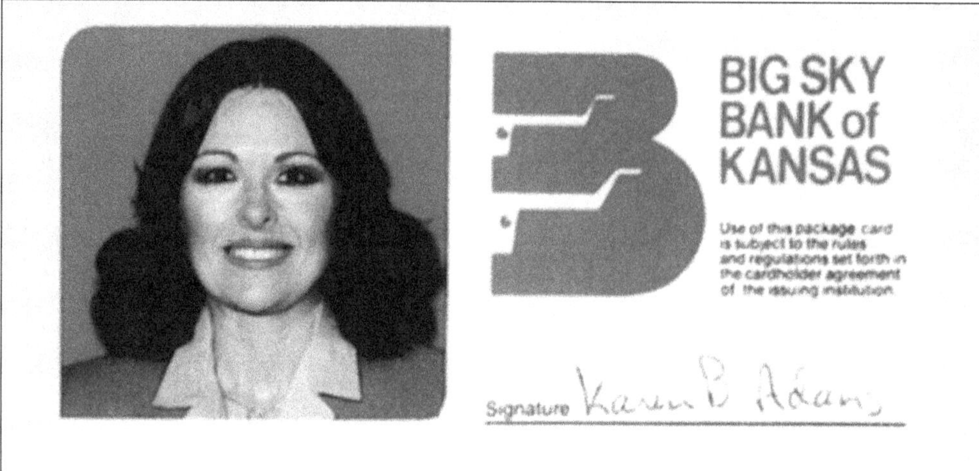

One of the most ubiquitous and long-lived applications for Polaroid instant photography was the business of providing identification cards and documents. Shown here is an identification card from 1968. In the early 1970s, in response to concern over apartheid laws in South Africa, Polaroid discontinued sales of its identification systems to the South African government. Later, concerned that its local distributor was not abiding by the agreement, Polaroid suspended all sales in the country by 1977.

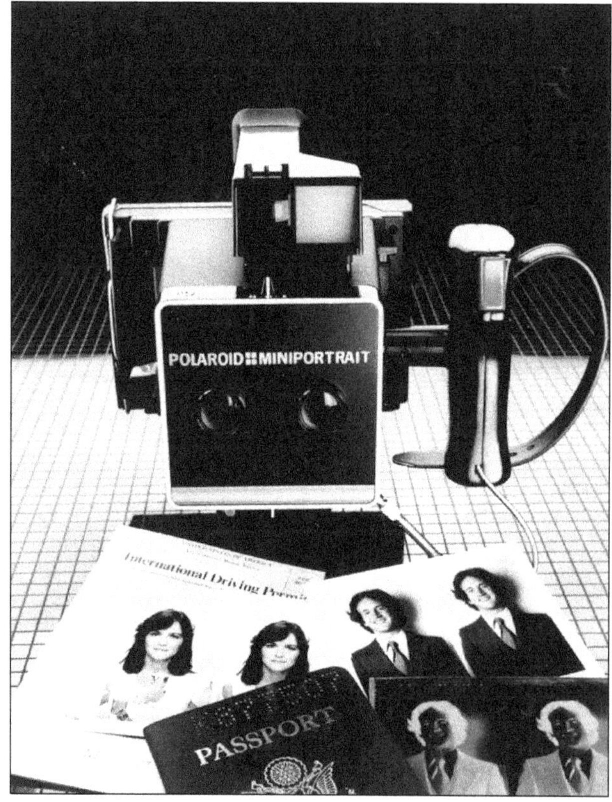

The Polaroid Miniportrait cameras were marketed for passport photographs. They produced two identical images at the same time. The U.S. Passport Office certified Polaroid Type 58 color film for use in passports in 1975.

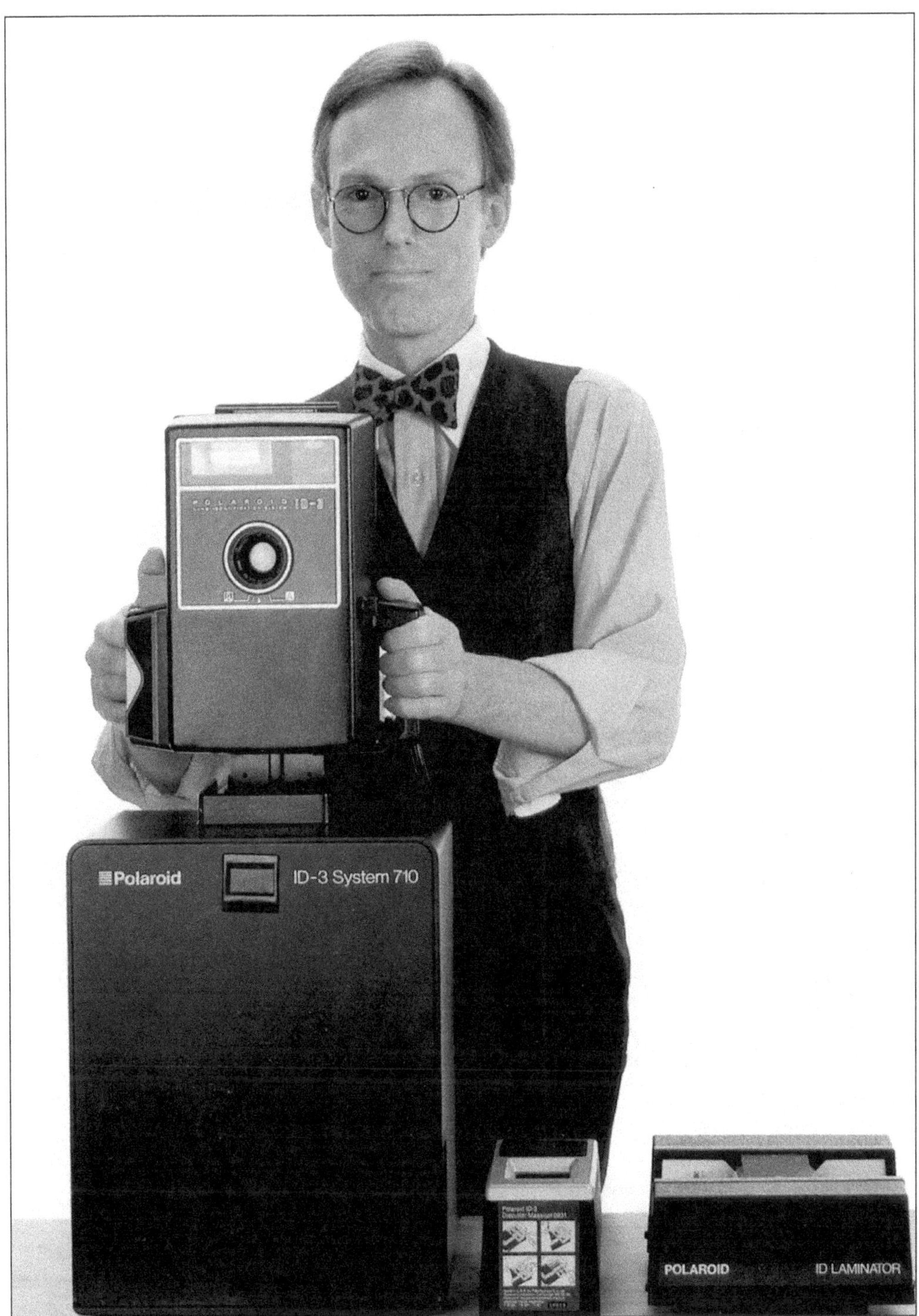

Worldwide, millions of employees and recipients of government identification cards (such as driving licenses) saw this view of Polaroid "instant identification" equipment and were rewarded with a completed card within a few minutes.

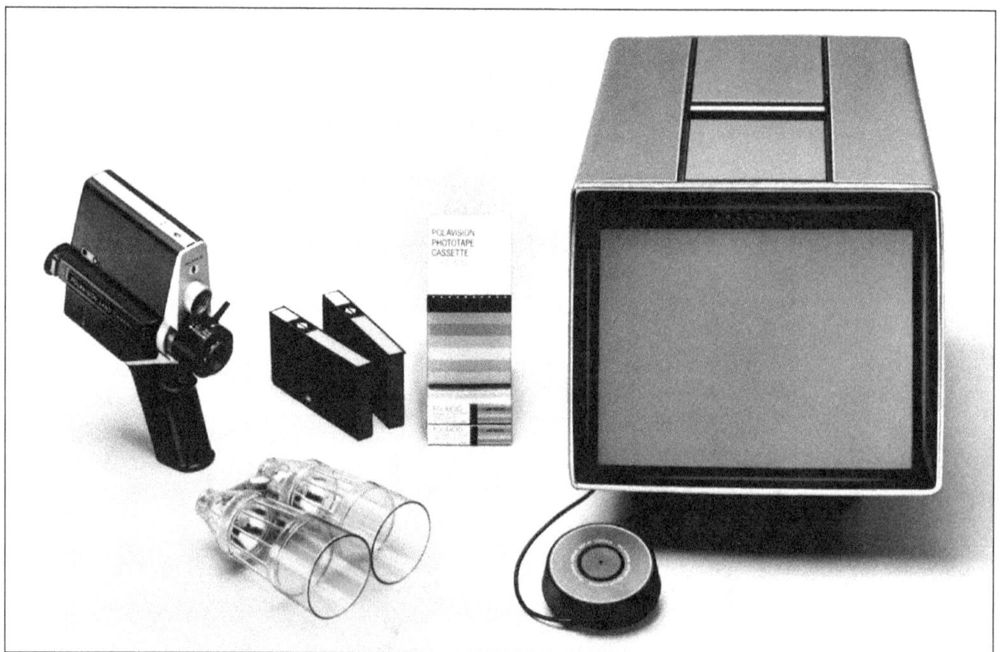

Hailed as a technological achievement, the Polavision instant-movie system (introduced in 1978) never caught on with the public, partly because of the emergence of more capable home video products at about the same time.

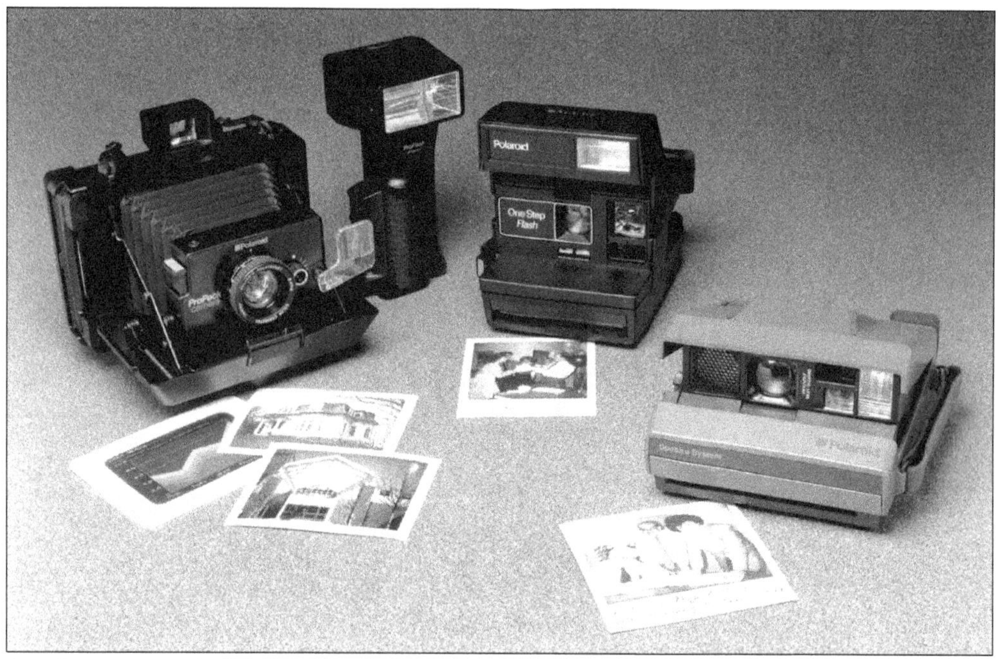

Another group of products rooted in the SX-70 technology, Polaroid ProPack (targeted at business users), the inexpensive Polaroid OneStep, and the Spectra cameras were all introduced in the 1980s. The Spectra camera debuted in 1986 at Boston's Jordan Marsh department store, 38 years after the introduction of the Model 95 at the same venue.

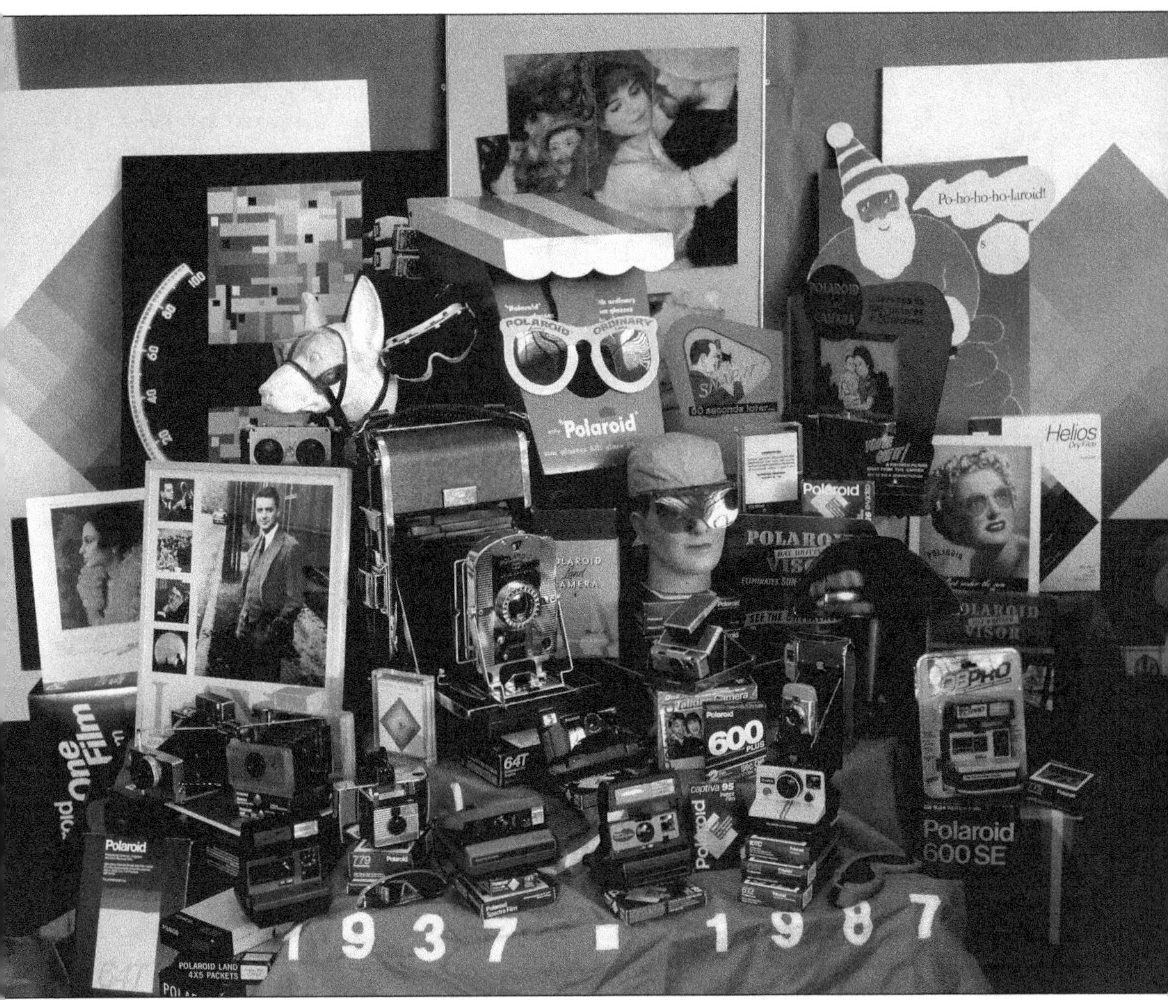

These artifacts from Polaroid Corporate Archives were assembled and photographed by Marie Cosindas in 1987 to celebrate the 50th anniversary of the company. An advocate of the American patent system, Edwin Land established the Polaroid Museum (attached to the patent department) in 1944. The growing museum collection, documenting the history of a unique American industry, later became source material and the basis for the corporate archives, which was established in 1984. Polaroid Corporate Archives, with over a million items (documents, photographs, and artifacts) in its collection, provided thousands of documents for the Kodak patent infringement case. Polaroid won the largest settlement in the history of patent infringement cases in 1991.

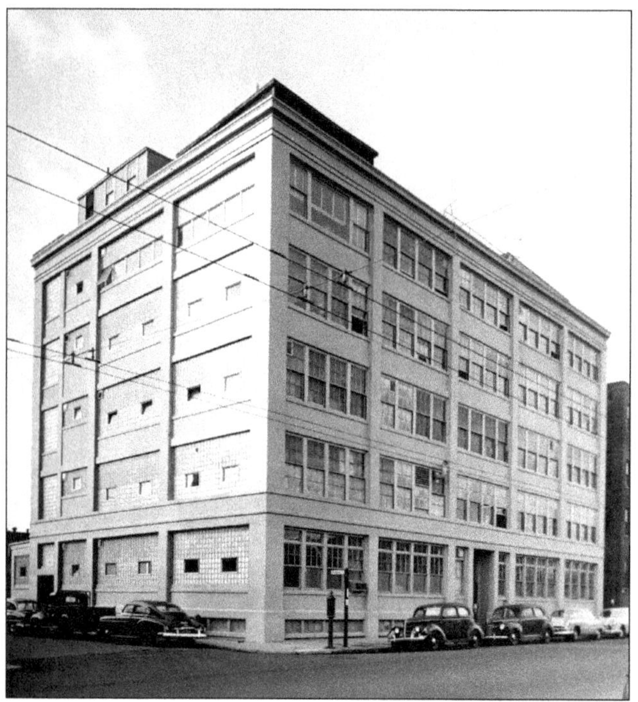

This photograph of 730 Main Street in Cambridge, Polaroid's primary facility for many years, was taken in 1950. Over the next four decades, Land always looked to nearby MIT and Harvard for the brightest scientists to join his company.

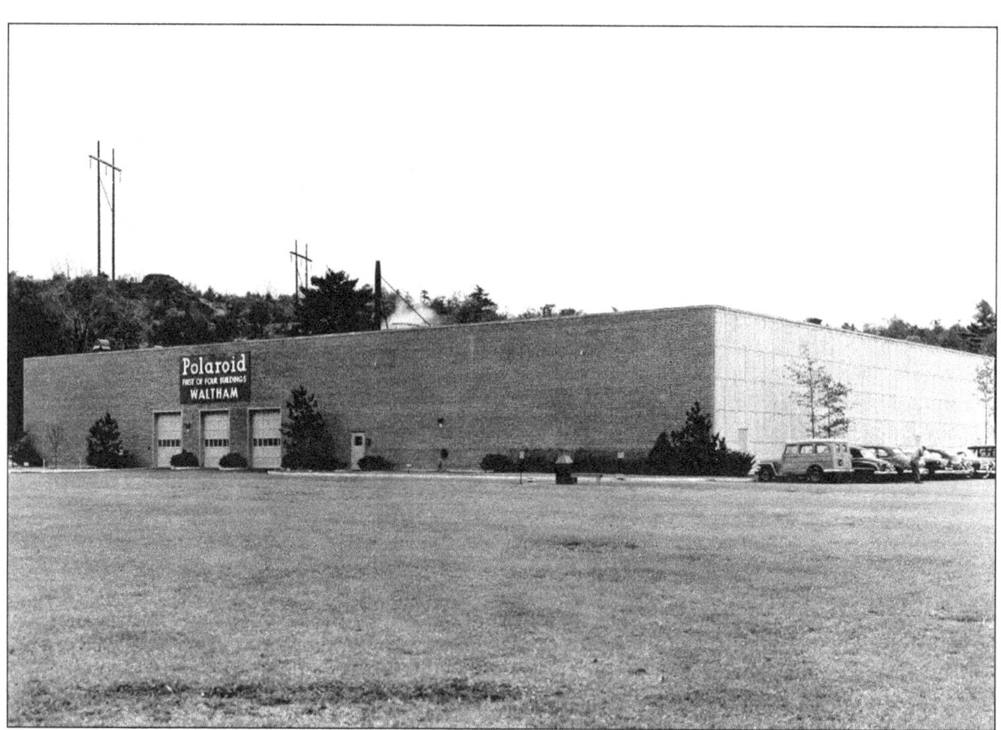

This mid-1950s image shows what the sign on the building describes as "the first of four buildings" planned by Polaroid for a large site on Route 128 in Waltham. This facility now houses the company headquarters.

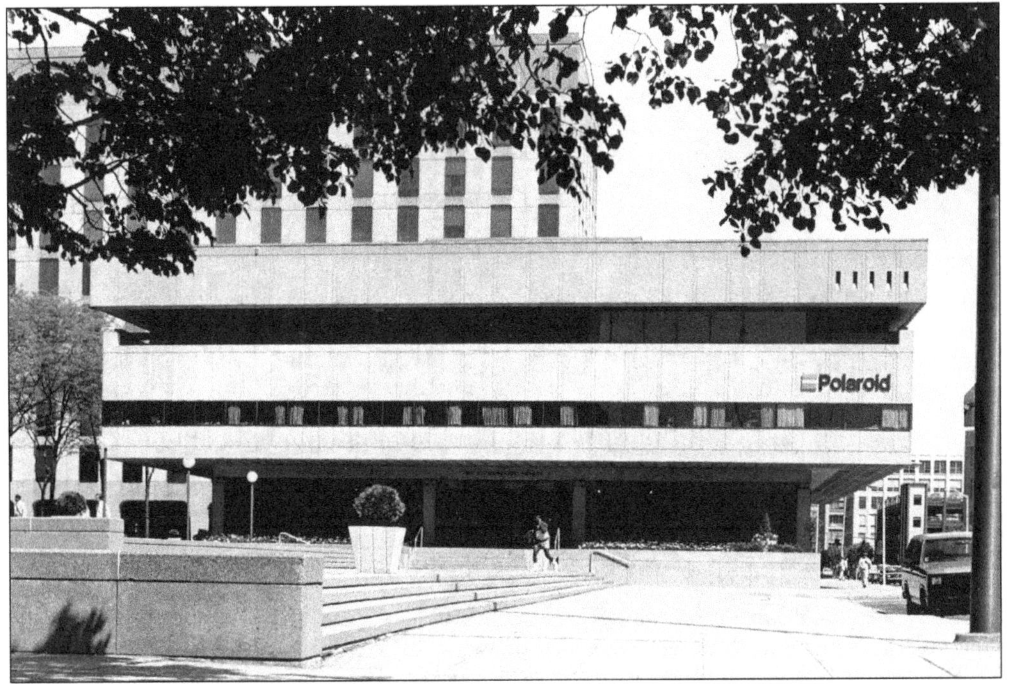

Polaroid's longtime corporate headquarters at Technology Square in Cambridge, adjacent to MIT, was surrounded by other Polaroid buildings in the neighborhood. The company occupied this facility in 1966. It was demolished in the late 1990s.

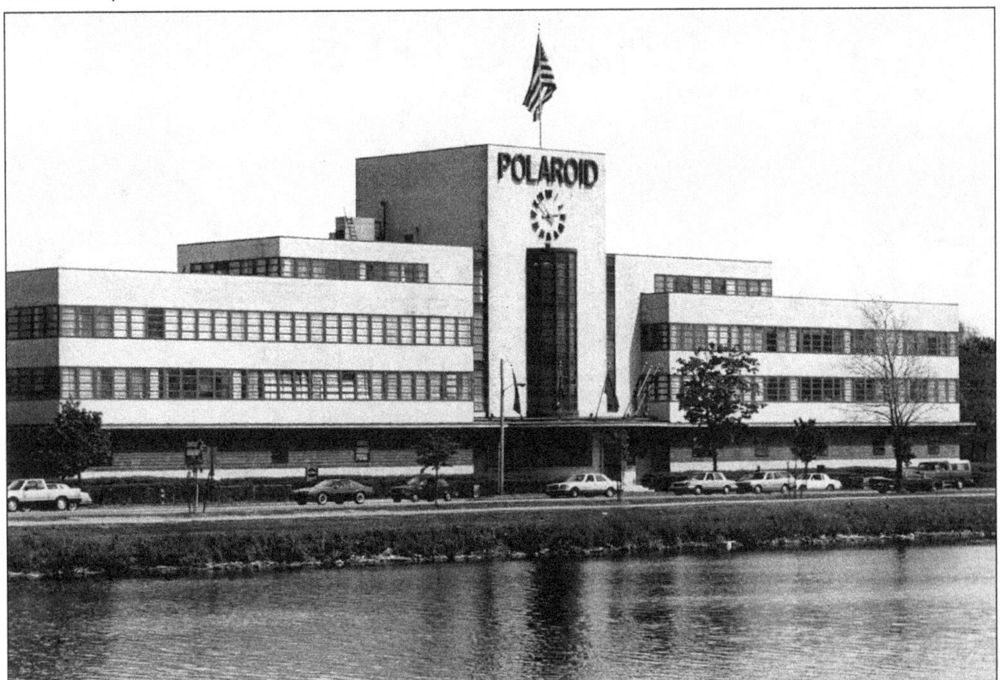

One of Polaroid's most visible properties was 784 Memorial Drive in Cambridge. Located along the Charles River, this landmark building served as the company's headquarters from the summer of 1998 through October 2002.

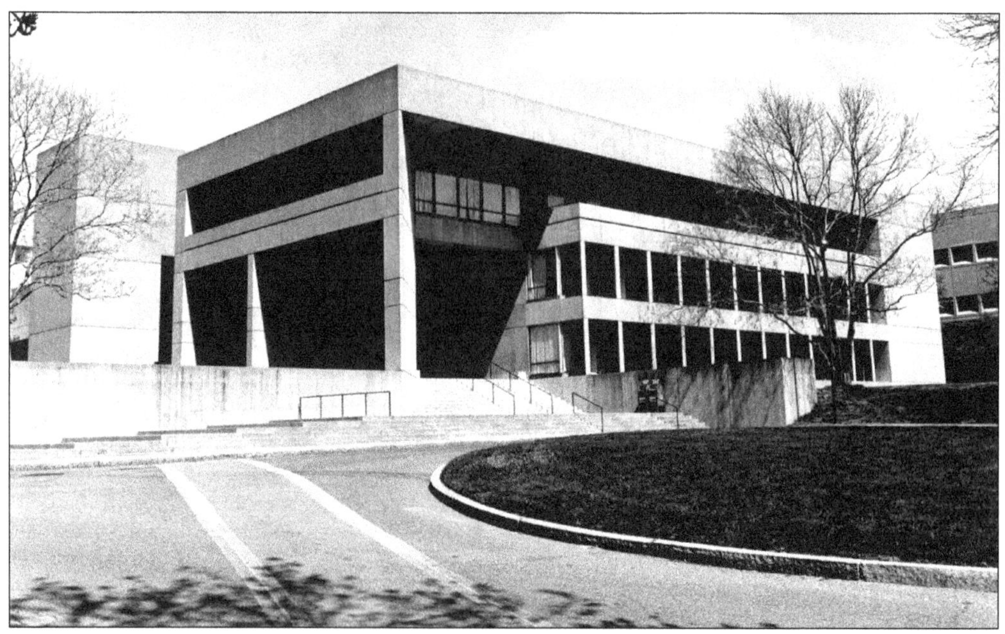

Polaroid's operations in Waltham expanded dramatically in 1968 with the addition of this I. M. Pei–designed facility near the Cambridge Reservoir. The building complex won several architectural awards and was selected by *Modern Manufacturing* magazine as one of the top 10 plants in the United States.

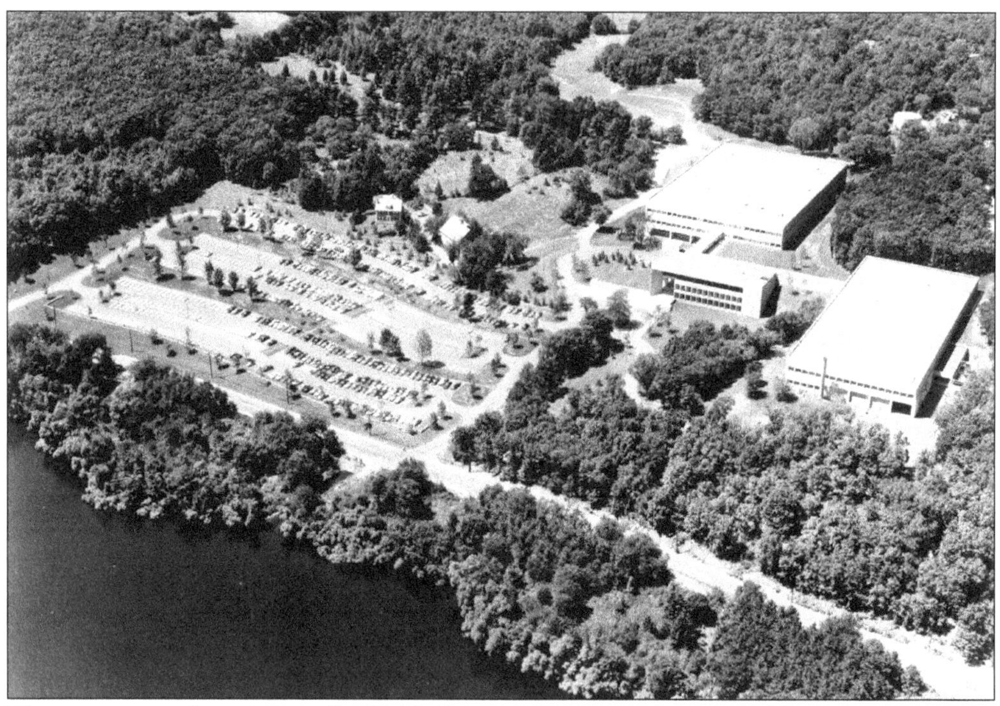

This aerial view shows Polaroid's SX-70 film-manufacturing plant at Waltham, located on the site of a 100-acre pre–Revolutionary War farm. Polaroid retained the original 1780 farmhouse and barn.

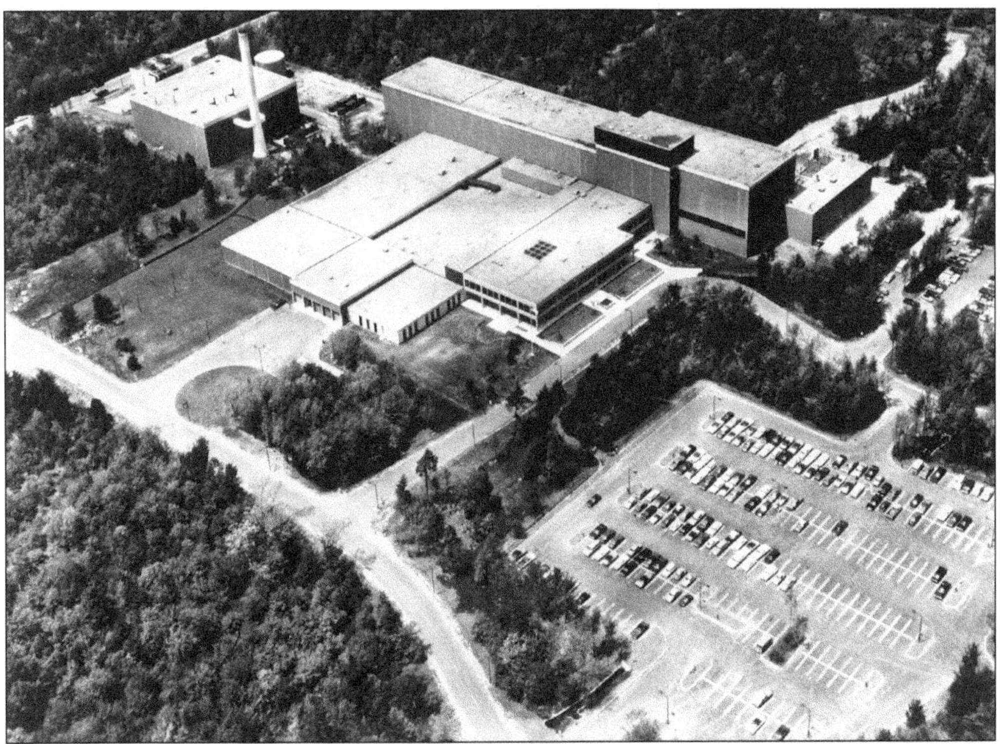

Another large manufacturing facility was set up in New Bedford, about 60 miles south of Boston.

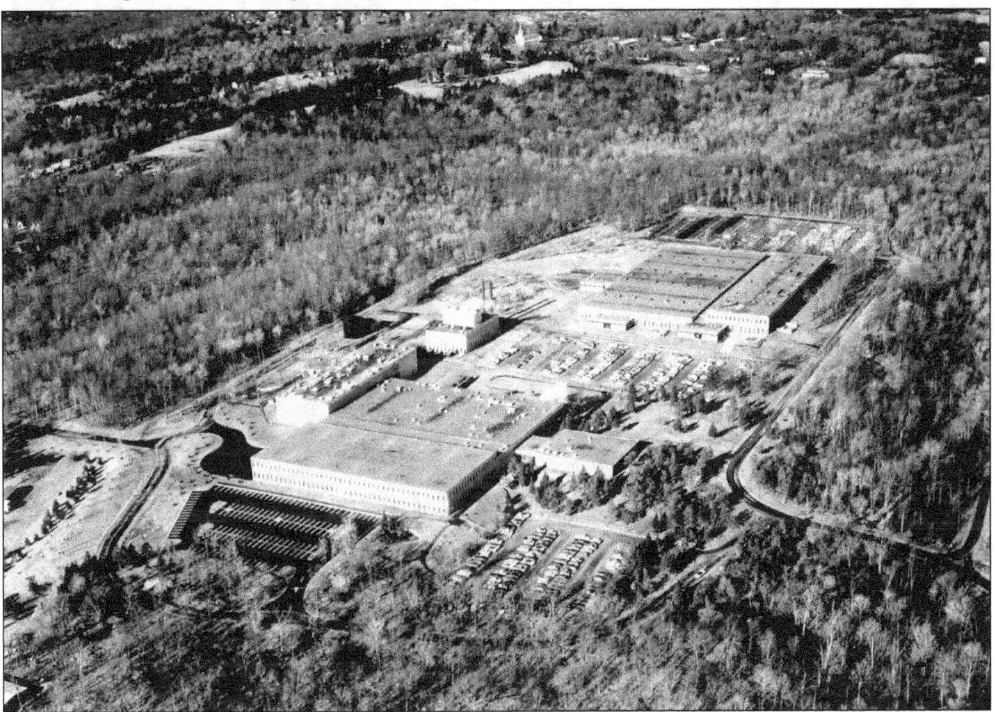

The SX-70 cameras required the establishment of a new facility in Norwood, a few miles south of Waltham.

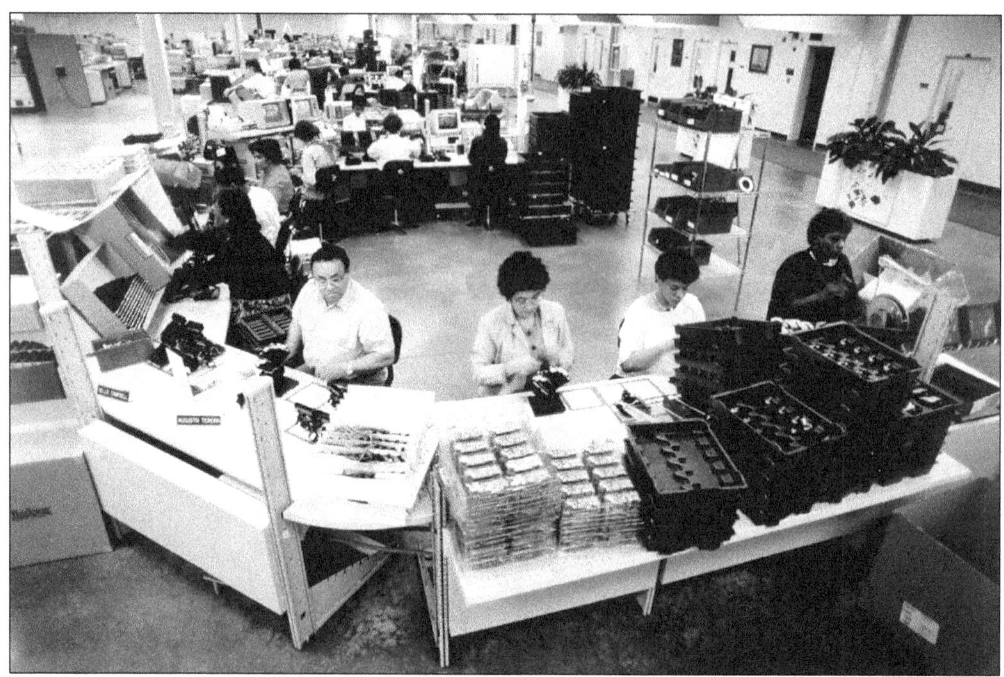

Camera-assembly work is being done in the late 1970s.

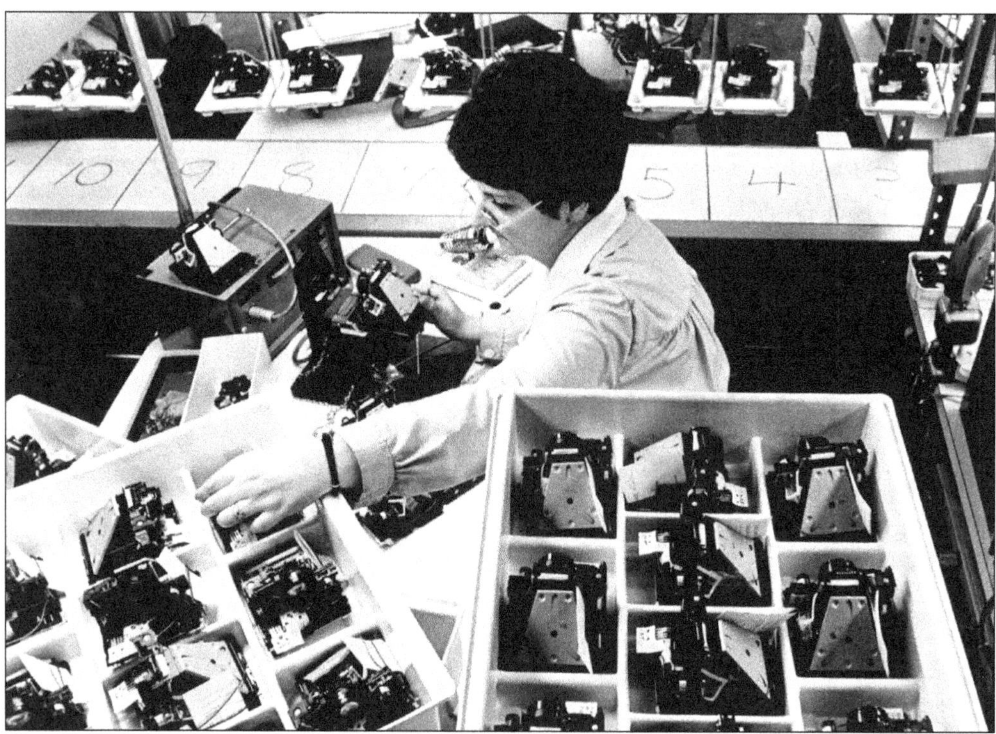

This is one of the many stages along the production line in Polaroid's Norwood facility, where components of 2,000 cameras were required to pass 100 percent inspection before being allowed to proceed to the next assembly operation.

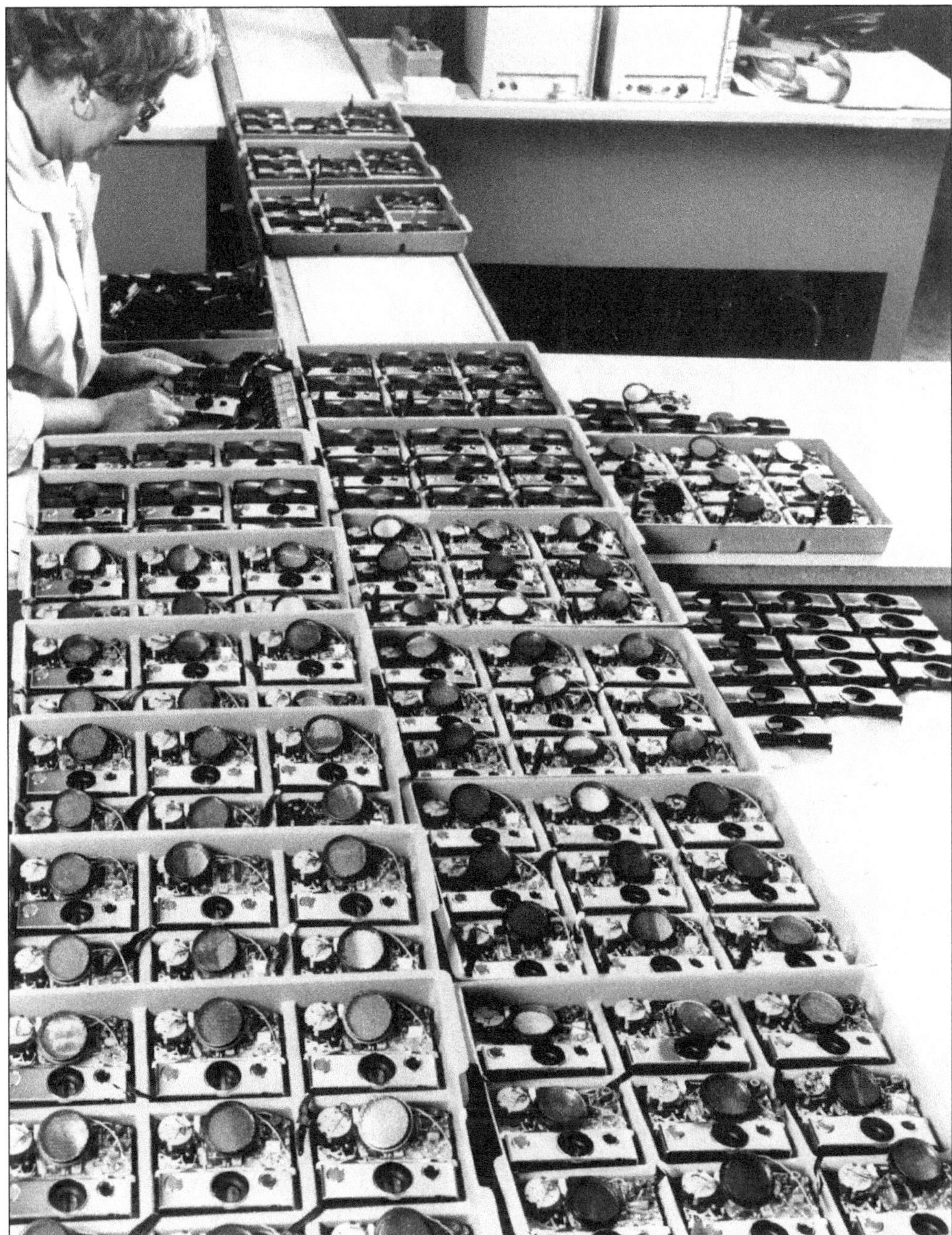

This is another view of manufacturing and inspection operations for cameras equipped with sonar for automatic focusing.

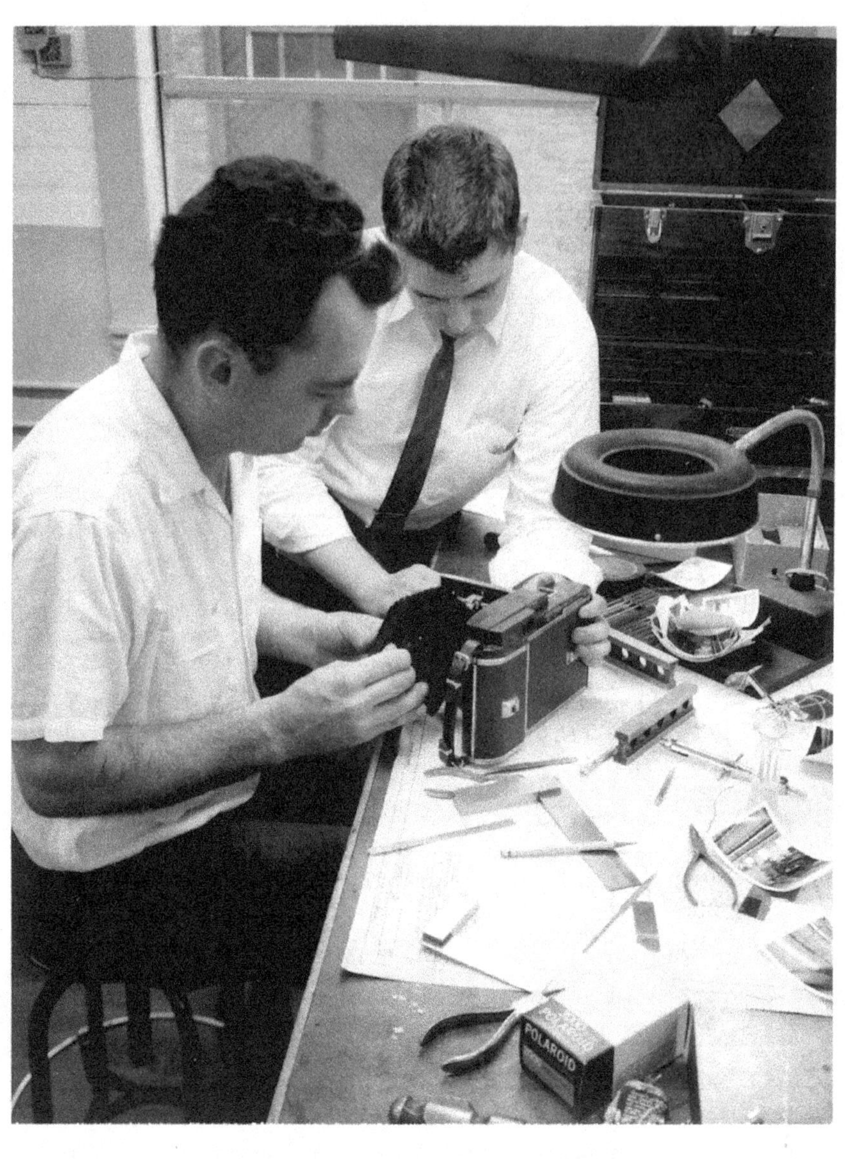

A Polaroid employee examines the workings of a Polaroid camera with an eye to product improvement.

Seven

The Intersection of Art and Science

Unlike many corporate leaders, Edwin Land was an active researcher himself. He sought the company of innovators. Those innovators included not just his fellow scientists but intellectuals, artists, and a growing number of photographers who found more than mere novelty in the products Polaroid produced. Polaroid and Land undertook efforts to sponsor photographers in exploring the new dimensions of Polaroid photography. In 1971, Land established the Polaroid Foundation, a charitable nonprofit organization that provided sponsorships in the art community as well. In homage to Smith College art professor Clarence Kennedy, a friend and inspiration to Land, Polaroid opened the Clarence Kennedy Gallery in Cambridge in 1973. The gallery's mission was to exhibit the works of emerging as well as professional photographers using Polaroid products. Among the many fine art photographers attracted to Land and Polaroid were Ansel Adams, Paul Caponigro, William Clift, Marie Cosindas, Philippe Halsman, David Hockney, Yousef Karsh, Arnold Newman, Andy Warhol, William Wegman, Bret Weston, and Minor White. Adams, who became close friends with Land, was hired as the company's first black-and-white photography consultant in 1945 and remained one for over 30 years. Cosindas became a color photography consultant in 1966. To the present day, the company maintains a significant collection of outstanding Polaroid photography by these artists and many others.

Perhaps informed by some of the same sensibilities and ambitions that compelled this connection with the arts, Polaroid invested in the best when it came time for the company to launch new products and leap into new markets. Well-known celebrities and top-rated network television shows were the typical venue for promoting Polaroid products from the 1950s to the present. Industrial designers such as Henry Dreyfuss made Polaroid cameras look as remarkable as in fact they were. And, notably, graphic designers such as Paul Giambarba put aside the original plain, businesslike Polaroid colors and product packaging for a series of strikingly bold designs whose impact reverberated across American industry for years after.

The net result was that Polaroid—founded on the technology of controlling light through polarization and having grown to greatness on instant black-and-white films—now became synonymous with color. The production of Polacolor films of ever greater fidelity ultimately led to the technological advances of the SX-70 system. It was a transition that the general public and the creative community experienced in equal measure. Casual photographers got quicker and more reliable results. Artists and professionals acquired access to rich, large-format films with outstanding sensitivity and fidelity—and, of course, the thrill of instant results. The great achievement of Polaroid was in satisfying the needs of both.

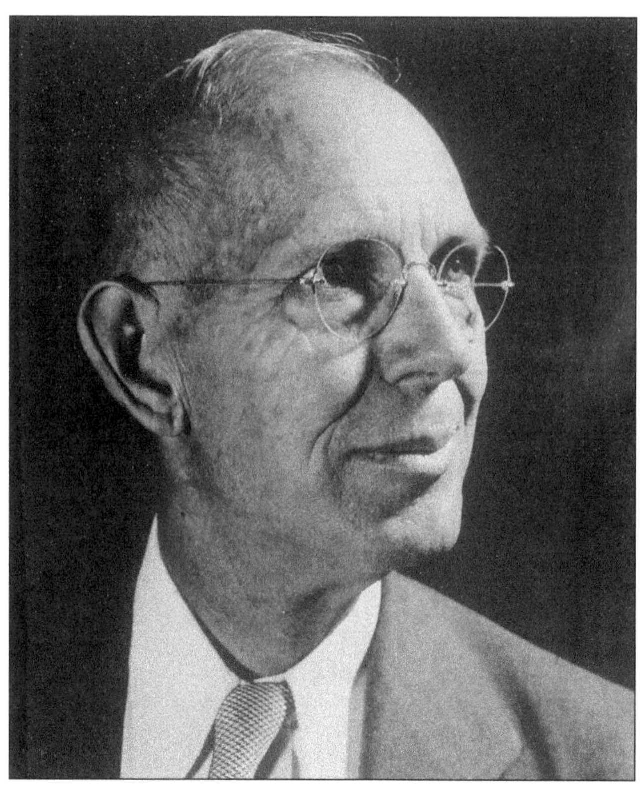

Clarence Kennedy encouraged the artistic side of Edwin Land. Kennedy, an art history professor at Smith College and the company's first consultant, encouraged Land to apply his polarizer technology to create three-dimensional viewing capabilities for the study of art, particularly sculpture. Land credited him with the idea for the name Polaroid. The company honored his memory when it opened the Clarence Kennedy Gallery in Cambridge in 1973 to exhibit the works of emerging and professional photographers using Polaroid products. This 1947 test photograph of Kennedy was taken by Meroë Morse.

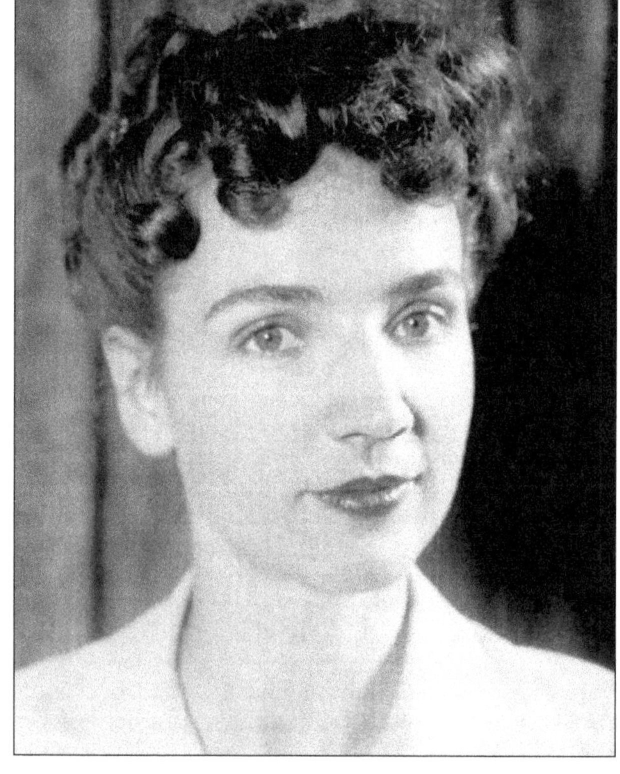

Meroë Morse was an art history student of Clarence Kennedy at Smith College. She was hired in 1945. A member of Land's inner circle and one of his top researchers, she was appointed as the director of the special photographic research division in 1966. She held 18 patents and was elected the first woman fellow of the Society of Photographic Scientists in 1969, just before her death. Meroë was also a liaison between Polaroid scientist and artists such as Ansel Adams. Meroë is shown here in a 1947 laboratory test photograph.

Ansel Adams served Polaroid as consultant, adviser, and artistic inspiration for more than 30 years. This photograph shows Adams on a visit to the Polaroid laboratories in 1949. It was made on Polaroid Type 40 Land film. During his long association with Polaroid, Adams, who became a consultant in 1945, sent thousands of memos reporting his tests results to Meroë Morse and Polaroid's scientists. Ansel Adams dedicated a chapter in his autobiography to Land, describing him as having "an extraordinary curiosity about everything and the discipline to satisfy it."

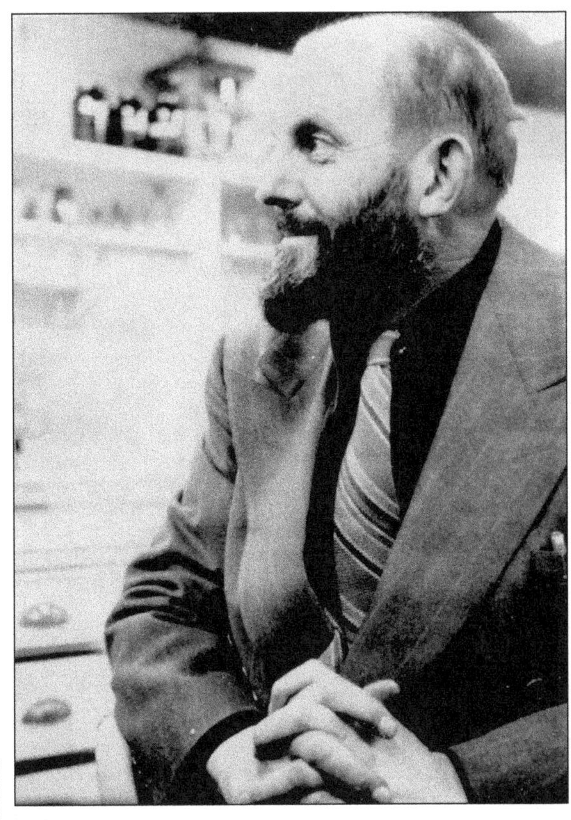

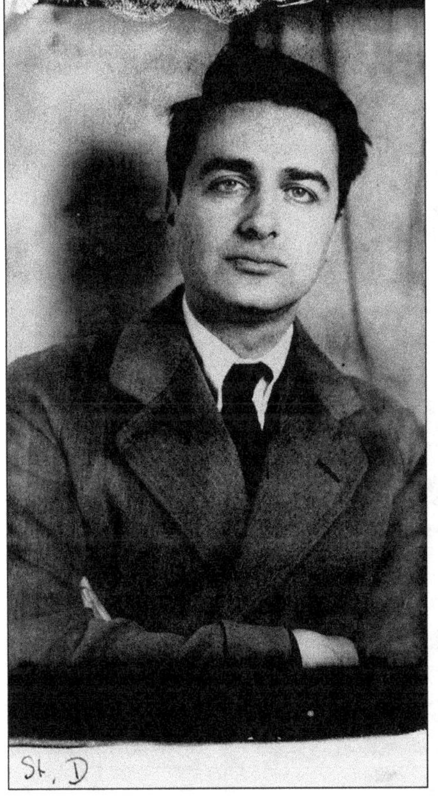

Edwin Land is pictured in 1945 in one of the earliest laboratory test photographs. "The beauty of the pictures by Kennedy and Adams played a striking inspirational role not so much in leading us to make beautiful pictures—though we tried—as to drive us toward 'beautiful' science as the basis for ultimate beauty in pictures. From this happy combination there arose a Polaroid culture which captivated the members of your corporation." —Edwin H. Land, in a 1978 letter to shareholders.

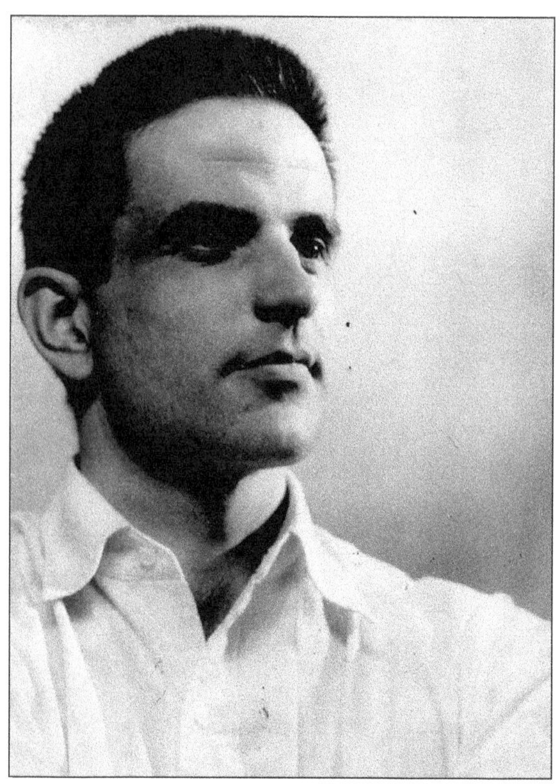

Howard Rogers, the inventor of the Polacolor film, is shown here in a 1946 test photograph taken by Meroë Morse. A Harvard dropout (like Land), Rogers joined the company in 1936 for lifelong work in research. Land praised Rogers in 1973: "In my life I've known few people who are saints or seem like saints."

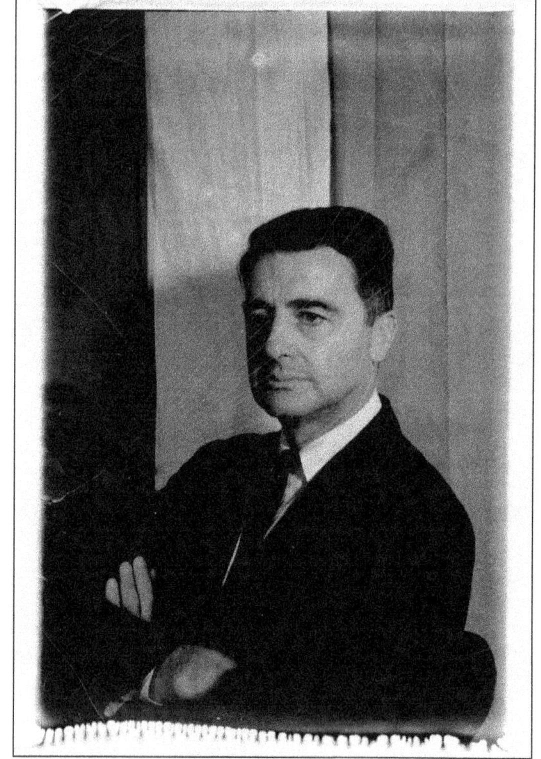

This Polacolor laboratory test photograph of Land was taken on September 27, 1962. "When I started the actual program of making black and white film for our camera, I set down the broad principles that would also apply to color. I invited Howard Rogers to sit opposite me in the black and white laboratory and think about color. For several years he assimilated the techniques we were using in black and white. Then one day he said, 'I am ready to start now.' My point is that we created an environment in which a man was expected to sit and think for two years." —Edwin H. Land.

The 60-second excitement

It's everywhere. Do you have your Polaroid Color Pack Camera? (Under $50.)

This advertisement features "the 60-second excitement" of the new Model 100. Launched in 1963, the Model 100 was the first automatic pack camera.

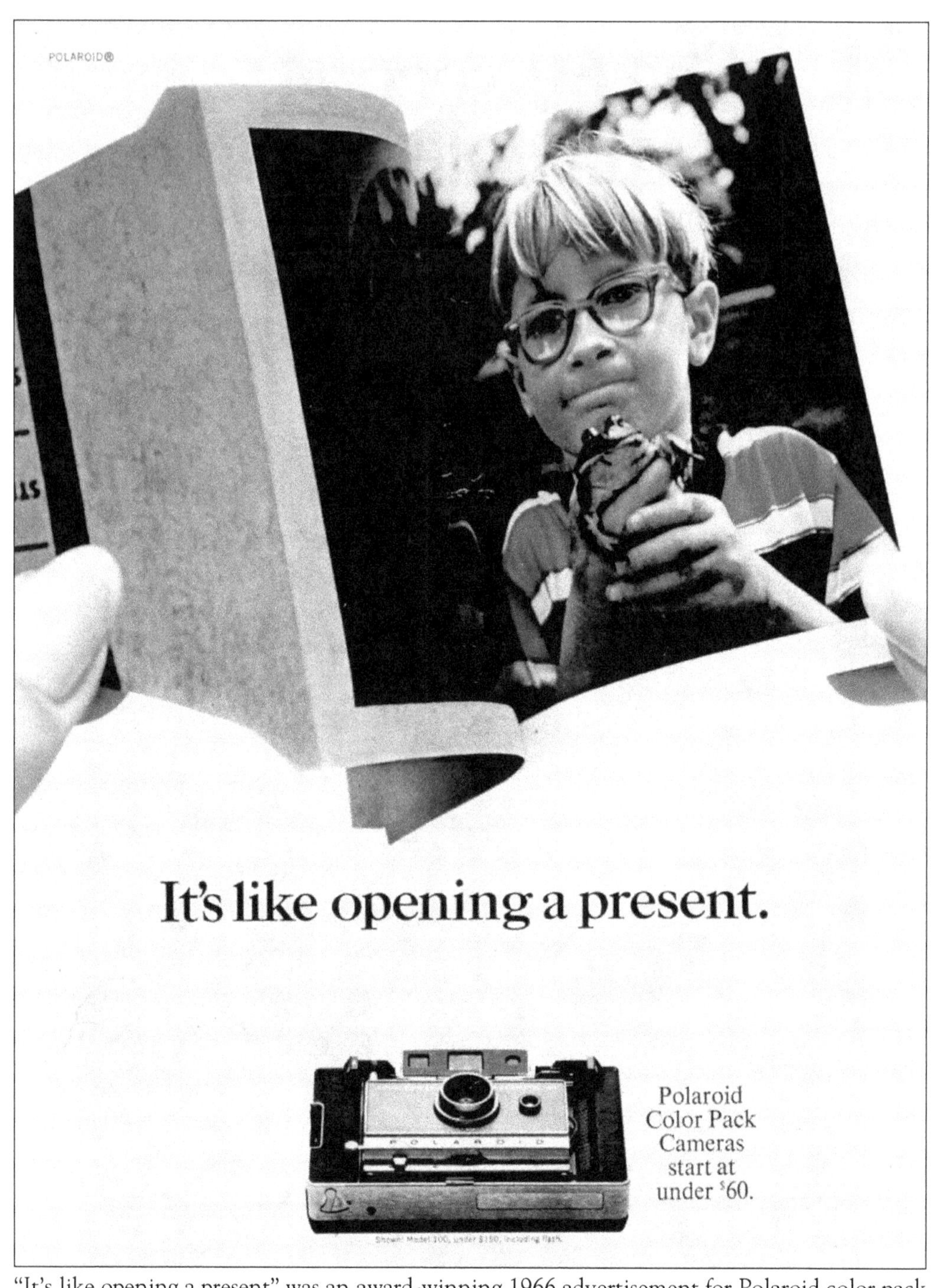

"It's like opening a present" was an award-winning 1966 advertisement for Polaroid color pack cameras. The firm of Doyle Dane Bernbach created award-winning advertisements that revealed the spontaneity of instant photography.

Polaroid invents The SX-70.

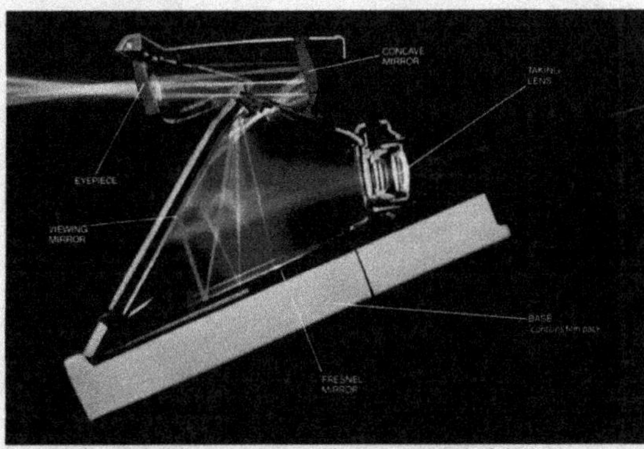

Cutaway photograph of the SX-70 using laser beams shows how you see precisely what the lens sees. When you touch the electric shutter button, the Fresnel mirror flips up and the film is exposed.

No matter how you've looked upon the act of taking pictures, instant or otherwise, picture-taking will never be the same.

A color photograph, which develops before your eyes outside the camera to a brilliance unparalleled in amateur photography, is only the *beginning* of the SX-70 experience.

The rebirth of a sense of wonder and an increased awareness of the beauty that surrounds you are the *true* end results of SX-70 picture-taking.

Watch it happen.

Remarkable as the Polaroid SX-70 Land camera is, what is important to remember is not what *it* can do, but what it enables *you* to do.

Touch the red electric shutter button and whoosh, the picture is automatically ejected from the front of the camera.

There is nothing to time, nothing to peel, nothing to throw away.

Your picture begins developing immediately beneath a transparent, protective plastic cover. You can stack it with other pictures, handle it, put it in your pocket. You can even spill water on it and still not hinder the development process.

As the image blooms before your eyes, you realize that this will be a color photograph such as you have never seen before.

Even after you have a beautiful picture, it keeps getting better.

Minutes later, you're looking at your finished picture. It is hard, dry, shiny, flat and extremely durable.

The image size of the picture is 3⅛ x 3⅛ inches.

The camera that makes it possible.

The SX-70 Land camera, closed, is 1" x 4" x 7". Wrapped in top-grain leather, it weighs only 24 ounces.

Inside, there exist over 200 transistors, a complex system of fixed and pivoting mirrors and a 12,000 r.p.m. motor, all working together to propel one brilliant picture after another into your life.

Yet all you have to do is frame, focus and touch the red electric button.

The SX-70 is a single lens reflex camera. Your eye sees precisely what the camera lens sees, because you're actually looking through the camera lens.

You can focus on a scene from miles away, down to 10 inches, and you can actually record far more detail than you can see without the use of a magnifying lens.

You can shoot up to 10 pictures, one every 1.5 seconds, to cover a full action sequence, like a baby's first jaunt across the room. Or you can take automatic time exposures up to 14 seconds long.

The scope of SX-70 picture-taking is as wide as your imagination will allow it to be.

Power from the film pack.

As amazing as the Polaroid SX-70 Land camera is, the story of the other

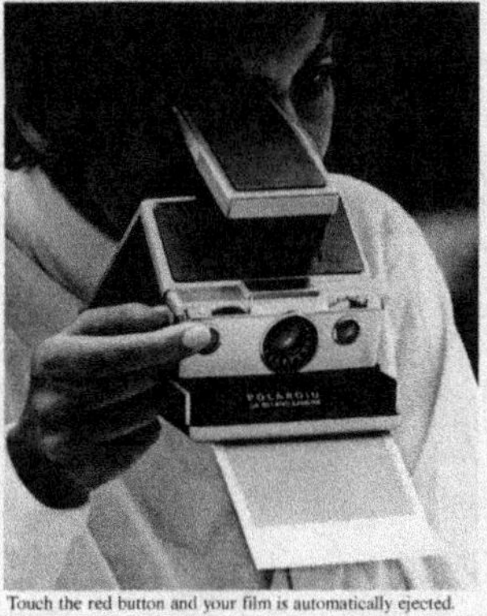

Touch the red button and your film is automatically ejected.

Dating from 1973, "Polaroid invents the SX-70" was another bold and, in this case, informative print advertisement prepared by Doyle Dane Bernbach for Polaroid. Noted filmmaker and designer Charles Eames made a film to introduce Polaroid's SX-70 photographic system, and Laurence Olivier became the product's first spokesman.

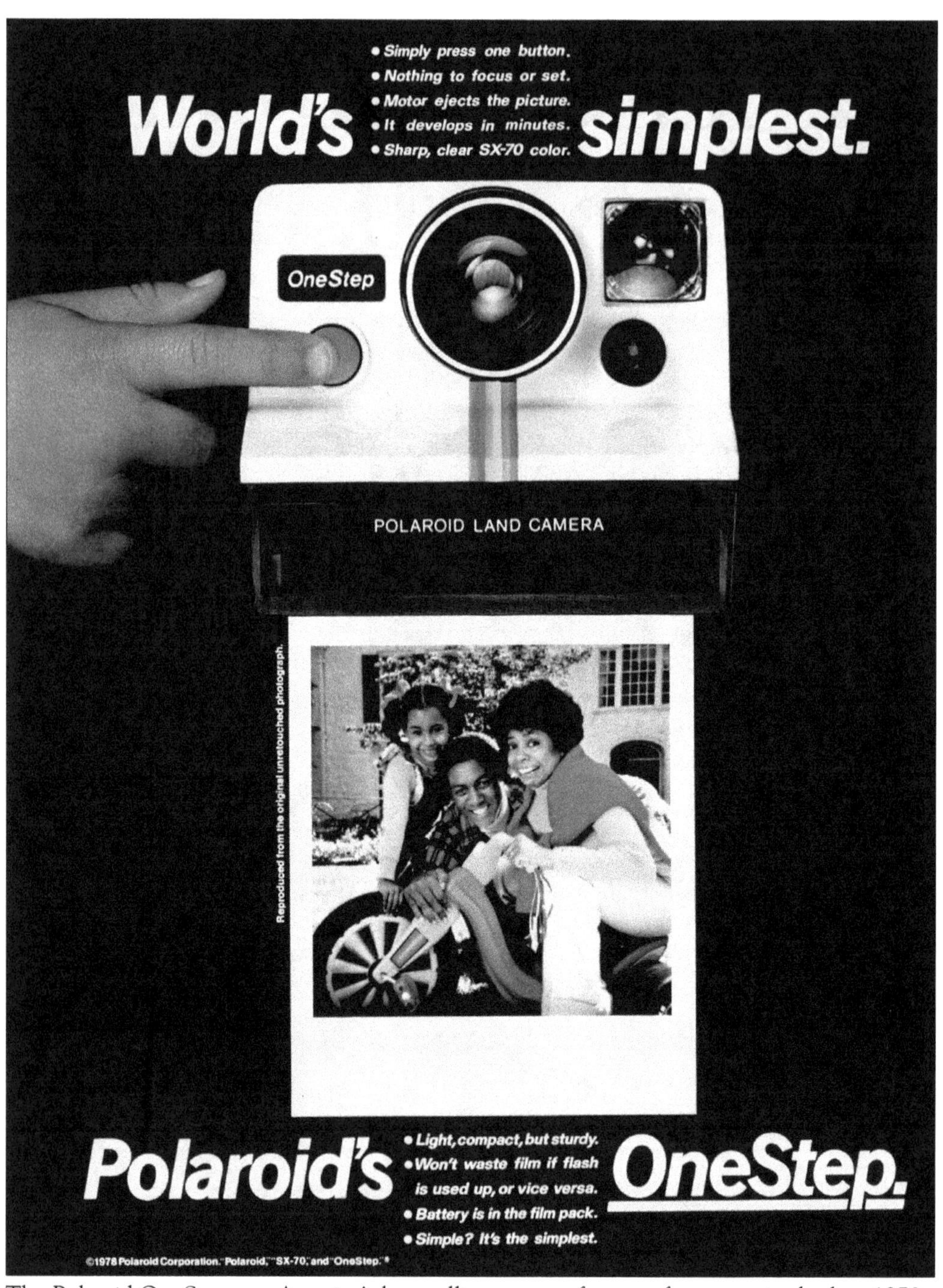

The Polaroid OneStep was America's best-selling camera for over four years in the late 1970s. Award-winning television commercials featured James Garner and Mariette Hartley.

Polaroid 600 System Photography The Film

Colors as rich as your imagination.

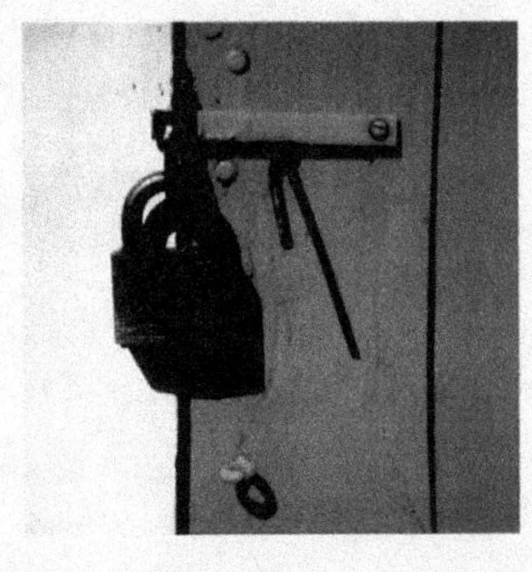

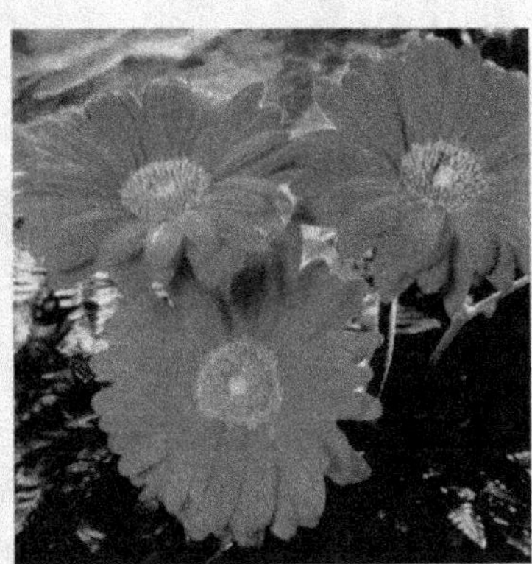

This advertisement promotes the Polaroid Sun auto-focus camera and Type 600 film (the fastest instant color film), introduced in 1981.

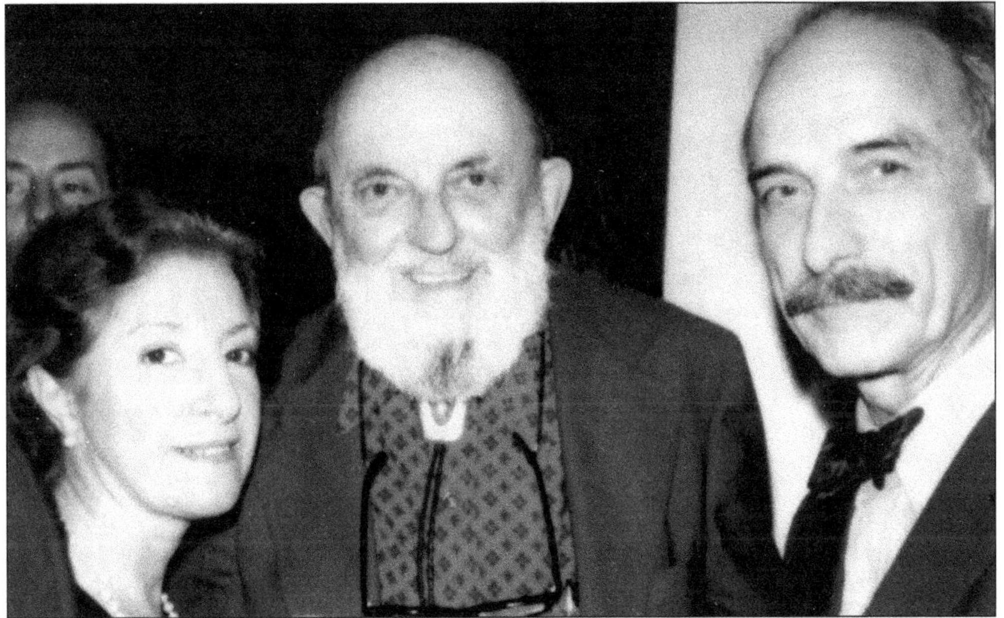

Pictured at a reception for Ansel Adams in the late 1970s are, from left to right, Marie Cosindas, Ansel Adams, and William McCune. In 1974, the Metropolitan Museum of Arts opened an exhibit of Adams's photographs, many of which were on Polaroid films. In 1979, Adams wrote an informative book, *Polaroid Land Photography*. Cosindas had her solo exhibition at the Museum of Modern Art in 1966 (the first time Polacolor film was shown there). This photograph was provided by Cosindas.

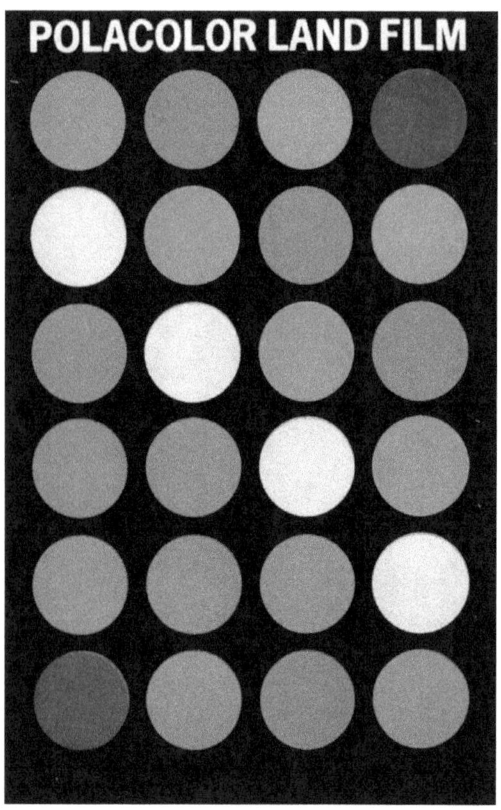

In addition to elegant product design, celebrity endorsements, and high-profile advertising, the company also made investments in striking product packaging. Here, the color scheme of the packaging for Polacolor Land film is on display.

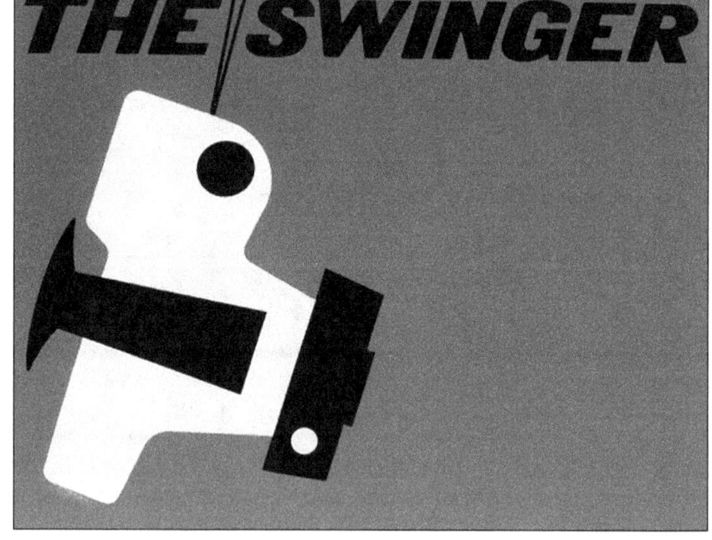

The award-winning Swinger advertising campaign was launched in 1965. This Swinger camera packaging captured the 1960s sense of style.

This Polaroid Type 88 Colorpack film packaging from 1971 defined a new look.

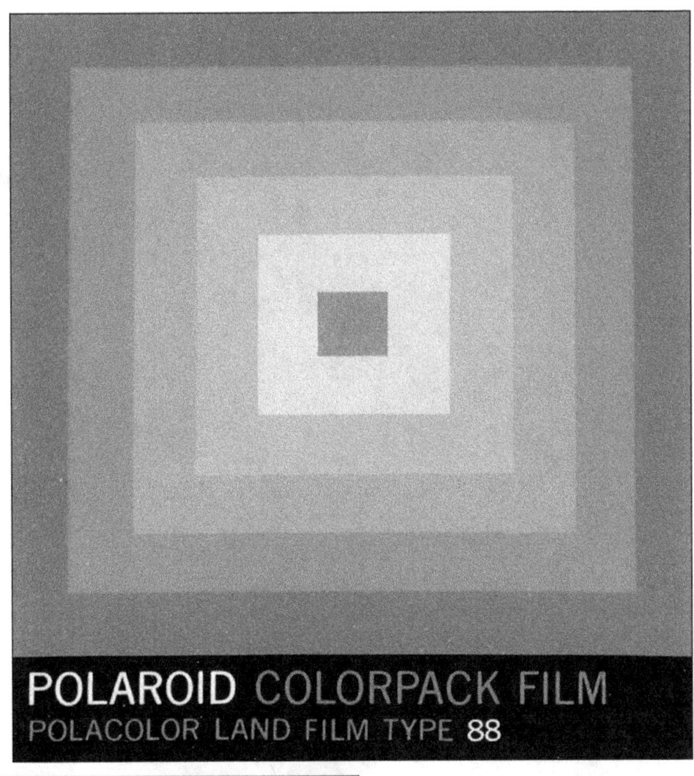

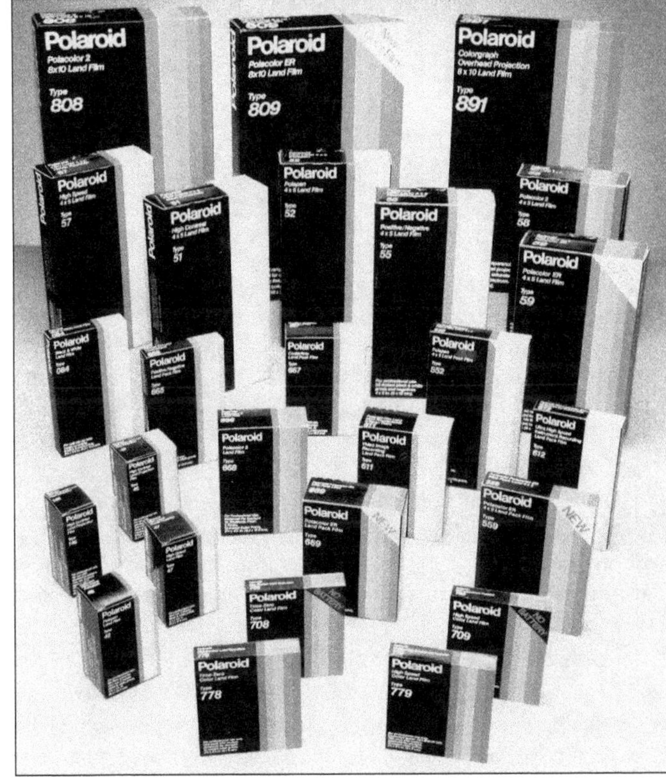

Film packaging from the early 1980s shows an array of Polaroid film products. By 1983, Polaroid was manufacturing 40 kinds of films for amateur and professional markets

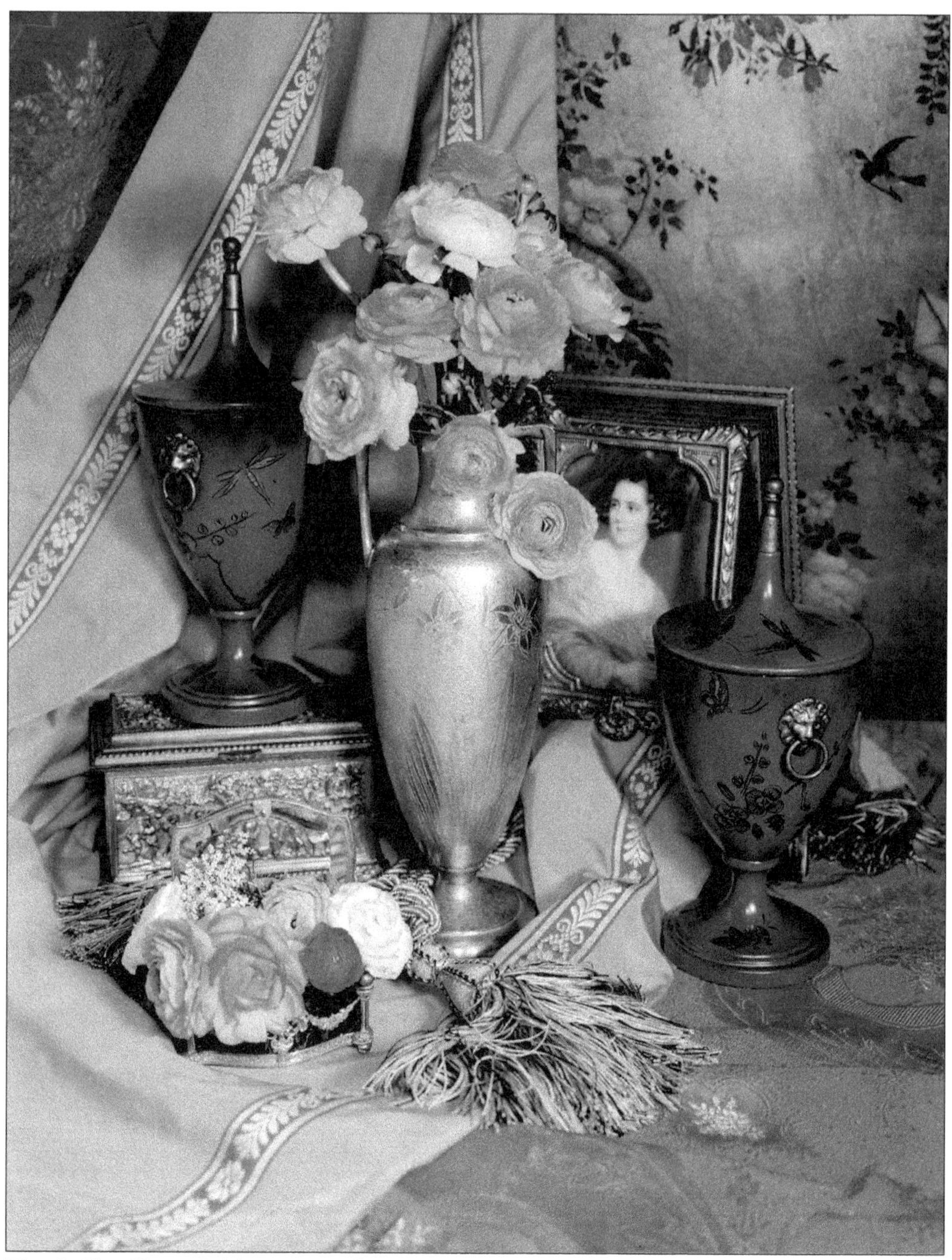

The Golden Vase, California was photographed in 1992 by Marie Cosindas using Polacolor ER Type 59 film. This formal arrangement and its rich colors are characteristic of the Cosindas signature.

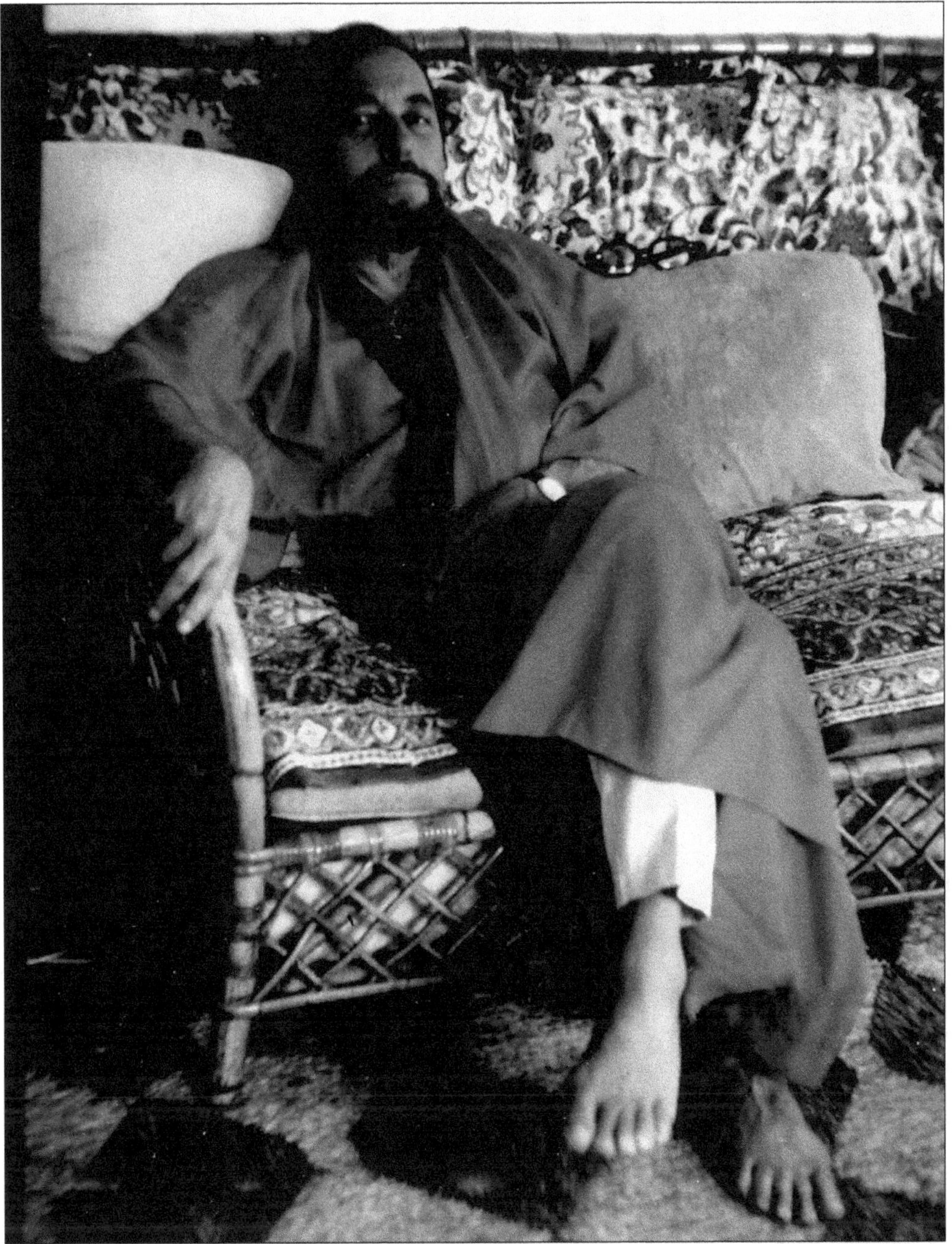

Even better known for her portraiture, Cosindas photographed a relaxed Tennessee Williams in Key West in 1974, using Polacolor ER Type 59 film.

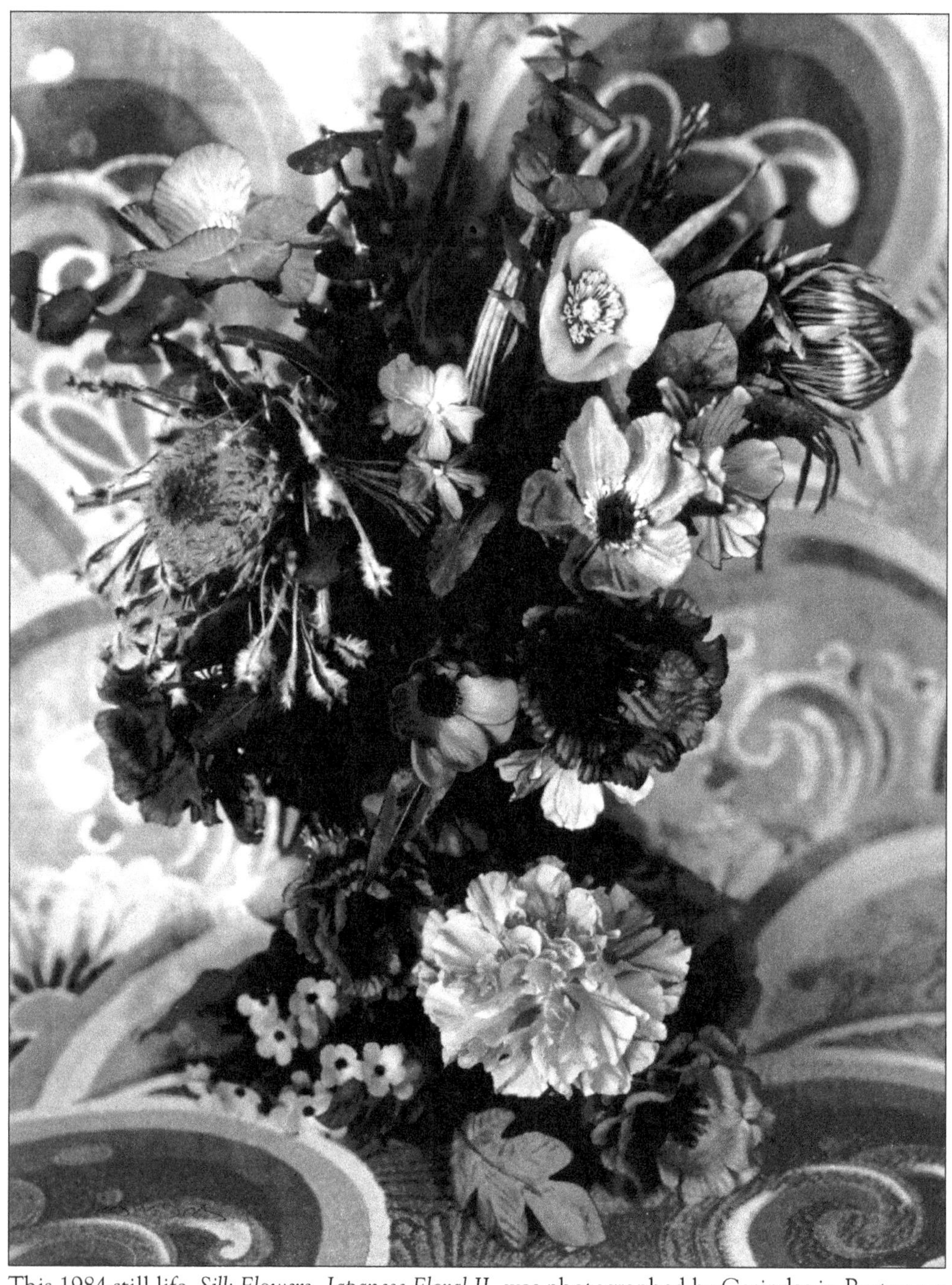

This 1984 still life, *Silk Flowers, Japanese Floral II,* was photographed by Cosindas in Boston on Polacolor 2 Type 808 film, an 8- by 10-inch instant color film.

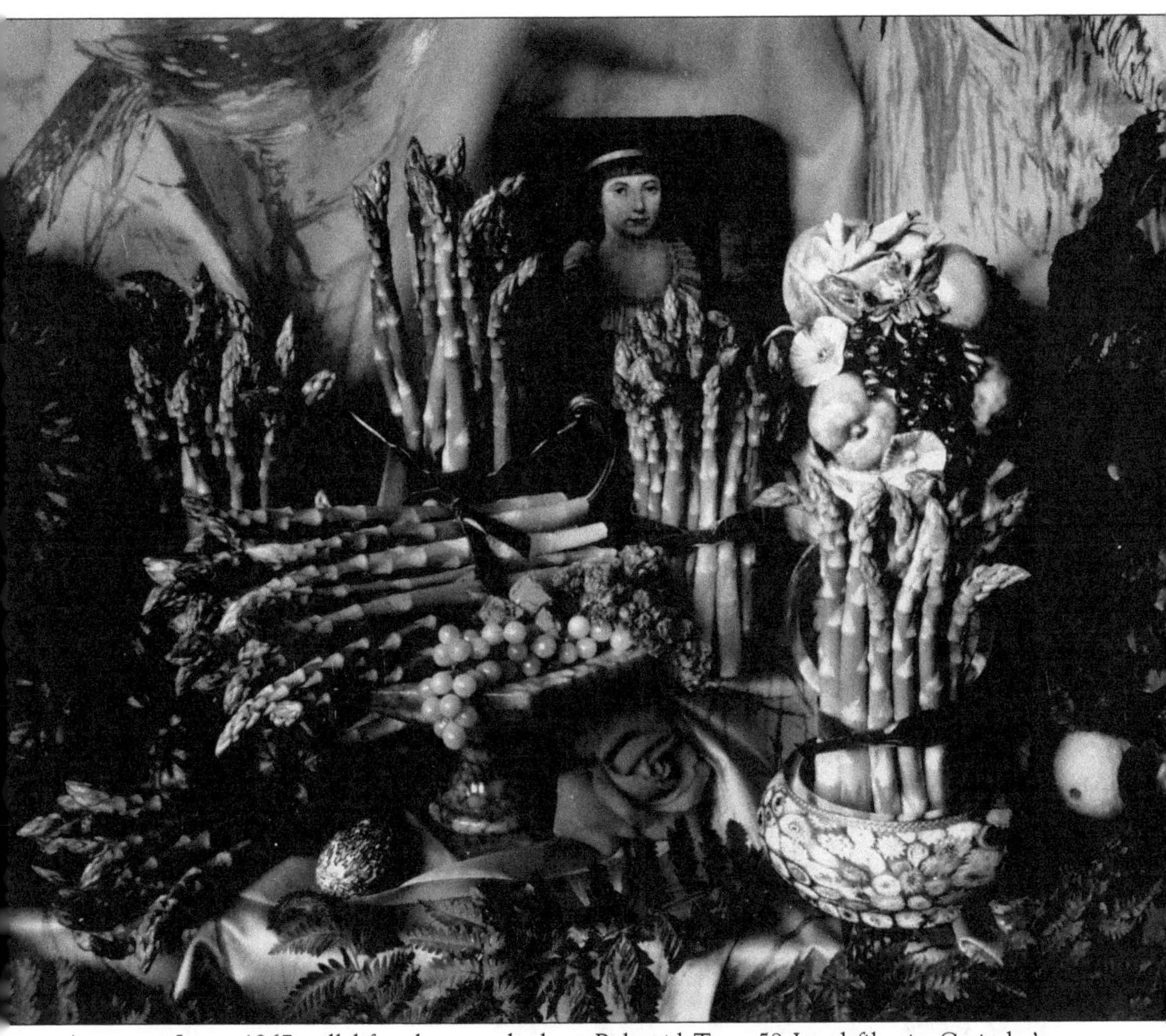

Asparagus I is a 1967 still life, photographed on Polaroid Type 58 Land film in Cosindas's Boston studio.

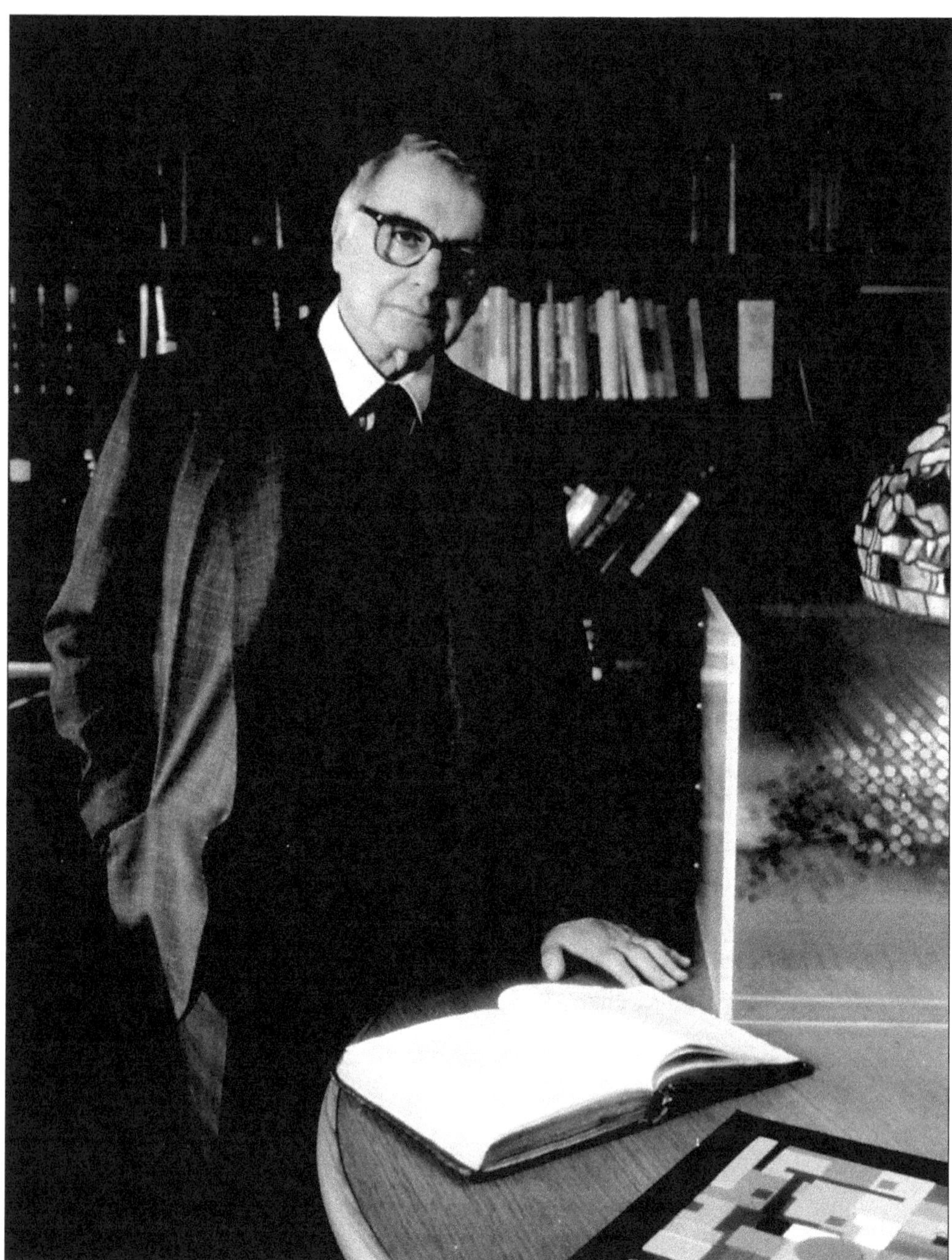

Edwin H. Land is photographed by Marie Cosindas at the Rowland Institute on his birthday, May 7, 1988. Taken on Polaroid Type 59 film, this is the last portrait that Cosindas made of Land (1909–1991). "Once in a long while one has an experience of overpowering clarity in suddenly seeing through a new face to the person within. Marie Cosindas has learned how to use photography reliably for this kind of penetration; when we look at her pictures, we are almost embarrassed by the intimate revelation of a stranger. It is clear that she could not work without beauty as one of her tools. What else she uses will remain as mysterious as art itself." —Edwin H. Land.

www.ingramcontent.com/pod-product-compliance
Lightning Source LLC
LaVergne TN
LVHW081552100826
845153LV00004B/369

* 9 7 8 1 5 3 1 6 2 1 7 9 7 *